'Keith Leslie has produced a very timely, well written and markedly useful book about leadership. It is stuffed with clear advice and important warnings for anyone involved in leadership, and manages to combine the lessons of a practitioner with the thoughts of an intellectual.'

Keith Grint, Emeritus Professor, University of Warwick
and author of The Arts of Leadership

'Grounded in fascinating research and practical advice, *A Question of Leadership* is an essential guide to compassionate and effective leadership.'

Dame Carolyn Fairbairn, Director General,
Confederation of British Industry

'Standing in the heat of leadership, you want a cool head at your side. I know. Keith Leslie was my mentor in leading change under pressure. I commend the wisdom of a working lifetime in this book to all who seek to lead their organization through crisis to good health.'

William Storrar, Director of the Center
of Theological Inquiry, Princeton, NJ

'In an age when change is relentless, and too many top leaders are blinded by ego, Keith's testimonies about what really works in leading organizations to success are most refreshing. This candid approach to mental health as a leadership issue could not be timelier.'

James Lahey, Visiting Research Professor and
Director of the Centre on Public Management
and Policy, University of Ottawa

'The pandemic has made a lot of us – business, politicians, public servants, teachers and parents – understand that leadership is not about the heroic individual firing out orders. This book explodes that myth and convincingly explains that real leadership is about asking powerful questions and accompanying others on their journey by listening, learning together and humbly promoting solidarity for the common good.'

Lord John McFall of Alcluith,
Senior Deputy Speaker of the House of Lords

'A refreshingly human, grounded, nuanced guide to leading sustainable change in a complex system. Keith Leslie's decades of wisdom and experience shine through on every page.'

Caroline Webb, author of How to Have a Good Day
and Senior Adviser to McKinsey & Company

'*A Question of Leadership* provides valuable insights for leaders across all sectors, and importantly highlights how leaders can effectively learn from one another.'

Lesley King-Lewis, Chief Executive, Windsor Leadership

'This book is packed with deep insight, applicable knowledge and advice gained through real-world experience. Keith's book delivers a valuable, timely and engaging view of the problems faced by organisations as they navigate change.'

Chris Cook, VP Engineering, Navarik, Vancouver

'This is a book for our times. With skilful use of the pandemic and other stories clearly laid out, Keith Leslie guides all of us as leaders involved in change. His people-centric focus on mental health is groundbreaking.'

Lieutenant General Richard Nugee CB CVO CBE,
former Chief of Defence People and Climate Change &
Sustainability Lead for the Ministry of Defence

KEITH LESLIE

A Question of Leadership

Leading Organizational Change in Times of Crisis

BLOOMSBURY BUSINESS
LONDON • OXFORD • NEW YORK • NEW DELHI • SYDNEY

BLOOMSBURY BUSINESS
Bloomsbury Publishing Plc
50 Bedford Square, London, WC1B 3DP, UK
29 Earlsfort Terrace, Dublin 2, Ireland

First published in Great Britain 2021

A catalogue record for this book is available from the British Library

Library of Congress Cataloguing-in-Publication data has been applied for

ISBN: 978-1-4729-8602-3; eBook: 978-1-4729-8603-0

2 4 6 8 10 9 7 5 3 1

Typeset by Deanta Global Publishing Services, Chennai, India
Printed and bound in Great Britain by CPI Group (UK) Ltd, Croydon CR0 4YY

To find out more about our authors and books visit www.bloomsbury.com
and sign up for our newsletters

Contents

PART ONE   CHANGE JUST CHANGED   1

PART TWO   'WHY DON'T THESE ORGANIZATIONS –
AND PEOPLE – BEHAVE RATIONALLY?'   19

  1   Change is an Accident Waiting to Happen   23

  2   Games Leaders Play   45

PART THREE   'WHAT DO I NEED TO DO – AND WHAT
SHOULD I EXPECT OTHERS TO DO?'   73

  3   Leaders' Journeys   77

  4   Finding the Answers on the Front Line   96

  5   Teams that Work   114

PART FOUR   'WHAT DO I DO WHEN WE MEET BUMPS
IN THE ROAD?'   131

  6   Learning from Leaders and Mistakes   135

  7   Tacking through Waves of Change   155

PART FIVE   'HOW DO I BUILD PURPOSE, BELONGING
AND MENTAL HEALTH?'   173

  8   Thriving and Belonging   178

9   Culture that Includes Everyone   198

10   Promoting Mental Health   217

PART SIX   'ALL THIS? ALL AT ONCE?'   243

The Author   253
Acknowledgements and Sources   254
References   256
Index   276

PART ONE

CHANGE JUST CHANGED

Leading change is no longer just for the manager, chief executive or consultant – we can all learn together and benefit from the stories of leaders at all levels. We need to understand why and when change works (and when it fails), what we can do, how we deal with adversity and how we build belonging, inclusion and mental health – not just survive change, but thrive with it. Originally I set out to write a book of stories and evidence on the principles of leading change, aimed at leaders in organizations. The experience of the onset of the COVID-19 pandemic of 2020 does not change these principles of leadership, but the context and scope were transformed and expanded:

> Leading change suddenly became everyone's role – in schools, small businesses, families, charities, community groups, faith groups, retail outlets, care homes ... as well as in the big organizations of companies, professional services, government, NHS and public services.
>
> Everyone had a shared experience of change and we all talked about the same issues – trust in our leaders, learning from front-line workers, unfamiliar new roles, experimenting with new processes and equipment, shortages, inequalities, promoting mental health, assuaging anxieties, dealing with loss, and supporting our communities.

My goal with this book is to help thoughtful people understand, lead, advise, avoid pitfalls and see the opportunities for *leading change*. It is for anyone who seeks to play a leadership role in organizations – whatever that role and whatever that organization:

> Whatever that role – whether making leadership choices as a new part of their informal roles at home, at work and in the community, *or* formally charged with leadership roles as leaders, directors, advisers, consultants, mentors, management team members, project managers or as front-line managers.
>
> Whatever that organization – from workplace to family through charity and street group. Organizations dominate our lives, whether tiny start-up companies or multinational or government behemoths or churches or charities. As soon as you try to do anything repeatedly – repeat events, consistent products, reliable support or resources – then you are organizing and you have an organization.

This book is not a comprehensive guide to leading people, organization design or project-managing change, where much is already written.[1] It is about the most challenging subset of leadership: leading change. There are, of course, many books already providing a formula for change management. Change management is an evergreen topic of interest to businesses and public services, because they embark on so many change projects – even though 60–70 per cent fail.[2] Change management is also fascinating for politicians and policymakers, who are frequently frustrated because they can see new policies that are needed, but organizations somehow stumble or frustrate the desired policy or strategy. The failures and frustrations are due to the static approach of traditional change management. Popular leadership books and autobiographies preach clear, passionate, insightful direction by the heroic leader, followed by tight project management and plenty of carrots and sticks. The reality is that such a simplistic formula cannot work when dealing with the complexity of human systems – in fact, it will exacerbate problems by encouraging people to play games within organizations. In the desire to give leaders a simple step-by-step guide, decades of high-quality research and thinking on change in organizations are frequently ignored. It doesn't help sales (whether of books or consultancy advice) to admit that leading change is about difficult, repeated, positive, long-term engagement of people.

For the sake of our society, economy, our organizational belonging and our mental health, we need to learn to lead change successfully in a complex and dynamic system. It can and has been done, often, so there are plenty of stories of success to be told. We all love hearing stories. Telling stories has always been a powerful means of shaping human behaviour and many organizations make deliberate use of stories to influence their people and leaders – especially because leaders learn from leaders. So every section of this book opens with a story, analyses what works and doesn't work, references the serious research and thinking we can rely upon – and closes with questions to ask. Reading this book will be worth your while – it will result in you asking better questions as a leader, rather than blindly issuing instructions.

CHANGE USED TO BE MORE CONTAINED AND MANAGEABLE

For decades we have been told that 'change is the only constant', that we live in times of turbulence, that more change has happened in recent years than in previous decades… or centuries… or since the Renaissance. The advent of globalization, the widespread enactment of liberal economic and social policies, and the rise of the Internet and instant communication have clearly transformed our societies and our lives as individuals and families. Commentators and advisers, especially in the business world, advocated many tools and approaches for coping and planning for change. Even in the field of pandemic planning, governments invested in preparedness and plans, while advisers like myself led 'wargames' for civil servants and business people on both long-term health crises such as obesity and short-term health crises such as new diseases – all as part of leadership development in businesses and in public services.

Despite this cataract of constant change, there was a key constraint in our experience that made change manageable for us – both in leadership of change and organizations' or families' experience of change. The constraint was that, for most of us, change used to come in only two flavours:

Up close and personal – but episodic and isolated

Our organizations – business, public service, charity, church or social group – embark on a new direction, self-selected by the leader or compelled by the market.

- If you are inside the organization, the impact is often direct and significant, demanding a response. For some there is an upside and opportunities to advance, for others there are losses – financial, reputational and emotional.
- Although some cycles of change repeat, most are programmed with a defined scope and duration. And – crucially – unless you are inside the organization, you are merely a bystander. Even within the organization, some people would feel impervious or indifferent to change – they had seen it all before and would see off this latest change attempt.

Incremental and impersonal – but continuous and relentless

Our society is continually changing with the constant impact of political, economic, health, social, religious, technological developments and trends. We all live in a world that is increasingly volatile, uncertain, complex and ambiguous (or VUCA, if we adopt the ugly acronym of many commentators) – but we adapt over time.

- For most of us, shifts in government policy or the growth of the Internet or the decline of traditional manufacturing or new health challenges are all issues that emerge slowly with incremental impact on our

4

lives. We recognize the impact after repeated media discussions and accommodate it in our choices as we change jobs, relocate or take family decisions. Yes, some may be reluctant choices, but we have time to choose our response and manage our reactions. Broader social or economic change could be treated by most people as an abstract, distant topic – especially if they are protected by established property or pension or employment rights.

- For a few of us, society-wide trends and events will have an immediate and often negative impact. In economics, the decline of manufacturing is devastating if a community relies on a mine or a factory and it closes suddenly. Deaths from new diseases are not so distant if it is your community that is struck by Ebola or HIV first – and before treatments become effective. But – crucially – unless you are unlucky enough to be singularly vulnerable, you have time and resources to manage your reactions.

This demarcated, limited experience of change enabled leaders within organizations to cope with change. The remorseless grinding of technological and economic change could be translated by leaders into manageable chunks for their populations or organizations to absorb. Where carefully scoped and phased, it could be led and managed and did not affect everyone at the same time and for an indefinite period.

Even so, setting out to change an organization was always the toughest sustained challenge for leaders:

Tough for the senior leader at the top of the organization trying to guide the change.

Tough for the front-line leaders trying to keep the show on the road.

Tough for the management teams allocating scarce resources and time to new pressing priorities.

WE ARE ALL LEARNING TO FACE NEW CHALLENGES OF UNCONTAINED CHANGE

Take off these limits – as the experience of the COVID-19 pandemic and its aftermath have done – and change is no longer contained and manageable.[3] We all face three challenges that in combination can overwhelm leaders:

1 *We are experiencing change that is simultaneously up close and personal – and also continuous and relentless.*
The economic, social and health consequences of the pandemic are still working through our organizations, societies and families, creating new issues for leaders of change. It is no longer good enough to deliver change in an organization and simply accept 'collateral damage' in the form of discarded people, broken commitments, social discord, inequalities and mental distress. During the peak of the 2020 crisis, taxpayers supported business and the economy as they had also done during the 2008 financial crisis. In addition in 2020, the health of the population relied on the effectiveness and, in many cases, the sacrifices of a largely low-wage workforce. However, in the absence of explicit action to close the gap, the 'haves' will emerge from the aftermath of the pandemic even further ahead of the 'have-nots'. Organizations need to act to ensure people thrive with change, not merely survive – which means change that builds positive organizational purpose and develops mentally healthy workplaces.

2 *There are no bystanders – instead we have many more leaders of change in more diverse organizations.*
At one level 'we are all in this together' because we share a universal experience of change, new to populations that have not experienced war or epidemic or famine. People have been called upon to exercise leadership of change in their organizations on a much bigger scale

than before the pandemic – in their families and schools, new workplaces, neighbourhood and community organizations, charities, faith groups, small businesses, people across public services and in commercial organizations working in new ways.

You can see from this that I apply a broad definition of 'leadership of an organization' to mean 'working with and influencing toward a common goal a group of people who are carrying out repeating activities that others rely upon'.

Many more people bringing different experiences of change before, during and after the pandemic want to know what it takes to lead change in their organization successfully. This is no longer the preserve of project managers and management consultants.

3 *Learning from effective leadership of change is vital – traditional leadership models have already failed.*
Even in the old context of contained change, traditional styles of leadership regularly failed across all organizations – commercial, government, health, local authority, charity, religious and start-up. During the COVID-19 pandemic crisis, we all observed careless, rushed statements and initiatives by governments and businesses that assumed 'business as usual' and relied on their leaders' past experience even where it was rapidly overtaken in the new situation. The pandemic and its aftermath called for leaders who could be open about the gaps in their plans, who could engage and learn from the front line and guide a population-wide change. Instead we had a plethora of plans that were discarded after weeks, denial and suppression of the voices of the front line, and failure to exploit a community willingness to volunteer and help out. Our universal experience of change across all organizations during and after the pandemic has made the challenges of leading

change more transparent. Leaders should feel pressure to be more effective in leading change and learn from successes and failures that are visible to a much wider audience and to participants who are more engaged.
We can see the failures of leadership that focuses on the individual leader at the top, in contrast to the vitality of 'positive deviants' in the form of front-line care workers and community organizers who worked out how to meet local needs despite the emergency and the absence of support.

Perhaps we should be motivated to learn how to address these challenges and how to be successful leaders of change because, quite simply, our society depends upon it. I think such abstract motivations belong to academics, advisers and authors. Wanting to learn about leading change is personal and compelling when:

1 *You have been plunged into leading change during and following the pandemic.*
   You might have thought that leadership was something the person at the top did while you got on with the real work – or that leadership requires buzzwords like *vision* and *charisma*. Then you discovered that you had to exercise leadership in your organizations – at work, at home (and work), in your family. Normal roles and boundaries dissolved: Who leads when working at home or home-schooling? Who leads remote worship? Who leads when the elderly in isolation were also the key volunteers in your charity? The list is endless.
2 *You were already engaged in organizational change in your workplace.*
   You probably already suspected that traditional formulaic models of leadership and change were unhelpful in your task and now, like the rest of the population, you know that formulae failed during the pandemic. Now you have shared and observed universal

8

experience of change and its consequences and choices
by leaders – and you are asking what is different
and what to learn to be more effective as a leader of
change, a consultant or a project manager in your
organization.

FOUR FUNDAMENTAL QUESTIONS OF LEADERSHIP

Successful leadership of change is not about taking lots of decisions; in fact jumping to issuing instructions will often be a mistake. It is about asking questions. Understanding is the first step towards finding actions that lead to successful change, including making mistakes, learning from others, adjusting direction and building belonging within the organization. Asking – and answering – four fundamental questions will equip you for the successful leadership of change:

- Why don't organizations always behave rationally?
  Explores the fundamental concepts of change in
  complex organizations and why rationally planned
  interventions produce unexpected results.

- What do *I* need to do – and what should I expect *others*
  to do?
  Walks through the roles and interactions of senior
  leaders, front-line leaders and management teams in
  delivering successful change in organizations.

- What do I do when we meet bumps in the road?
  Because there will inevitably be mistakes and switches
  of direction, we need to learn together and develop a
  common language of change.

- How do I build purpose, belonging and mental health?
  Successful change is not just about strategy and financial
  returns, it is about purpose, belonging and mental health
  in the organization.

'Why don't these organizations – and people – behave rationally?'

Becoming a leader for the first time is a moment of truth. You may be asking yourself 'what do I do next?' or thinking 'It's obvious what is needed – let me just explain and they will do it'. When I first led a team of people, I experienced both simultaneously!

The messy reality of workplace change is that 'effective leadership' is much less about strategic logic or positional authority or following a change formula than one would think from studying most leadership or change books. It is much more about the essential building blocks of satisfying the human needs for 'a good story' and for discovering the pattern or meaning in behaviours of these creatures that we call 'organizations'. In 35 years as a front-line manager, chief executive, chair, volunteer, Dad and consultant, I observed that every initiative is followed by anxieties and frustrations – whether from 'experienced leaders' or 'new leaders':

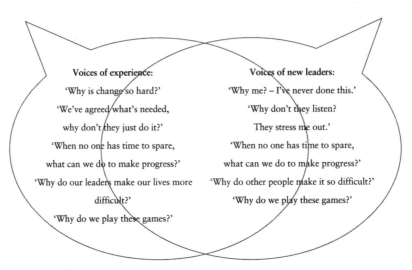

Voices of experience:

'Why is change so hard?'

'We've agreed what's needed, why don't they just do it?'

'When no one has time to spare, what can we do to make progress?'

'Why do our leaders make our lives more difficult?'

'Why do we play these games?'

Voices of new leaders:

'Why me? – I've never done this.'

'Why don't they listen? They stress me out.'

'When no one has time to spare, what can we do to make progress?'

'Why do other people make it so difficult?'

'Why do we play these games?'

Our understanding of how *individuals* make judgements and choices has improved enormously over the past 20 years, but our understanding of the behaviour of *organizations* has not improved at the same pace. Organizations exhibit patterns of behaviour that resist change because they overemphasize internal conversations at the expense of external reality. When abused, this internal focus results in the loss of trust in institutions – from banks through parliament and church through Google to Oxfam – evident during the past decade. Understanding repeated behaviour patterns in the real world of organizations and how to influence organizational behaviour is an essential – but neglected – leadership capability.

Organizational life is not simple and consequently it does not respond predictably to simple leadership or change prescriptions. Before turning to what senior leaders, front-line leaders and management teams *should* do, the complex realities of what leaders *actually* do, even in small organizations, are described in Sections 1 and 2:

1 *Change is an accident waiting to happen: complex systems and new language*
This section analyses how change often goes badly wrong despite the best of intentions, because different leaders within organizations are working to inherently different agendas. The most ironic example is how initiatives to improve safety end up causing unavoidable accidents, in part because the complexity of interventions are obscured by apparently simple language. Senior leaders are introducing change while front-line leaders remain focused on keeping day-to-day operations stable. The resulting instability leads to frustrated leaders, undelivered change and potentially serious failures.

2 *Games leaders play: over-relying on experience*
This section asks why leaders often make the wrong choices, even when these decisions are known to be wrong from the outset by the wider organization. Leaders struggle to meet performance expectations

while working with chronically fragmented time and some leaders consequently fall back on familiar routines or 'games' that worked for them in the past – but are unlikely to fit the new situation. The organization is experienced in managing leaders and promptly 'plays the game' but it can all end badly for everyone.

'What do I need to do – and what should I expect others to do?'

On becoming a leader – or realizing you have been a leader – among the most powerful questions to ask are: *What should I do because only I can do it – and what do I need to engage others in doing because only they bring the perspective and capacity? I cannot – and should not try to – do their job for them.*

Organizational reality is complex and leadership has to shape conflicting organizational behaviours while acting within the limitations on each leader's role in the organization. Leadership is exercised at all levels within organizations – by senior leaders, by front-line managers and by management teams. All these leaders lead fragmented, time-starved working lives and take most decisions based on patterns or 'games' that they learned within the organization.

Effective leadership varies by leadership role – different opportunities, constraints and approaches apply – but the common theme is one of challenge and struggle:

- Many *senior leaders* struggle with leading change in their organizations despite valid economic and strategic thinking, personal integrity and sound project management.
- *Front-line leaders* struggle to keep operations stable when new directions are issued from the centre, as they make essential trade-offs between change and continuity.
- *Management teams* struggle to allocate scarce resources against competing priorities.

12

The roles of senior leaders, front-line leaders and management teams differ – but each is essential for successful change – as laid out in Sections 3 to 5:

3 *Leaders' journeys: adapting to the real world*
This section focuses on the senior leader – the one or the few who are responsible for overall direction. Senior leaders cannot just tell their people what to do, they need to be 'on the journey' with their organization. Rather than providing the answers, leaders need to ask powerful questions, bringing experiences and ideas from the real world inside the organization, testing them and adapting them to fit the situation. When change demands a big adaptation in people's behaviour, then they need time and support to change at the pace they can – the 'adaptive' role of leaders. That role is balanced by the 'programmatic' role of leaders in providing clarity and structure so people can start the journey with confidence and initial successes, learning as they go.

4 *Finding the answers on the front line: leadership at all levels*
This section focuses on front-line leaders – the corps of people leading sales teams or depots or surgeries etc. Leadership at all levels in the organization is critical and front-line leaders need to be equipped and engaged early – to keep the show on the road day-to-day, making the unseen trade-offs, and to innovate. This crucial front-line leadership role, badged 'positive deviance', is the constant search for new ways to do the job better or differently for customers or users.

5 *Teams that work: getting the real work done*
This section focuses on the management teams in organizations – the groups of key people who get together and sort out conflicting priorities, needs and shortages across the organization. Management

teams do much of the hard work within organizations, prioritizing limited resources and embedding new ways of working. Investing in these groups of leaders pays off handsomely, but it is not about training or off-site events – it is about doing real work together, in cycles of action and reflection.

'What do I do when we meet bumps in the road?'

It will not be plain sailing. Judgements and direction will need to be adjusted or compensated for when results or events do not turn out as expected. Outright mistakes will be made quite often, leaders will fail in their roles every so often. Looking back over 35 years, I cringe to think of my mistakes as a leader.

It makes sense to think about learning from the experience of others and planning for likely adjustments and changes in direction. After all, it would be illogical in a complex environment to think that everything can be fixed from when you set out on your chosen road – or that everything can be accomplished in one project. Change will keep happening.

Some bumps in the road can be steered around by clarifying expectations from the start. People need to know where and when to expect adjustment and the next phase of the journey. Leaders need to be clear about:

Where this project or this particular road gets us.	*versus*	*The vision or the ultimate destination after all these twisty roads.*

Almost all successful leaders of change bring together the leaders across their organization to learn together. By doing real work together, they are clear about challenges ahead, recognize adjustments as they happen, learn from mistakes and share stories.

Language can be a huge barrier *to effective leadership*
Perhaps some insecure leaders and consultants use management buzzwords like 'transformation plans' and 'KPIs' and 'agile' as

a crutch, demonstrating their superior knowledge, avoiding acknowledging mistakes and controlling debate. The frequent overuse of military and sporting analogies is usually tangential, unhelpful, exclusionary – and often covers up a power play. I have tried to avoid jargon in this book, but I deliberately emphasize a few key phrases that are loaded with meaning – leadership at all levels, real work, the real world, storytelling.

Language can be a huge asset *to effective leadership*
Ordinary language might not suffice to concisely convey issues, direction or style. Sometimes you need effective, brief phrases that convey a lot of meaning to you and others who use them regularly. This does not mean we all need to become wordsmiths on a par with Churchill or Shakespeare. It is about sharing learning with the key people involved in change at all levels in the organization, allowing new stories and a common language to emerge.

Once again, there are stories of successful change that address the challenges of learning from experience and shifts in direction – described in Sections 6 and 7:

6 *Learning from leaders and mistakes: creating common language and a community of peers*
Failures of leadership are common but often concealed, and this is a missed opportunity to learn. Almost every successful organizational change builds in an element of group learning. Although content and style varies enormously, it reinforces that 'we are all on the journey together' and encourages the telling of new stories of change within the organization. Quite quickly, a common language of change is developed by the people that need it.

7 *Tacking through waves of change: ambition, pace and capability*
Leaders need to strike a balance between containing change to manageable chunks that people can cope

with and also recognizing that the ultimate goals
may be many years and phases into the future. Like
sailing a boat, you have to tack back and forward to
reach a destination that is upwind. Successful change
programmes take time and waves of activity that work
indirectly towards the ultimate goal, building the
organization's capabilities with each wave. At times,
your people need the reassurance of an immediate
project – at other times, they need the reassurance of a
worthy and ambitious ultimate goal.

'How do I build purpose, belonging and mental health?'

Positive pressure for change comes from ambition, expectations,
peers, real-world events or personal development – but when it
becomes stress then it damages individuals and organizations.
Change can alienate individuals, the culture of the organization
can frustrate desired change, and the working environment can
threaten both the organization and individuals' health. During the
peak of the pandemic and its aftermath, we have seen the power
of increased organizational purpose and belonging, the potential
of positive organizational cultures and the need to protect and
support the mental health of the population. Although radical,
these are not new priorities – we tell stories of leaders and
organizations already on this path in Sections 8 to 10:

8 *Thriving and belonging: individual psychology and*
   organizational purpose
   Human beings have amazing capacity for survival in
   adversity. But merely surviving is not good enough,
   especially following the contradictions we observed
   during and after the pandemic. For us to be truly 'all in
   this together', leaders need to be constantly nurturing
   organizational purpose and belonging. This investment
   does pay off, both in thriving human potential and also
   in thriving organizations because people are then willing

to 'go the extra mile', to put in the discretionary effort necessary for successful change.

9 *Culture that includes everyone: changing the powerful and invisible*
Cultural norms of 'this is how we do things here' can be a power play to frustrate change that challenges established leadership groups within an organization. To achieve positive change and organizational belonging, leaders need to understand the unintended impacts of organizational culture – then change unhelpful or outdated ingrained behaviours, create new peer groups and include previously excluded groups and cadres.

10 *Promoting mental health: the leadership opportunity*
Mental health rose up the public agenda over a decade and the pandemic and its broader effects demonstrated just how wide its impact is across the population and how we need leadership attention to protect and support mental health. Costs and damage can be averted: leaders can mitigate the epidemic of stress and ill health in the workplace that is both costly economically and slows momentum for change. There is also upside for us all and for leaders: as individuals and organizationally we can be more productive and more fulfilled.

All this? All at once?

It might be daunting, but the good news is that a powerful model of leading change is available – one that:

...was already emerging from organizations experiencing successful change in the old world.
...is reflecting the continuing consequences of the pandemic.
...will ensure organizational purpose and mental health.

Leaders can – and do – lead successful change in their organizations. Organizations and people thrive with change that builds human effectiveness over time and works with the complexity of organizational systems, rather than imposing a deceptive simplicity on change and leadership.

Stories from the real, messy world of leaders introduce each of the following sections with the authentic voices of leaders from the corporate, government, public services, education, church and voluntary sectors from the 1980s through the early stages of the COVID-19 pandemic to the time of writing.

PART TWO

'WHY DON'T THESE ORGANIZATIONS – AND PEOPLE – BEHAVE RATIONALLY?'

Organizational life is not simple and consequently it does not respond predictably to simple prescriptions of change. Before turning to what senior leaders, front-line leaders and management teams *should* do, the opening chapters of this book describe the complex realities of what leaders *actually* do, in both large and small organizations. Myths around the role of the individual leader are deeply embedded in our thinking about organizational life:

The decision-maker...	...who makes a rapid impact...	...and is in control
When I ask groups of managers or consultants 'What is the role of the leader?' or 'How does the leader lead?', the most frequent answers are 'Give direction' or 'Take the big decisions' including 'Appoint the key people'.	Popular management books read as if the heroic leader singlehandedly innovates, convinces others and creates new business in rapid succession. Stock market investors have expectations of improving earnings – delivered quarterly. Media coverage of business change focuses on the arrival of a single new leader and attributes short-term success or failure to their insights, drive and skills. Consultants emphasize the importance of 'quick wins'.	Leaders don't just give direction and leave the organization to it. They secure buy-in and set up structures, processes and incentives to drive the organization in the given direction.
So why does this clear role not result in the organization following the given direction in so many cases? Outright sabotage seems unlikely... Serious managers at different levels are making choices (consciously or unconsciously) to adjust or compromise or only pay lip service to senior leaders' direction.	So why do organizational insiders (and serious research) almost always tell a different story? Intuitively, it is likely that 'transforming' organizations takes time.	But this frequently does not deliver the desired results. Especially when organizations stray into abuse of their power, we see regulators, media and senior leaders being charged with incompetence – 'How could you not have known what your organization was doing?' Hindsight bias tends towards an individualistic approach to cause-and-effect investigations, rather than a systemic approach.
We need to understand how and why leaders at different levels of the organization choose to make trade-offs in how they implement a given direction.	We need to understand how leaders actually shape change that delivers short and long term.	We need to understand what is really going on within organizations that don't deliver or that behave dysfunctionally despite all the modern control apparatus.

The *realities* of organizations are a web of complex relationships, implicit deals, roles, common behaviours and influencers. The organization and the relationships among its members are much more than a simple economic or contractual relationship and go well beyond what can be measured and assessed in a control mechanism that focuses on the individual. Organizations are more than the sum of the individuals who make them up. Perhaps it is the individualistic success story of senior leaders that predisposes many to read across from an individualistic model of change to how an organization actually behaves. And therefore they are *misled* as to how the organization will react.

Organizations are influential, they behave differently from the individuals who make up the organization – and we have underinvested in understanding them: 'All important social processes either have their origin in formal organizations or are strongly mediated by them.'[4] A major reason for failed change programmes is that leaders do not understand how to influence their organizations effectively and do not understand the limits to traditional power. The realities of organizational life are set out in the following sections:

1 **Change is an accident waiting to happen: complex systems and new language**
Organizations are complex systems and working in complex systems means tensions between change and continuity and between front-line management and the centre. Senior leaders and front-line leaders are simultaneously exercising valid leadership roles, but they are often inevitably in conflict. This conflict leads to unavoidable or 'normal' accidents when leaders do not understand the reality and therefore miss the opportunities for sustainable change.

2 **Games leaders play: over-relying on experience**
Leaders are time-bereft and their attention is fragmented, while pressure for short-term results is intense. As a result of this stress, some tend to fall back

on heuristics that worked for them in the past. This can go badly wrong when they face an unfamiliar context and the heuristic is inappropriate. Major change in organizations is unfamiliar almost by definition and leaders have undue confidence in their experience. They end up 'playing games' and their organizations respond in kind and, at times, dysfunctionally.

* * *

These first two sections set out the fundamental concepts of:

- Complexity and unforeseeable consequences of change initiatives.
- The three categories of leaders – senior leaders, front-line leaders, management teams – who need to work together to deliver successful change.
- The cognitive traps – optimism bias and the planning fallacy – that result from leaders' over-reliance on past experience when under pressure for results and bereft of time.
- Games played by leaders and organizations – what gets measured gets gamed.
- The impact of the language we use, the missed opportunities to bring in the real world and the need for leadership at all levels.

1

CHANGE IS AN ACCIDENT WAITING TO HAPPEN: COMPLEX SYSTEMS AND NEW LANGUAGE

STORIES OF ACCIDENTS WAITING TO HAPPEN – PEOPLE MAKE MISTAKES IN NEW SITUATIONS AND ACCIDENTS KEEP FINDING NEW WAYS TO HAPPEN

'Change is an accident waiting to happen' – exaggeration, surely? Let's test by looking at some accidents. Statistics tell us that fishing is the most dangerous occupation and that scaffolding is the technology most often implicated in accidents. However, for truly spectacular accidents, you have to turn to the oil industry – which has generated its share of headlines, condemnation and search for the guilty parties. Some of the worst accidents come readily to mind:

- Leaks from tankers and subsequent ocean pollution, from the *Torrey Canyon* in 1967 through the *Exxon Valdez* in 1989 to the *Braer* in 1993.
- Explosions and deaths at every stage – during project development at Deepwater Horizon in the Gulf of Mexico in 2010, during production at Piper Alpha in the North Sea in 1988 and during refining at Texas City in the United States in 2005.

Even the threat of possible environmental damage roused public anger and boycotts when, in 1995, Shell considered disposal of the North Sea Brent Spar installation in line with the then best scientific advice.

By the early 1980s, when I was working for Shell, safety was top-of-mind for all of us – safe practices codified and mandated, 'near misses' reviewed, accident protocols enforced. The industry policy was that 'accidents shouldn't happen' – but they did:

The ridiculous incident of the one-legged man falling off a ladder

Painting was not done by oil company staff – it was contracted out to a painting firm, who were required to follow the same safety standards as company employees. Our team was stunned when we heard that a painting firm had sent a one-legged man up a high ladder to paint a tank – and he had, unsurprisingly, fallen off. Happily, he suffered only minor grazes. Was it the company's fault for not checking up – or was it the contractor's fault? In future, we checked.

The serious leakage of 1 million litres of jet fuel into a harbour

The jet fuel storage tanks at the Shell depot in Auckland city centre were decades old and not fitted with the latest measuring devices because a brand-new high-tech industry depot was being built on the edge of the city. Instead of being continuously electronically monitored, they were 'dipped' daily and the stock checked against deliveries into the tanks by ship and deliveries out of the tanks by road tanker. The system was inherently inaccurate and when it showed a loss of 10,000 litres one day, the supervisor dismissed it as a measurement error, given there was no visible leak. The next day the dip showed a loss of 200,000 litres and management reacted immediately by transferring the remaining fuel to ships and other tanks. This incident is documented in safety reports from the time, it was a typical accident and current Shell safety reporting shows that, over the last decade, there is a steady incidence of accidents in the industry at around 1 accident per million hours worked – even following 30 years of improved practice, investment, training and tighter regulation.[5]

Investigation found that a hole had developed in the floor of the tank due to an engineer using the wrong steel to repair a fault a year earlier. As a result, the tank had slowly leaked over 1 million litres over months and it had only been noticed when the leak developed into a large enough hole for losses to be apparent. Head Office managers and international investigators turned up to ask why front-line managers had made the initial wrong judgement.

I look at an old leather boot with a wooden sole that sits on a shelf in my office. It is about 100 years old, one of a pair issued as safety footwear when Shell's Auckland depot opened. Shell has since sold its refining and marketing businesses and left the New Zealand market.

As the little plaque on the heel says, it was a farewell gift from my staff to remind me of my time as their manager, of what I learned, of them and of safety. But the learning hadn't finished.

Throughout my career, I looked closely at accidents that my employers and clients endured, asking 'Why do accidents keep happening in well-run organizations?'

Accidents cluster around non-routine tasks

An operator doing annual maintenance was dismantling equipment that was out of service and had been isolated, but he forgot that it was held in position by a powerful spring and he suffered serious facial injuries when the equipment moved unexpectedly. How could we prevent this recurring? A new protocol and additional supervision was added.

Accidents are frequently associated with downtime or maintenance, when people are not performing their typical daily operating tasks – interestingly, the fire at Notre Dame in 2019 also happened during renovations. Even routine tasks in a new situation can present an opportunity for an accident.

WHO'S TO BLAME – HUMAN ERROR OR SYSTEM FAILURE?

Now, at this point you may be concluding:

Either I was simply an unlucky/incompetent manager. It is hard to convey the frustration for oil industry managers – including me at that time – everyone was committed to 'zero accidents', but they kept happening.

Or you may be thinking that this is just how it is – daily operations are a challenge and accidents just happen. Protocols and checks depend on people getting it right every time, but they won't. The best that can be done is to engineer out as many potential problems as possible, so we don't rely on unreliable humans.

Or you may conclude in favour of more regulation to control and safeguard activity in what is obviously an industry dealing with inherently dangerous products.

The default thinking tends to be all about who is to blame. In the heat of a crisis following an accident, the human tendency is to rush to allocate fault rather than stand back and ask: what was really happening here? And crucially: why did an inherently dangerous operation run *without* accidents for long periods – what did that safe operation rely upon and why did that change? Rather than thinking about blame, we should focus on what keeps us *more* or *less* safe.

Day-to-day operational judgements keep complex systems going

It is the job of front-line leaders to make the daily trade-offs to keep the complex system of oil production and distribution happening in a safe and profitable operation. They had to decide routes for road tankers to fill stations and customers, decide when and how to shut tanks and tankers and depots for repairs and cleaning, choose materials and contractors to conduct repairs, train new staff etc. It was all largely invisible to the senior leaders of the companies, but the system relied on these hundreds of front-line leadership decisions.[6]

Operational judgements are not the job of senior leaders

Managing operations to minimize safety incidents (as well as satisfy customers and turn a profit) was a daily or hourly task for front-line managers – but it wasn't one that senior leaders engaged in until there was a problem. Similarly distant from the day-to-day, BP's Group Chief Executive of Refining and Marketing, John Manzoni, responded to the Texas City refinery deaths in 2005 with: 'I wasn't aware of the problems before the explosion occurred.'[7] Getting involved in detailed operational issues unnecessarily is also a problem, as we saw during the pandemic when ministers talked up their efforts to negotiate protective equipment from Turkey, which arrived late and promptly failed quality/safety checks.[8] What *is* the job of senior leaders is to understand how their system relies on front-line leadership and to build that into their thinking about change in the organization.

Unfamiliar operations increase the probability of accidents

Front-line managers will tell you that the safest operations are those that are repeated again and again or when the process is kept running. The riskiest moments for accidents or breakages are when the process is stopped or being repaired or improved or restarted. During operations in Afghanistan, Royal Air Force maintenance personnel learned to run their Merlin helicopter engines continuously, rather than shutting down as soon as flights ended – the engines suffered fewer breakdowns. Unfamiliar actions – including new people appointments or improvements that change the process – will always increase the risk of unforeseeable untoward events.

Illustration: Protect the NHS – central intervention during the COVID-19 pandemic with unforeseen consequences

As the pandemic began to take a grip in the UK during March 2020, the NHS feared that its acute hospital beds would be overwhelmed by the sheer number of patients, as had been seen in Italy. In response, spare capacity was created. First, the military were brought in to build the Nightingale temporary hospitals. The second structural solution was an instruction to clear all dischargeable elderly patients to care homes immediately. The clearing of capacity was important in ensuring the NHS was not overwhelmed at the peak of infections during April and the Nightingale capacity was almost unused. Unfortunately, in the absence of testing capacity for the 25,000 vulnerable and untested patients discharged into care homes, the structural solution seeded the virus into many of these facilities, where the majority of deaths then occurred.[9]

Don't do anything to obscure the front line's view of the system

By the 1980s, the oil industry was on the second or third generation of safety management – and today they are on the ninth or tenth. But there had been earlier blind alleys – most notoriously the introduction of safety officers. It might seem an obvious response to a safety problem to appoint someone to focus on safety, but it was a serious psychological and system error. The psychological error was that, implicitly, safety was 'their problem' as safety officer – when it needed to be 'everyone's problem'. The system error was that it added a layer of opacity to the system and gave a false certainty to the organization.

Hindsight bias and the 'blame game'

When an accident happens, and especially when it attracts attention, the senior leaders engage and typically ask 'How did this happen?' and some variant of the blame game is inescapably played out. Of course, mistakes happen and sometimes an individual was at fault, but more typically there was a system failure that caused an accident – for example, a lack of training or continuing use of old facilities without modern monitoring kit while awaiting new facilities coming on-stream.

Psychology explains that, once we know the outcome, we are biased to believe that the chain of events was foreseeable and preventable, rather than a reasonable trade-off in the circumstances as they actually were when the decision was made. Hindsight bias was frequently evident during the immediate aftermath of the pandemic as ministers' and officials' decisions were criticized for failures in stockpiling equipment and the prioritization of hospitals over care homes. We understand the past less well than we believe because we assess the quality of decision-making by whether the outcome was good or bad, not by whether the process was sound and the beliefs reasonable when the decision was made.[10] And the worse the outcome, the greater the hindsight bias we suffer, as evident with 9/11 in New York when there were 'faint signals' of an imminent attack on the United States[11], the Grenfell Tower fire in London in which 71 died in June 2017 after long delays in implementing improvements following an earlier London tower block fire, the many sad cases of victims of complex hospital systems[12] and the pandemic that cost over 500,000 lives globally in the first six months of 2020 alone.[13]

It turns out that the reality of 'managing to avoid accidents' has much to say about all change in organizations. When change in complex systems goes wrong, the dynamics are similar to accidents – i.e., the system is stable until an external intervention that *both* destabilizes the system *and* creates opacity that makes it harder for front-line managers to correct and re-stabilize the system. Finally, with the benefit of hindsight, it appears obvious how the instability should have been planned for and corrected. Change *is* an accident waiting to happen and, as we are about to explore, one that is obscured by the language we use.

MANAGEMENT-SPEAK LOADS FALSE CERTAINTY INTO ORGANIZATIONAL LIFE

The dynamics of complex systems have been concealed or obfuscated through careless use of language when discussing major change projects. This is where corporate jargon and buzzwords, usually associated with the latest management fad, do most harm – they give false certainty, reduce honest discussion of trade-offs and minimize the role of front-line management in keeping the overall system stable.

'Management-speak' is a butt of media and water-cooler humour[14] and is usually disparaged as an attempt to obfuscate or to lend pseudo-scientific credibility to banalities, common sense or the latest fad.[15] You know when you are dealing with a management fad when its advocates assert that 'this changes everything', when it is not enough that the new idea is 'correct', but that everything that went before has to be 'wrong' – and usually accompanied by an unhelpful military or sporting analogy.[16] Like many, I have my personal list of fads and management buzzwords that raise my hackles and that I never choose to use – notably 'benchmarking' and 'culture change' – because they are shorthand for creating false precision and excuses for avoiding difficult judgements. However, the game of spotting amusing buzzwords is usually just that, a trivial game. Much deeper rooted and more serious, there is a language challenge in leadership and management – our loading of false certainty into our inherently subjective debates, through our preference for terms that in common parlance connote tangibility and tractability and normality. Prime examples are the words 'project', 'plan' and 'team'. 'Plan' comes up in the next section and 'team' in Section 5.

So let's start with a key management buzzword: 'project' – a word that in ordinary language connotes:

- A planned, managed approach with a clear start and a clear end.
- Using mainly technical rather than judgemental skills, with dedicated resources put in and outcomes delivered.

The implication of this ordinary language is that the failure to deliver a project simply means a lack of competence – and so someone should be held accountable. A whole philosophy and code of practice, training and accreditation institutes exist to promote 'delivering projects to time and budget' and 'project controls'. The true experts in project leadership know the limitations of project thinking and the need to closely manage the scoping, resources and engagement of employees and stakeholders – and they recognize that much of the value embedded in any project is actually the real options it creates for next-phase value creation.[17] The potential for project delays, cost overruns and undelivered benefits – 'accidents' – increase when senior leaders over-rely on opaque project reporting rather than testing the front-line progress.

'Projects' have become the typical vehicle for introducing change in organizations, with vaunted early examples having lodged deep in our conscious leadership models, like the Manhattan Project 1942–45 that built the first nuclear weapons, dropped on Japan, and the Project Apollo 1961–72 that landed men on the moon. During the 50th anniversary celebrations of Apollo 11, many commented 'If we can do that, why can't we adopt the same approach to do...' It is rarely pointed out that, even after the billions of expenditure and comprehensive planning, most Apollo flights had more than 150 technical failures per flight; Apollo 1's crew died in a fire, while Apollo 13's crew nearly died in space – and two space shuttles with their crews never returned.[18]

The danger does not lie in projects and their engineering, it lies in our false optimism when we discuss them, our tendency to equate engineering language with precision and reliability, and the difficulty of translating a winning approach from one project to the next one. Problems can begin when organizations create a project as a default response when leaders want to demonstrate serious commitment and taking charge of a problem:

'Let's set up a dedicated project to solve the problem – ideally with a foolproof technical solution – then roll it out. It's a logical response and demonstrates that we are on top of this.'

It's not bad as a media message or a short-term holding position, but there are two major problems with applying the project mindset to leading change. First, leading change in organizations is fundamentally about people and treating people as if they behave like machines or can be engineered into predictable behaviour is wildly inappropriate. Second, it turns out that the project mindset doesn't actually work well for large-scale engineering either.

COMPLEX SYSTEMS ARE INHERENTLY UNSTABLE – WE CAN'T ENGINEER OUT THE HUMAN BEING

While it's sad that such disasters have occurred in the first place, we fortunately have great research and insights into complex engineering projects that went wrong – plane crashes, nuclear power station meltdowns, dam collapses, shipping collisions etc.[19] It turns out that engineering-led projects can be 'accidents waiting to happen' just as much as change-led projects. In fact, they acquired their own academic term – 'normal accidents'.[20]

The Second World War stimulated new thinking that grew into the fields now known as 'operations research' or 'decision analysis' or 'management science'. The US Department of Defense developed techniques such as linear programming, decision trees and simulation to take complex logistics decisions, to develop new equipment and to allocate scarce resources across competing needs.[21] One example of early scientific management was the analysis of human error and plane crashes:

- Rapidly growing the number of military pilots was a huge wartime programme with careful selection and training of pilots in the US, UK and Canada. Despite this training, mistakes by trained pilots during active operations led to many allied aircraft being lost due to accidents. For example, it is estimated that 30 per cent of Royal Air Force aircraft losses during the Battle of Britain were due to 'pilot error' including failures during take-off, landing and formation flying. Research showed that the Royal Canadian Air Force trained its pilots for much longer and suffered much less attrition – the Royal Air Force refused to learn from their experience.
- Similar examples in the US Air Force included Boeing B-17 'Flying Fortress' bomber pilots who repeatedly caused their aircraft to crash on landing after long raids by mistakenly retracting the undercarriage when they had intended to adjust the flaps after touchdown.

  The analysis pointed out that the two handles of the undercarriage and flap up/down controls in the B-17 aircraft were very similar; moreover, they were next to one another in the crowded cockpit – and tired pilots could easily err in selecting the correct one. Noticing that other aircraft did not have the same cockpit layout and did not suffer the same systemic accidents, the engineers' prescription was to improve the cockpit design to eliminate this 'human error'.

  Improving the cockpit design reduced the frequency of that specific pilot mistake in future aircraft.

33

Across industries, the goal of safety engineering became to 'design out' the possibility of human error, to create safe systems, either through automated machines, safety valves etc. or through IT systems that prescribed, channelled or facilitated human actions.[22] The engineering or machine model was the answer – and for decades accident reports focused on creating 'fail-safe' systems and minimizing the human role.

Debriefing some of the research and literature on accidents in complex systems

BEHIND HUMAN ERROR by Woods, Dekker, Cook, Johannesen and Sarter, 2nd edition (2010, Ashgate)

Complex systems have a 'sharp end' of operators interacting with the business process, who have to adapt to a 'blunt end' of regulators, policymakers, leaders and HQ who set resources, constraints, goals and incentives. The adaptations are typically not transparent and create systemic vulnerabilities deep inside the organization.

Research, notably into the Three Mile Island nuclear accident in 1979 and the Challenger and Columbia space shuttle accidents in 1986 and 2003, led to the emergence of Normal Accident Theory:[23] 'Eliminating (errors) becomes the target of more rigid rules, tighter monitoring of other people, more automation and computer technology all to standardize practices ... Ironically, such efforts have unintended consequences that make systems more brittle and hide the sources of resilience that make systems work despite complications, gaps, bottlenecks, goal conflicts, and complexity.'[24] Operational, system and engineering barriers actually add complexity and increase opacity so that, when even small things start going wrong, it becomes exceptionally difficult to get off an accelerating path to system breakdown.[25]

The source of accidents are frequently the policy changes by leaders that create dilemmas for the sharp end, through goal conflicts or losing attention or oversimplification or

---

> design-induced error. Instead, leaders should be looking to
> reduce systemic vulnerabilities, tame complexity and avoid
> creating new paths to failure. Potential failures cannot be
> designed out – complexity means many 'normal accidents' are
> possible and are likely to happen eventually.

The ugly problem with the engineering model was that, despite using
technology or IT to 'eliminate' potential human error, accidents
kept happening. As fast as old opportunities to make mistakes
were plugged, new opportunities emerged – if humans were not
deliberately risk-seeking, what was going on? What was happening
was that the systems were becoming more complex, less transparent
and less intuitive, with the result that the humans operating them
had to learn to cope with increasingly complex interfaces – and
take the blame when things go wrong. Even in industries subject
to intense scrutiny and regulation, such as nuclear and defence, the
same blind spots have arisen in the US, Soviet Union, UK and Japan:

- The Three Mile Island nuclear accident in Pennsylvania
  in 1979 came down to operators ignoring and covering
  up the crucial warning indicator because they believed it
  was the indicator that was malfunctioning, not the plant.
  Similarly, the Chernobyl nuclear accident in 1986 was
  due to reckless behaviour by the management (who were
  prosecuted) – but only led to a catastrophic explosion
  due to a fundamental flaw in the reactor design that had
  been covered up.[26] The nuclear industry has a history of
  over-reliance on technology and blame as a response –
  in Japan, the Fukushima accident in 2011 relied on
  out-of-date seismic analysis that led to inadequate safety
  margins at the plant and the industry had suffered
  scandals over falsified safety data, while the UK had also
  simply covered up the scale of the Windscale fire in 1957.
- The destroyer USS *John S. McCain* collided with the
  freighter *Alnic MC* off Japan on 21 August 2017, killing
  10 crew. The officers and helmsmen gave orders during

a three-minute period that they thought would avoid the collision, but a new computerized helm and propulsion control system did not behave as they expected and in fact steered the ship into the collision. The old electro-mechanical system of 'mainly knobs and dials' had been replaced by a new, touchscreen-based system with a graphical user interface 'like a video game without instructions'. The new system had five modes of operation and allowed the Navy to reduce costs by allowing one fewer person to stand watch. After the accident it was discovered that some modes of operation were undocumented, that training was inadequate and that some parts were non-compliant.[27] The US Navy subsequently issued warnings and then replaced the new helm system with an older system – but proceeded to court-martial the officers for negligence in applying a system they did not understand.

It turns out that trying to engineer out the human being runs up against the risks that are bound to be present when making any change in complex systems – the implementation challenge is underestimated, operators simplify their choices in order to cope with routine pressures, people defer to their leaders, who make rushed choices and over-rely on past practice.[28] Pressure to 'just do it' affects even trained professionals who should know better: the airline industry identified a class of plane crashes caused by crew failing to speak up when they saw their captain making an obviously dangerous mistake – deferring to their superior's rank and assuming he knew better – with fatal consequences.[29]

MORE SOPHISTICATED APPLICATION OF TECHNOLOGY WILL INCREASE 'NORMAL ACCIDENTS'

The consequences of engineering project failures are so catastrophic, costly and high-profile that huge effort has gone into understanding why they happened and how to prevent them. Less visible, but much more part of life in organizations, are the 'accidents' caused by the bumpy transitions to new IT systems and the difficult mating of traditional large-scale IT with modern agile developments.

For most organizations, 'engineering out risk' means IT solutions rather than heavy machinery. Mention 'big IT project' and many managers roll their eyes, doubtless thinking of long-delayed over-budget new IT projects (e.g. the major NHS-wide IT systems of 2000–2010) or the disruption as new systems transition into operation (e.g. TSB's migration from its old Lloyds IT backbone to a new system developed by its new parent, Sabadell, in 2018).

Illustration: Phoenix – the payroll system for public service employees in Canada[30]

In 2011, the Canadian government decided to use customized, off-the-shelf software and consolidate pay centres for all public service employees. The new technology and centralized system would allow the government to lay off hundreds of compensation advisors across Canada and eventually save about C$700 million. In order to keep project costs within budget, Phoenix was de-scoped and some losses of capability (such as inability to cope with retrospective pay changes, the norm in public service) resulted in wide-scale implementation problems. When launched in 2016, the technology did not work as expected, with tens of thousands of public servants underpaid, overpaid or not paid at all – with many distressing cases, including repossessed houses when public service employees could not pay their mortgages. In the end, more compensation advisors and satellite pay centres had to be established. An independent report[31] found that a lack of proper definition, oversight and accountability plagued the project from the start. While there were people inside government who had concerns about the unfolding Phoenix process over the years, there was a fear to communicate those concerns. It notes the lessons have not yet been learned, but it will be critical for the Canadian government to apply the lessons in future transformations.

In addition to failed big-IT projects, operator ignorance or misunderstanding or refusal to use new IT capability or outright misuse has led directly to accidents. The latest example is the Lion Air Boeing 737 Max 8 crash in October 2018, where initial investigations have identified the potential cause as being the new MCAS (manoeuvring characteristics augmentation system) that is designed to prevent stalling – and resists pilots' commands even if they are flying manually. The MCAS issues are being lost in debate over whether the FAA and Boeing were at fault in the development process – the most important issue is that the change in a complex system rendered the experience of the front line ineffective. That is the lesson for leaders of organizational change. Like many users of new software, pilots are wondering what other default settings will drive unintended results. Analysis suggests 'The systems designed to make flying safer are confusing pilots ... automation is eroding the old-fashioned skills that pilots used to keep planes in the air', with the most notorious incident being the loss of Air France 447 off Brazil in 2009 due to a brief computer malfunction that misled the pilots, who failed to understand that their Airbus was in a stall.[32]

The implementation of increasingly complex IT-enabled systems creates new error modes, especially as operators typically ignore the new capabilities to focus on the old information that they were used to getting. An extensive research base in medical practice shows that doctors tend to ignore most of the wider range of information offered by new IT systems.[33] They often revert to the narrower range of data provided by the predecessor system because of familiarity – or they work to a few heuristics as to likely diagnoses/treatments and limit their use of the technology to confirming those assumptions. Doctors are highly intelligent and highly trained; this is a normal human response to technology.

The fourth industrial revolution includes the widespread adoption of automation (driverless vehicles, drones, artificial intelligence, algorithms, cognitive tools for decision-makers) and this will change the operating environment for leaders again. Front-line leaders will need to be even more responsive and understand all the factors driving the automated responses, correcting for unforeseen implications and conflicts of goals. Senior leaders will need to understand the limitations of automation and resist any temptation to under-invest in skilled and insightful front-line leadership. Both senior leaders and front-line leaders need to make informed trade-offs of stability versus change, because the lesson of the last 50 years of large-scale IT investment is that unforeseeable incidents actually increase with greater complexity and opacity.[34]

IF ACCIDENTS ARE 'NORMAL', THEN PREPARE FOR THEM TO HAPPEN

Despite its prevalence in every corner of organizations, it turns out that 'project language' with its implication of machine-like predictability is inadequate to describe the challenges of leading major technical projects such as aircraft operations, far less the behavioural challenge inherent in change in organizations. 'Project' distances us from the realities of organizations where front-line management is continually making trade-offs by balancing change and continuity to keep operations stable. Conventional 'change management' language of 'change tools' and roles such as 'head of change' and strategies built around 'seven-step programmes' falsely suggest that change is a predictable, defined task.

Instead, leaders need to assume accidents *will* happen: leaders at all levels need to explore the vulnerabilities of their organization – whether in customer service, production, systems or key people. The philosophy has to be to ensure there is capacity and capability to remedy potential incidents, rather than trying to eliminate all risk. When incidents occur, you should escalate quickly and without recrimination, while also demonstrating and rewarding candour. Defensiveness is never a good strategy – as we observed during the Number 10 daily briefings during the height of the pandemic,[35] and also with the slow and painful extraction of the truth about Post Office Horizon new technology – i.e., that an impenetrable new IT system caused multiple post office owner-operators to be wrongly convicted of theft and deprived of livelihoods.[36]

Because change potentially destabilizes complex systems and because technology makes risks opaque, leaders need to learn to ask more powerful questions rather than jumping to the default 'human error' answer:

Don't ask:
What caused the failure?

Do ask:
What kept the system stable for so long when it was clearly prone to failure?

Don't ask:
What went wrong?

Do ask:
What changed to catalyse the failure?

Don't ask:
What did the front-line operator do or omit to do?

Do ask:
What is the balance of central versus front-line action required to keep the system stable?

Don't ask:
Why was the strategy not being implemented?

Do ask:
How can this system change without inevitable failure?

The realities of organizations going through change are that things inevitably go wrong in unforeseeable ways. We do not help ourselves by (mis)using language that gives the impression of greater certainty – or by asking the wrong questions and pursuing human error when change goes awry.

THREE CATEGORIES OF LEADERS THAT NEED TO WORK TOGETHER FOR SUCCESSFUL CHANGE

Research into 'how complex systems fail' summarized succinctly that 'change introduces new forms of failure'.[37] We will only learn how to exercise effective leadership of change if we are clear on the fundamentals of how organizations behave as complex systems:

1 *Complex systems are inherently unstable and will tend to fail unless continually corrected.*
2 *Front-line management are pivotal to making the continual adjustments necessary to keep complex systems stable.*

3 *Central interventions into complex systems, however well-intentioned, risk destabilizing complex systems.*

Successful delivery of change is, therefore, a task for three categories of leaders, who need to be aligned in leading change – no single leader or single category can make it happen alone:

Senior leaders	The person(s) at the top of the organization, providing overall direction and strategic justification.
Front-line leaders	The managers making the daily trade-offs to keep the operation stable – e.g: • In oil companies: refinery managers, regional managers and business unit managers. • In hospitals: the operating officers who allocate available beds. • In professional services: the partners dealing with clients (complicated by them also being owners and electing senior leaders). • In power companies: power station managers and customer/service managers. • In care homes, the nurse on shift who sets standards for safety and care. • In technology firms: website and marketing managers.
Management teams	The groups of peers who make organizations work as entities, allocate scarce resources and set priorities across organizational units.

Organizations need their senior leaders to design changes with the front line in a complementary system, their front-line leaders to focus on keeping the organization stable, and their management teams to test for and invest in system resilience.

Senior leaders need to do more than just ask what the unintended consequences or second-order implications are of

41

their strategies, appointments and decisions. They also need to recognize that the same strategies can, over time, build up to create non-transparent inherent risks in the organization – often visible only after the event as goal conflicts between 'smooth and safe operations' and 'do more with less'. Pressure 'from the top' to improve system outputs will place front-line management in the position where they have to risk increased occurrences of system failure. Similarly, cost reduction programmes focusing on resources at the front line reduce the focus on system stability or the margin available for system correction. Another typical intervention, increasing IT investment and automation of front-line management, risks opacity of system risk and lack of focus on system stability.[38]

Front-line leaders make the trade-offs that maintain organizational stability, but they can often turn a blip into a crisis unknowingly. Design your strategy with and for front-line leaders in order to design change that complements the system and runs no knowable risks. Organizations need to understand what the front line rely upon and provide some reserve to deploy in crisis. One of the reasons that there was a crisis over protective equipment during the 2020 pandemic was that front-line managers reacted to central shortages by trying to create a protective reserve and the entire system promptly collapsed.

Management teams do the hard work of prioritization and allocation of resources to keep the whole organization in balance between its strategy and its capabilities. Their role is to ensure that resilience, training, spare capacity and technology are lined up to support senior leaders' aspirations and the front line's realities.

It is evident from these stories of leading change that leaders at all levels in an organization need to evolve a different language and a different way of thinking about change:

Senior leaders saying...	*This is where we need to go – how do we get there without crashing the system?*
	What are the known unknowns here? How do we test what we believe?
Front-line leaders saying...	*What keeps the operation stable is... Here's how we can bring this in without risking day-to-day operations.*
	Our contingency and resilience plans are...
Management teams saying...	*How do we reduce system vulnerability? How do we enable people to address issues? How do we learn from unexpected events?*
	How do we build scarce capabilities and reinforce key processes?

Summary   *Organizations are complex systems that depend upon day-to-day operational judgements and interventions to keep the system stable, safe and routinely productive for customers, suppliers, staff, regulators. Accidents are much more likely to happen when unfamiliar interventions – change – are introduced to a stable system. Even changes designed to make day-to-day operations safer can increase the probability of unforeseen consequences, if they make the linkages more obscure between front-line action and results. Technology-driven change is prone to this kind of 'normal accident'.*

Three categories of leaders need to work together to enable successful change within the complex system of the organization:

- *Senior leaders set context and direction.*
- *Front-line leaders make daily trade-offs to keep the operation functioning.*
- *Management teams allocate resources and prioritize.*

When unforeseen accidents happen or change fails to deliver the expected results, the unavoidable reaction is to ask who is to blame. Hindsight bias fools us into believing accidents are foreseeable and therefore we attribute blame to 'human error' instead of system failure. Rather than asking why the system failed, we should ask what kept it running successfully and what changed to cause the failure.

The language that leaders use – for example, 'project' or 'plan' – deceives us into assuming greater certainty than exists in the complex systems of organizations. To manage the inherent uncertainty, leaders fall back upon their experience – but change makes that experience unreliable.

Action

Expect unforeseeable consequences of change.

Recognize the key roles in leading change for front-line management as well as senior leaders and management teams:

- *Design change with and for front-line leadership. Understand the vulnerabilities of day-to-day operations.*
- *Plan for unforeseeable accidents, especially with technology-enabled change. Build organizational stability and capabilities.*
- *Ask the right questions to get the right actions, rather than giving answers that (falsely) transmit certainty in a complex system.*

2

GAMES LEADERS PLAY: OVER-RELYING ON EXPERIENCE

STORIES OF ORGANIZATIONAL GAMES – PLAY THE GAME, BUT NEVER ADMIT THAT IT IS A GAME

Like most long-established industrial companies, Shell has pursued cost reduction through every imaginable technique over the decades – from annual budget reductions to periodic campaigns or new technologies or out-sourcing. Recently, a senior Shell leader described the latest approach they are now taking and its promising results so far[39]. So when, back in 1983, Shell's senior leaders – the Committee of Managing Directors – decided to systematically reduce the cost of its central offices, then it was unsurprising that many Shell managers treated it as just another change initiative that they had to survive.

The Shell Group was highly decentralized and operations were run through operating companies in almost every country in the world, while central corporate services were provided through service companies based in London and The Hague. The central services included an enormous range of activities, including the R&D programme, technical advice for the operating companies on everything from production to distribution, commercial strategies, branding and administrative functions such as finance and legal. The cost base was huge; it was funded (with considerable complaining) by the operating companies and they, as well as Shell's senior leaders, wanted change – downwards.

The senior leaders had to decide the approach to make the cost reductions happen. Should they:

- Cut the budgets and leave it to management down the line to find the savings?
- *Or* set up a project team with authority to find the savings?
- *Or* set targets for different services depending on how the top leadership – and the operating companies – valued the services provided?

All options had upsides and downsides and all had to overcome the natural resistance within central offices to shrinking their resources and, with it, their influence.

Shell's senior leaders chose to retain a consulting firm, supported by a Shell project team, and adopted a methodology still in use today (but then quite new) called Overhead Value Analysis (OVA).[40] The process balances all the options of setting targets, engaging line management and using operating company input. Each organizational unit would catalogue all its activities and analyse their cost, then the unit management would propose ideas to change or reduce activities in order to meet a 40 per cent cost-reduction 'ambition'. The ideas would be tested with relevant operating companies and other users of services, then finally these ideas would be adopted or changed or rejected by a panel of senior managers to deliver a 25 per cent actual cost reduction. But it is vulnerable to corporate game-playing...

I observed a typical response to OVA in Shell and later in many companies that also used the OVA methodology or its many variants. Having been instructed in the methodology, many managers in these companies would state baldly: 'Here is how we shall present our cost-saving ideas to ensure we do not end up losing any of our resources.' In other words: A clear message as to how managers were to play the game to outwardly comply but, in reality, to resist and survive. Typical tactics included carefully defining and bundling up the unit's activities in order to make it difficult to tease out activities that were vulnerable. Then a mix of ideas was put forward – there were a few sacrificial lambs offered up to be cut, but most of the activity reductions were set up to be unacceptable, usually because they diminished the quality or frequency of inputs that senior leaders were known to value. Of course, the end result of managers 'playing the OVA game' in similar ways was that companies ended up making only a minimal cost reduction.

Naively, I wondered if this game-playing would be called out or the low results deemed insufficient, but nothing happened other than the OVA being declared 'successfully completed' and everyone getting back to 'normal life'. A decade later, when discussing the Shell experience, I heard the OVA described explicitly as a gesture or a game – the service companies were pressing operating companies to cut costs and therefore the OVA was needed in order to visibly demonstrate that service companies' costs were under the microscope too. The game was to be seen to be doing something and to engender a sense of 'we are all in this together, reducing costs'.

During the 2020 pandemic, shortage of testing for the virus was a major problem in dealing with the crisis – and became a major credibility problem for governments. In the UK, the government set a target of 100,000 tests per day to be met by 30 April. Setting targets (as we shall see) can be an appropriate means of galvanizing effort in the short term to meet a vital goal. Targets become a problem when they are overused – or treated as totemic. The UK grew testing capacity rapidly as 30 April approached and that should have been treated as a triumph and a vindication of the strategy of setting a clear bold target. Instead, the media handlers gamed the numbers, producing implausible analyses showing the target was met on the very last day – and earning a reprimand from the UK Statistics Authority.[41]

In some cases, the game can be to chase a target, without any necessary connection to what people actually do. In professional services firms, the annual target-setting process has, since the 1990s, been treated with great seriousness and goes on for many months. It is accompanied by books of analysis and spreadsheets, with extended meetings debating the impact of an extra percentage point here or there, and an accompanying ritual in the form of interrogation of abstruse assumptions about potential market developments over the coming years. Participants hedge their real opinion and bid only what they have to, until either everyone is worn down or a preconceived total is hit. At the end of the process, a set of targets is fixed and thereafter treated as unchangeable – although the underlying assumptions would have been rendered out of date during the long debating process. This is the 'holding to account' game and will be a familiar experience for leaders who engage in annual budgeting processes in companies, government or charities.

During the target-setting or budgeting process, it is simply unacceptable to admit that so much time and effort is going into a game. Leaders can be criticized for 'sandbagging' (management-speak for lobbying to artificially reduce) targets to make them easier to exceed. On rare occasions I observed senior partners and business leaders who lost patience with the process and stated, 'Just tell me the number you want.' They were promptly accused of 'not playing the game' – or alternatively told, 'This is not a game!'

The Italians have a word for this: *gattopardismo*, which means creating reforms that are only apparent rather than real.[42] The term 'game' is already a loaded word in the management vocabulary. It is sometimes positive: one might encourage a peer 'to play the game', and 'gamification' is the latest trend in recruitment, training, online engagement etc. But it is usually negative: 'gaming the system' connotes cheating or the behaviour of a bureaucrat pursuing an internally focused game rather than the ostensible purpose of the organization. The characteristics of games in organizations are that they are known phenomena with accepted rules – just rarely admitted to – and the same games appear to be played again and again across many different organizations. Game-playing is the result of performance pressure on leaders who are already short of time – games can look like an attractive shortcut to 'just do it'.

THE TIME DILEMMA AND FRAGMENTED EFFORT

Senior leaders are desperately short of time – in two senses: the turnover in senior roles is high, with leaders given only a short time to prove themselves, and also leaders' days are packed and fragmented. Investors can drive commercial senior leaders to decide quickly on business initiatives, while the media can drive public sector senior leaders into rapid policy initiatives – with neither given time to be well thought through and tested before launch.

Performance pressures are intense

Companies – and therefore chief executives and their teams – are on an expectations treadmill. Failure to meet 'profit guidance' or competitors' results can result in swift punishment. Data for chief executives of companies show a steady decline in tenure, so corporate leaders feel they have to make a big impact or decide on a big move quickly.[43] Pressure from investors can force commercial leaders into actions that they might not choose. For example, the US sub-prime mortgage market was always fundamentally a bad business, long before the crash of 2008.[44] Selling financial products to those least likely to afford them was initially profitable because of the higher margin achieved by selling to less sophisticated buyers, but ultimately it was bound to go bad. One of the last banks to enter the sub-prime market was HSBC. I quizzed a top executive as to why HSBC had entered, given that they had always viewed it as a bad business. He replied that he had not changed his view on the sub-prime market, but that it was impossible for HSBC to continue to resist the pressure from shareholders to participate in a profitable market that was (then) boosting other banks' share prices. HSBC felt that it had to act in line with expectations – even against its own better judgement.

Similarly, in public services, some key roles (NHS Trust chief executives, directors of care services etc.) are expected to satisfy rising need for the service from a budget that reduces every year. In government, some cabinet ministers barely have long enough in the job to master their brief – and some key White House jobs turn over every few months. The impact of the 24-hour news cycle and the responsiveness of social media via mobile technology means that issues can go from initial complaint to full-blown crisis in hours; new 'facts' (accurate or 'alternative') can appear at any point – and the leader of the organization has to respond and 'take charge' of the issue. Frequently, the confrontation becomes personalized around the senior leader and the game is all about deflecting blame – or blaming the messenger or anyone else nearby! During the height of the pandemic, media questions focused on key choices by government. Instead of making clear that the best judgements were made in the face of uncertainty, the deflection was frequently: 'We are following the advice of scientific/medical experts.'[45] However, there are limits to science: conclusive expertise is usually delayed beyond the moment of crisis, behavioural issues cannot be subject to randomized control trials,[46] causation is frequently unclear and average results conceal huge variation and inequalities. As described in Section 7, scientific knowledge does not progress by logic, but through revolutions – it is contested.

Time is fragmented

Almost every day in a senior leader's diary is hopelessly fragmented, moving rapidly from issue to issue. The picture of the top person being the one taking big decisions, maintaining the strategic overview and reflecting on the long term is entirely false.[47] In many organizations across all sectors, few people spend even 50 per cent of their time on their primary task – the task that defines their role. In fact, most people spread their time extraordinarily thinly, and the most important tasks are often spread over scores of people who each make tiny contributions, and senior people are excessively engaged on lower-level tasks due to low capability levels resulting from high staff turnover and poor systems.

Fragmentation is a fact of life in public services as much as in companies. Defence Equipment & Support (DE&S) – the Ministry of Defence organization responsible for £16 billion per annum of spending on defence procurement and in-service support – is one of the few organizations that has analysed in detail what the entire organization of 16,000 people actually spends its time doing. It asked consultants to 'provide a report with high quality baseline data to answer the questions "what does everyone do?" and "what output do we get from each person?" in relation to staff in DE&S; then define the priorities and value of these outputs from staff'.[48] DE&S leaders subsequently commented that the organization's fragmentation, with too much time spent on administration and too little delegation, seriously affected morale and productivity and accentuated the shortage of key skills.[49]

Summary of pioneering research into what leaders actually do

THE NATURE OF MANAGERIAL WORK by Henry
Mintzberg (1973, Harper & Row)

Mintzberg's path-breaking empirical studies of what top managers actually spend their time doing replaced worn-out theories of 'managerial work' as being 'planning, organizing, co-ordinating, controlling'. He described the reality of managerial work as long hours, few breaks but frequent interruptions, with typical calls or discussions to cover the biggest issues lasting no more than 6–12 minutes.

Much of managers' work is challenging and unprogrammed. They choose brevity because they prefer action over reflection, they value their personal input highly and want to maintain

---

breadth of contact across their organization. Much of managers' power derives from their exclusive information, mostly received verbally via a network of external contacts and therefore hard to disseminate, in turn making delegation difficult. This reinforces managers' perceptions of their superior experience, insights and solutions.

The prime occupational hazard of management is superficiality, unrelenting work pace and work activities characterized by brevity and fragmentation. 'The job of managing does not develop reflective planners; rather it breeds adaptive information manipulators who prefer a stimulus-response milieu.'[50] 'Furthermore he is driven to focus on that which is current and tangible in his work, even though the complex problems facing many organizations call for reflection and a far-sighted perspective.'[51]

Mintzberg's research pre-dated the impact of mobile technology, email and the Internet on managers' time. Interestingly, when he repeated the research in 2011,[52] the findings had changed little, suggesting that managers choose fragmentation – and use the technology available to match.

Relying on past experience is a seductive coping strategy

The myth of the 'first hundred days' is perpetuated in much modern advice to new leaders – 'you have to launch your big ideas while you are new in post' – and adds to the pressure to 'just do it'. Because of their desperate time shortage, many senior leaders feel compelled to act quickly. The most reliable way for leaders to act quickly is to reach for formulae or heuristics that have worked for them in the past – even if that may be to risk oversimplifying or applying a mismatched solution.

We know from behavioural science, from observation of senior leaders and our personal experience, that pressure results in most people falling back on default behaviours. For leaders in particular, their route to the top has been one of accumulating experience and severe winnowing of a crowd of contenders down to this one individual – encouraging a belief in one's own achievements and judgement. People who acquire more knowledge develop an enhanced illusion of their skill and become unrealistically overconfident.[53] But that is not how some senior leaders see it – they are often unaware of the pitfalls or gaps in their experience. For example, few senior doctors have deep expertise in elderly care, and scientists advising governments during the pandemic wrongly relied on their experience of flu epidemics rather than the rarer SARS/MERS experience.[54] Leaders' past experience may be less complete than they know – e.g., they may have moved on before the negative results emerged; they may be making unrealistic assumptions about the capabilities of their current organization to implement what their previous organization succeeded with; or they may be unduly optimistic about recruiting new capabilities. Research indicates that error denial increases as one goes higher in the organizational hierarchy.[55]

Problems loom for this approach – organizations are complex systems where untailored initiatives are likely to have an unforeseen impact. Significant change in organizations takes time to accomplish, so pretending otherwise is likely to end in disappointment. And past experience tends to be overvalued by all of us.

WHAT GETS MEASURED GETS MANAGED

Why would you change the formula that has brought you success so far? Smart, ambitious senior people know they are under pressure and they know the kinds of messages/strategies that will buy them the time and space to act but, unfortunately, those strategies all rely upon simplifying the real problem.

Relying on past experience is not usually as simple as the senior leader saying 'I've got the answer' – although that is one variant that can emerge. *The root of misapplied experience is mistrust of how the organization currently works.* Senior leaders will observe the front-line leaders and the management teams accommodating central initiatives with daily trade-offs to avoid destabilizing operations and systems. If they have not invested the time to understand the organization, then senior leaders are likely to misinterpret the continual trade-offs as suboptimizing and under-delivering on the central initiatives. So, a senior leader setting about 'correcting' this under-delivery will begin controlling or limiting or changing what front-line leaders and management teams do.

Misapplied experience + distrust = three typical centralized initiatives or 'games'

1. I want to focus on execution:
Controls and indicators to limit the discretion exercised through the organization.

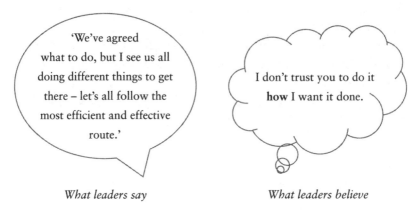

'We've agreed what to do, but I see us all doing different things to get there – let's all follow the most efficient and effective route.'

I don't trust you to do it **how** I want it done.

What leaders say   *What leaders believe*

Execution is part of the *lingua franca* of management – key performance indicators, targets, what-gets-measured-gets-managed. The commercial world adopted this approach in the 1990s – BP under John Browne was the poster child for performance contracts, KPIs, benchmarking and performance reviews.[56] The corporate sector had moved on from a pure targets approach by the time the public sector adopted 'delivery units and Public Service Agreements' under the Blair governments in the 2000s, which lives on with NHS Trusts currently being measured on multiple KPIs.[57] During the pandemic, daily KPIs in the NHS became visible to the public in the form of hospital admission figures and spare intensive care capacity. Even the charity world is steadily adopting the language of execution. In particular, many social enterprises use the full apparatus of sales pipelines, indicators and revenue models as they demonstrate investable propositions to potential social investors or operate with the discipline of paying regular capital returns.

2. I have the plan:
Allocate resources and rewards in line with the central priorities.

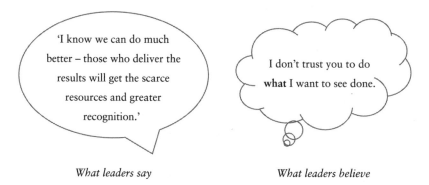

'I know we can do much better – those who deliver the results will get the scarce resources and greater recognition.'

I don't trust you to do **what** I want to see done.

What leaders say   *What leaders believe*

A classic paradigm of managing large, diverse organizations is that senior leaders allocate resources and promise results based on devolved delivery, following a detailed corporate plan. It appeals to the same sense of certainty as we saw earlier in our discussion of 'project'. Commercial leaders such as Arnold Weinstock and Harold Geneen managed conglomerates of unrelated businesses against 'the Plan',[58] while professional services firms try to manage individualistic partners against 'the Plan'. Not only does the government seek to manage complex systems such as the NHS against 'the 10 Year Plan' but, during the pandemic, we had a plethora of 'plans' like the four-phase 'contain-delay-research-mitigate' plan of February 2020 that was abandoned by March.

3. I want to make a big move that changes everything:
Change the context and expectations for the organization.

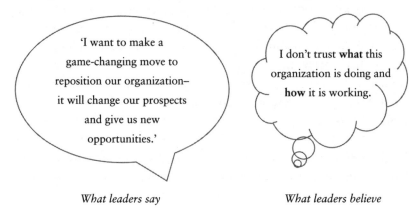

'I want to make a game-changing move to reposition our organization– it will change our prospects and give us new opportunities.'

I don't trust **what** this organization is doing and **how** it is working.

What leaders say   *What leaders believe*

This is part of the mythology of the senior leader taking big decisions – the one big move that will transform the fortunes of the organization. This approach has major variants:

1 External restructuring through the 'transforming acquisition/partner'. Examples range from ICI's acquisition of speciality chemicals to attempts by Defence Equipment & Support to create a GOCO – a government-owned contractor-operated procurement outsourcing partner.

2 Internal restructuring through 'reorganizing'. Examples abound from corporate life where some executives believe one 'should reorganize every three years' and from government tinkering with the 'machinery of government' – a telling phrase betraying the engineering/ machine mindset in dealing with complex systems.

3 Process and system transformation or the 'one new way to work' (often technology driven) with too many examples from 'quality' in the 1980s through 'core process re-engineering' in the 1990s through 'lean' in the 2000s to 'agile' now.

4 A single 'game-changer'. Examples range from a pivotal new model vehicle to, during the pandemic crisis, a technical breakthrough in the form of a vaccine or treatment that would obviate the need for the hard grind of long-term behavioural change to deal with the threat of the virus.

Of course, there will be many variants on these three broadly described games. I call them 'the games leaders play' because the games are played again and again (sometimes repeatedly in the one organization). The 'rules' of these games are broadly understood; people across the organization tend to comply and – finally – the senior leader knows that the game will work... for a time.

Depending on the context, there will be times when one of these broadly described games will be right – and most organizations will be applying elements of them effectively in parts of their business. However, they are typically reached for too often and too early, because leaders (and shareholders and ministers and trustees) prefer the big, visible actions that present decisive action[59] – they want to 'just do it'.

LEADERS PREFER BIG, VISIBLE ACTION – BUT 'JUST DO IT' WON'T DO

A classic example of preferring a big, visible act was a chief executive who met with me because 'I want to reorganize my company and introduce a new structure that means all my senior people will have to change jobs'. At the time, I was a partner at McKinsey and known for having advised on many restructurings. On the only occasion we met, he opened the conversation by repeating his planned big move and, retrieving drafts from his briefcase, he suggested we review his proposed new organization charts. We would have settled down to a lengthy discussion of options and project planning that might have resulted in a lucrative and challenging assignment for me and the firm in which I was a partner. A hunch made me hesitate and instead I asked him what he was trying to change in his organization – 'just to check that the goal matched the plan'. He replied that he wanted to make his senior people focus on his priorities – he was frustrated that they seemed to be pursuing a range of activities, only a few of which matched his priorities as chief executive. So we spent the rest of the conversation discussing how to build alignment and team dynamics. We never looked at his proposed organization charts and that restructuring never happened, saving all the disruption and distraction from day-to-day operations. The chief executive left with an outline plan to improve how his senior team would work together – and we didn't need to meet again. He did not require an intrusive, expensive and lengthy intervention – he got on with what helped him with his senior team.

Many chief executives would not have been so flexible in their thinking. In 20 years of consulting practice, I found clients remarkably resistant to recommendations of lower-profile projects or no action. Clients *want* to play a game even when advised that it may not be effective, because of their preference for tangible action, as highlighted in Mintzberg's research. Some of the most difficult client situations I ever experienced involved clients who did not want me to put anything in writing that warned them that a visible programme of action was ill-advised – they much preferred to pay the fee, keep us quiet and play the game!

ORGANIZATIONS RESPOND BY PLAYING THE GAME – WHAT GETS MEASURED GETS GAMED

People in organizations know that a new leader will make changes and that they, as followers, need to demonstrate their positive response. Academics have documented this tendency of organizations to conform to the expressed priorities of senior leaders – even when it is an indirect expression of intent. Research into media companies demonstrated 'that reporters are more liberal in their views than are the owners of the paper, and thus a subtle censorship is at work ... they write what they know will be accepted. The editor does not have to tell them ... it becomes apparent.'[60] So the initial positive feedback will reinforce the choice of the game and, almost by definition, leaders who rely upon familiar games will succeed – initially.

Sometimes the game is an appropriate match to the situation and overwhelming leadership focus on one measurement mobilizes an entire organization for a limited time. When the UK government set a target of 100,000 virus tests per day at the height of the pandemic crisis, then it was both a vital step forward and an organizational compulsion – the Civil Service, industry, local authorities, Public Health and industry all mobilized to deliver on the target and collaborated in ways that previously had been managerially impossible.

The problem comes when the game becomes the driving leadership focus for measurement of success over the long term – simplification has been taken too far – and the organization responds by gaming the chosen measures. Most people in organizations are smart when it comes to their personal survival and therefore they follow the mentality of 'If the leader wants to play this game, then I will play it if that's what it takes to keep my job'. For many questionable goals, compliance is the default response and various management-speak responses do the rounds – e.g., BOHICA 'bend over, here it comes again'.

This non-compliant compliance or passive resistance is most common in highly siloed companies, where there is usually a strong element of groupthink and wilful blindness to the bigger picture. Despite easier communication and adoption of smart technology, silo behaviour remains one of the major obstacles to successful change programmes – the focus on the internal world blinds organizations to market realities, discounts the views of other organizational actors, blocks information that does not fit the established view and minimizes collaborative working.

Silos affect individuals' behaviour through information that is only held or circulated within that silo, affiliation to that silo through working relationships and training/development and inducements, financial and otherwise, to prioritize time within the silo.

Interestingly, the academic research and description of the 'organizational gaming' phenomenon sees it mainly from the perspective of the senior leader who is being deceived and defeated by disingenuous underlings! In a masterly understatement, a principal academic study of complex organizations suggests 'we should always examine the possibility that organizational masters prefer unofficial goals over difficult ones and may even make sure that official goals are not achieved. We should then search for extra-organizational interests that are served by what appears to be, from a leadership perspective, drift or goal displacement.'[61] Actually, 'goal displacement' is a game played out between leaders and organizations – and a game where senior leaders take undue risks by over-relying on their experience. It is not a matter of 'people are not up for change'; instead, it is organizations that are unprepared for change, because the root causes of problems and the fit of the proposed solution have not been addressed.

The systemic problem with 'playing the execution game' is that other important performance measures are neglected by front-line management – as one commentator put it, 'what gets measured gets done' has become 'what gets measured gets gamed'.[62]

BP	Smart managers began to manage expectations downwards so they would be promoted despite failure to deliver against KPIs. In response, an 'analysis group' came into being to track and comment on performance against ever more ornate KPIs.[63] The intense drive to meet a handful of production and cost KPIs meant that *inter alia* safety practices did not receive equivalent attention.

GE, Microsoft   The annual cycle of ranking every employee according to their performance then firing the bottom 10% of performers (known as 'rank and yank') was undermined by smart managers hiring relatively poorly performing people just to provide fodder to the corporate process.[64]

NHS   The introduction of KPIs for waiting time in Accident & Emergency (A&E) resulted in the data being gamed, including by keeping patients in ambulances lined up outside A&E wards and by shuffling patients into temporary facilities.[65] The Chair of NHS England, Lord Prior, stated that targets, competition and reliance on inspection all led to a disjointed system and demoralized staff.[66]

al-Qaida and Islamic State   Even in terrorist and criminal organizations such as al-Qaida, the execution game plays out. As found in a raid on their Algerian operation, al-Qaida's central organization had written to their Algerian unit, complaining that they were not maintaining expected performance in appropriate KPIs like stores of explosives and ammunition, achieved kidnappings etc. In response, the Algerian unit of al-Qaida had fobbed off their 'head office' with distracting and unquantified claims of performance against alternative measures.[67]

The systemic problem with 'playing the plan game' is that the plan can assume the status of dogma, when usually most plans are quickly overtaken by events and become increasingly irrelevant as the months pass. This is not to suggest that organizations should not be planning – the thinking process is hugely valuable to prepare leaders for decisions that need to be taken – 'planning is everything, the plan is nothing' is a useful catchphrase.

Tech start-ups	Remaining tied to 'the plan' under pressure from investors risks the long-term customer position of the firm – and frequently the motivation and retention of talented young people.
NHS	In most NHS Trusts, a mass of one-off cost savings were adopted in order to hit 'the plan' with two consequences for the next plan – first, costs tend to bounce back higher after being temporarily squeezed and, second, one-off savings usually build in higher whole-life costs.
Contracting businesses	Companies in long-term contract-based businesses in (e.g.) construction or facilities management or outsourced services can be tempted to hit short-term plans at the expense of long-term financial sustainability. Companies like Carillion and Enron artificially boosted their short-term performance by *inter alia* deliberately underpricing to win contracts (hoping to win add-on work to rescue the contract later) and/or accounting for contracts by recognizing the entire revenue in the year it is signed rather than over the life of the contract. Business strategy turns into a Ponzi game of running ever faster and runs the risk of running out of cash – both Enron and Carillion went bust.

The systemic problem with 'playing the big move game' is that it shuts down debate and thinking. There is frequently a lengthy delay while senior leaders seek out 'the big deal'; often there is pressure to make it happen even if it is apparent that the move is no longer (or never was) attractive; and, after it has died as a strategy, leaders then scrabble around to find a replacement.

BT	When the telecoms giant announced that it would progressively divest itself of traditional line businesses and only acquire and retain mobile-technology-based businesses, it was not in the least surprising to find how many old businesses were quickly repositioned and sometimes rebranded as a fashionable 'i-business' to meet the new corporate requirement. Corporate support functions quickly demonstrate how their resources are deployed to deliver the big deal.
DE&S outsourcing	Defence Equipment & Support pursued a GOCO (strategic outsourcing) strategy 2010–14 that excluded other options, leaving the department short of options after four years' distraction when the sole bidder withdrew.[68]

Games that have not been well thought through for the specific context of the organization, but instead rely only on personal experience and past success, will ultimately break down. Organizations are complex systems so one big idea will have an effect – but an effect that is not wholly predictable. The answer may be simply wrong in a new context – and neither the organization nor the leader seriously confront the mismatch or test the proposition against reality. This is frequently the case when the senior leader deploys an approach that worked well elsewhere.

Illustration: General Electric (GE) senior leaders transplanting experience that failed

Although it has fallen on hard times since the 2008 crash, GE was the epitome of 'best practice' for many decades. One element of GE's success was the widespread adoption of 'Six Sigma' – a quality and efficiency improvement technique based on statistical control. When GE's legendary chief executive Jack Welch stepped down in 2001, the competition to succeed him was won by Jeff Immelt, and his two rivals, Bob Nardelli and Jim McNerney, left GE to become chief executive in other big companies. Nardelli went to run Home Depot, McNerney to 3M – and both quickly introduced Six Sigma as 'one big move' across their new companies, regardless of the significant differences in their businesses. Six Sigma is attuned to the manufacturing and repeat processing that dominates GE, but Home Depot is a retailer and Six Sigma encouraged a decline in customer service. At 3M, applying Six Sigma to its innovative development activity encouraged a decline in the pipeline of new products. Relying on experience didn't work.[69]

GAMES CAN END BADLY – WITH EVERYONE A LOSER

Many will say that a lot of this is 'just organizational politics' and that canny organizational operators know how to play these games – indeed, that 'playing the game' is a key management skill. But playing games can end up in dysfunctional compliance across the organization and cause real harm:

1 Dishonesty and lip service at middle management levels breeds acceptance that 'what I say is not my responsibility'. People whisper in corridors about tactics and subterfuge:

> *'It's not about what's right, it's about what John wants'* BP

> *'The Minister simply won't accept it'* Whitehall

*'I am not bound to follow the decision because
I remained silent'* An Air Vice-Marshal on leaving a
management team meeting

This is the reason that the OSS – Office of Strategic
Services, now the CIA – included in its Simple Sabotage
Field Manual in 1944 a host of apparently legitimate
questions and delaying tactics that could be used to slow
down munitions production without drawing undue
attention to the saboteur.

2 Front-line management levels keep their heads down
   and 'just keep things running while head office play their
   games' because 'this fad will blow over and be forgotten
   when the next new one comes along'.

3 A sustained pattern of game-playing makes dishonesty
   acceptable or even encouraged. Consequently, trust is
   breached with the public, customers and regulators. In
   most organizations, people defend the status quo[70] –
   including the authority of the leader. The power of the
   senior leader can lead to compliance with plans that
   generate short-term profits or meet political slogans – but
   are in breach of acceptable behaviours towards customers
   or citizens. Companies have a long record of rewarding
   systems failures such as the PPI scandal. Government does
   the same, as illustrated by the Windrush official enquiry,
   which concluded that the Home Office's target-dominated
   environment in immigration enforcement demonstrated
   'ignorance and thoughtlessness consistent with some
   elements of the definition of institutional racism'.[71]

A major contributor to loss of trust in institutions – banks, retailers,
the NHS, police, parliament, churches and charities – has been
the exposure of informal organizational games. Games played
to rules such as: 'Don't undermine the leadership', 'Keep up with
expectations', 'Protect one of our own' and 'Above all, protect the
institution' and 'Just hit the target'. Even allowing for hindsight

bias, it is shocking to see how responsible people avert their eyes from uncomfortable acts or omissions known to them – explored further in Section 6. Senior leaders can obfuscate what they knew and when they knew it – wilfully blind when the game turns sour, but content when it generates positive numbers.[72] Management writers and regulators have neglected the social pressure to conform that affects all complex organizations.[73] The financial crash of 2008 is a classic example: media and general commentary focuses on irresponsible behaviour of the banks, with a few being mildly critical of regulators, while the behaviour of the banks was driven by pressure from *consumers* for ever cheaper deals and pressure from *regulators* to provide credit to lower-income groups.[74]

In the final phases of the game, as performance expectations are publicly missed, organizations seek things and people to blame. Scapegoating is a normal human response to failure and groupthink decays into a 'not one of us' whispering campaign against the designated scapegoats, with truth being an early casualty: 'Truth is an organizationally established frame of reference, independent of courageous or timid members.'[75]

AVOID GAMES BY BRINGING THE REAL WORLD INSIDE THE ORGANIZATION

Our understanding of how *individuals* make judgements and choices has improved enormously over the past 20 years, but our understanding of behaviour of *organizations* has not improved at the same pace. Organizations exhibit patterns of behaviour that resist change because they overemphasize *internal* conversations at the expense of *external* reality – and few have the independence or foolhardiness to make criticisms that would equate to telling a leader 'your baby is ugly'. Failing to bring in the real world results in blind spots and misplaced assumptions and reinforces the confirmatory biases within the organization – leaders read the material that confirms their experience.

Many apparently logical and necessary major change programmes fail in poor practice. Middle management pay lip service and front-line management ignore the programme due to silo behaviour and the internal organizational world being prioritized over the real world. As a result, the alarms are not heard and 'normal accidents' happen without being treated as serious signals that something is amiss. This is why so many post-collapse reports comment on the number of warnings not heeded and the opportunities to intervene spurned.

Bring in real-world perspective to balance the internal conversation

Game-playing is inauthentic, and so is best addressed by exposing it to reality. Leaders can dig into others' experiences within the organization, or bring in outside views – business partners and commentators, or invite criticism and contribution. Understanding repeated behaviour patterns in the real world of organizations and how to influence organizational behaviour is an essential – but neglected – leadership capability. The 'real world' comes in many sources, perspectives and formats:

From *internal* sources ...in informal conversation, workshops or sitting in on actual customer service.	*Front-line people* can bring a perspective on what works – and what will not work. They may be innovating and delivering in ways not visible to senior leaders.
From *business* sources ...in facility visits, service reviews, planning meetings or workshops.	*Customers, suppliers and partners* can challenge preconceptions and stimulate innovation. They may also offer comparisons with competitors and perspectives on regulators.
From *external observers and experts* ...in learning events, workshops, leadership conferences, or designated 'critical friends'.	*Industry experts, researchers and journalists* can introduce new perspectives and potentially disruptive trends in economics, technology and politics. They may prompt radically different thinking.

It may literally be about bringing in an outsider to give the perspective, it may be about designating an individual with that role. The Vatican has appointed a 'devil's advocate' to oppose every beatification proposal over recent centuries precisely in order to challenge groupthink. More modern examples include how Shell treated Pierre Wack and subsequent planning co-ordinators as a licensed 'court jester' (original purpose: to deflate the pompous) to think the impossible and challenge assumptions, while British Airways reportedly did appoint an official corporate Fool.[76]

Mobilize the management teams across the organization

Critical prioritization and resource allocation decisions are taken routinely in management teams across the organization, when heads of business units or functions or regions or practices come together. The wider organization is acutely tuned to the actions and omissions of these management teams. People will be watching to see if the teams blithely ignore the senior leader's 'new direction'. If it is just 'business as usual' for these teams, then it will be for the wider organization. On the other hand, if the management teams shift resources to new activity – or move away from old practices – then 'it's serious: we'd better pay attention'.

Acknowledge the games that get played and guard against groupthink

One of the most effective counters to game-playing is simply to name the behaviour. By doing so, leaders equip and give permission to other people to call it. By acknowledging people's negative behaviours at work and obstruction of goals, leaders can reinforce those who are more likely to listen, ask questions and challenge. One of the most effective actions is to broaden the range of inputs to decisions. A few companies set up competing strategy teams to test the potential for different approaches; public entities are subject to quadrennial reviews to test their ongoing purpose; the UK Ministry of Defence and US Department of Defense use 'tiger teams' or 'red teams' to challenge groupthink.[77] Sometimes consultants or academic experts are retained to inject new thinking.

Make candour the norm and reduce the risk of honest misjudgements

Organizations have difficulties being straightforward about failure, especially when senior leaders apply hindsight to focus blame on the front line. The National Health Service in the UK responded to a cover-up at the Mid-Staffordshire Hospital Trust when professional staff failed to speak up about patient maltreatment, by putting in place a 'duty of candour' programme – complete with processes and contacts rather than values and behaviours that one would expect in caring organizations.

Blaming the messenger suppresses the psychological safety required for organizations to get the best ideas and constructive criticism from their people. A psychologically unsafe working environment trains people to adopt survival strategies for their protection against vengeful bosses. Senior leaders need to match actions to words when learning from accidents, encouraging open debate and setting about system improvements.[78]

Buy time to master the organization's complexities

More than anything, senior leaders need to invest the time to master the organization as a complex system – the critical trade-offs made by front-line leaders to maintain continuity, the weaknesses to be addressed, the risks of change. Buying the time to do so can be accomplished by testing front-line capability to launch experiments and the time needed to scale up successful pilots, learning to ask a better class of question and listening carefully, comparing across the organization and externally.

During and after the pandemic crisis, the UK government rarely bought itself time. There was clearly a communications strategy to use only the language of certainty and control, rather than buying time through using the confident language of dealing with the unknown, trying measures only some of which would succeed, learning from what works and what doesn't work. It only added to media pressure when the government declined to examine uncomfortable international comparisons or participate in debate on challenging media programmes.

The realities of organizations are that they are complex systems, where interventions can destabilize operations. Senior leaders need to resist relying upon past experience that is only rarely an accurate guide to a new situation. They need to engage front-line leaders in designing initiatives that balance change and continuity, while management teams reallocate resources against new priorities, building the processes and capabilities that enable results. So, leading change requires participating leadership at all levels in the organization.

Senior leaders saying…	*This is the context and where we need to go – do we have all the options on the table? What happened last time we did something like this? What can we learn?*
Front-line leaders saying…	*These are the games people will play… Here is what we shall do to get people on side.*
Management teams saying…	*This is how we are going to shift resources… assess risks…*

Summary   *Leaders will sometimes play games within their organizations – apparently a serious change initiative but, below the surface, the rules of the game are understood and the impact is limited.*

Leaders are time-bereft and consequently rely on heuristics that worked for them in the past, rather than taking the additional time and effort to create the right initiative for the situation – akin to the psychology classic Games People Play.[79] *The catch for leaders in organizations is that past experience is unreliable when applied to non-routine issues – and all change is by definition non-routine.*

Most of these leadership shortcuts are rooted in mistrust of how the organization works and fit into three broad types of centralized game:

- *The 'execution game' limits discretion across the organization.*
- *The 'plan game' directs resource to central priorities.*
- *The 'big move game' changes both what the organization does and how it works.*

When leaders start a game, then organizations quickly work out the rules and play the game back – what gets measured gets gamed. Most game-playing is unproductive and sometimes dysfunctional. At the least, effort is going into game-playing rather than productive work. At the worst, games can end badly with dishonesty, suppression of failure and loss of trust.

Action   *Win respect and commitment by articulating the real purpose of initiatives and decisions, and by working through the realities of organizational complexity.*

Guard against your own experiential shortcuts by testing fitness for purpose:

- *Make candour the norm and reduce the risk of honest misjudgements.*
- *Bring the real world inside the organization to counter groupthink.*
- *Mobilize management teams across the organization.*
- *Never rely on wholly central initiatives – engage locally.*

PART THREE

'WHAT DO I NEED TO DO – AND WHAT SHOULD I EXPECT OTHERS TO DO?'

Change is messy – complex and destabilizing, over long periods of time, with leaders and organizations vulnerable to game-playing rather than doing real work. Successfully leading change is achievable and practical in most organizations, but it cannot be led by 'the leader' alone. Change requires complementary action from senior leaders, front-line leaders and management teams. It requires 'leadership at all levels'.

Knowing the untidy reality of life in organizations, it is highly unlikely that there is a tidy formula for the work of leadership of change. However, two principles underpin successfully leading change:

- Each of the three different categories of leaders within organizations needs to do what only they can do ...without a detailed prescription and without someone trying to do their job for them.
- Collaboration is necessary across the three different categories of leaders so that the work they do gets

traction across the organization rather than being dissipated in silos

...without being dictated in detail through the formal apparatus of control.

Abandoning the single-leader focus does not mean we replace it with a general aspiration for everyone to 'be a leader'. Instead, different categories of leaders within organizations need to lead in specific decisions, change activities and relationships/roles:

Senior leaders	*Decision-making:*	Defining context and goals
	Activity:	Asking the right questions
	Relationships:	Influencing stakeholders
Front-line leaders	*Decision-making:*	Making trade-offs to maintain core operations
	Activity:	Experimenting
	Relationships:	Developing networks of customers, suppliers, influencers
Management teams	*Decision-making:*	Prioritizing scarce resource
	Activity:	Planning and optimizing
	Relationships:	Building internal coherence

Depending on your context as a leader, you may find yourself playing multiple leadership roles at different times. For example, a headteacher may play all three leadership roles at different times of a single day in combination with the school's teachers, admin staff, PTA, board, local authority etc. – as might a community organizer or charity leader or priest. In the aftermath of the pandemic, successful organizations have retained the decentralized leadership that was forced on them by the crisis of the virus – people who previously thought of themselves as 'just one of the workers' have realized they are actually 'front-line leaders' making daily trade-offs to keep the operation running.

The real work of senior leaders, front-line leaders and management teams – and their collaborative endeavours – in successfully leading change is set out in the following sections:

3 **Leaders' journeys: adapting to the real world**
   Senior leaders need to be personally on the journey of change, as well as the organization being on the journey. In contrast to the myth of the leader with 'all the answers', asking powerful questions is a critical skill for successful leaders. Engaging the organization in debating these questions is part of a key task for senior leaders: bringing the real world inside the organization and thereby limiting internally focused game-playing.
   In practice, leaders need to balance two approaches:
   · The 'adaptive approach', where they enable their organizations to come to terms with the behaviour changes that they face and work out the answers for themselves.
   · The 'programmatic approach', where they give confidence to the organization by providing initial structure to the challenge.

4 **Finding the answers on the front line: leadership at all levels**
   Front-line leaders are a neglected source of the energy and ideas needed in organization-wide change, because they:
   · Make the trade-offs necessary to keep routine operations performing.
   · Discover the change solutions for themselves, especially when it is enabled by technology.
   · Provide a flow of innovative experiments and pilots on the front line by tapping into the 'positive deviants' within the organization – i.e., the people within the organization who are already finding better ways of working.

5 **Teams that work: getting the real work done**
  Management teams across the organization provide
  essential co-ordination and embed change in processes
  and systems. However, most teams are less than the sum
  of their parts and improving their performance is a vital
  investment, by:
  • Doing real work together, in cycles of action and
    reflection, and ensuring alignment.
  • Sharing stories of change that demonstrate that
    everyone is on the journey of change.

3

Leaders' Journeys: Adapting to the Real World

THE GENERAL'S STORY – EVERYONE (ELSE) HAS TO CHANGE

The General described the radical change that he was looking for in his organization and asked for advice on how to structure a transformation programme. As one would expect, he had spent his entire career in uniform, in a culture dominated by rank and where military effect is achieved by a balance of centrally determined mission with decentralized leadership on the front line. Already over the 30 years since the end of the Cold War, we have seen the role, size, capabilities, support, finances, equipment and training of the armed forces change radically. The next phase of transformation would be the most challenging yet to deliver – it focused on changed behaviours among the leadership, with most of the easier changes having already been delivered. How the General planned to set about his transformation was therefore a highly relevant question to answer.

When asked questions about his personal role and priorities in leading the change, the General was unimpressed. He was looking for examples from the private sector of alternative structures for the programme; he was not inviting discussion about how he would lead the change in behaviours. We turned to case studies from industry and they provided some useful pointers. However, they also led us back to choices the General would need to make about his own priorities, the leadership role he would play and the role model he needed to become for the behaviour changes he sought among his officers.

At this, the General repeated quite forcefully that he was not open to thinking about or discussing changing his role. He wanted to match the best programme structure from the commercial sector, but he would not be changing. The conversation promptly ended.

Subsequent conversations with the General's leadership team revealed their disenchantment with the transformation, especially that the General insisted that *they* all change, while he stated that *he* had all the answers already. In fact, they were *all* correct: the General was right in asking for more structure in the programme, but he was deluding himself thinking he could issue orders and expect people to adapt long-established behaviours.

The General and his leadership team were looking at two different but equally essential elements of major change – a programme structure that gives confidence plus leaders' personal journeys to adapt behaviours over time. It can be hard to move on from issuing central directives in a hierarchical and traditional organization, but people have learned that 'When somebody has an answer for every question, it is a sign that they are not on the right road' (*Pope Francis*).[80]

COGNITIVE TRAPS FOR SENIOR LEADERS: OPTIMISM BIAS AND PLANNING FALLACY

The General was not on the journey with his senior officers, in part because his optimistic certainty in his programme of work betrayed two cognitive traps common to senior leaders who have to come to grips with behaviour change across their organization:[81]

Optimism bias

'Most of us view the world as more benign than it really is, our own attributes as more favourable than they truly are, and the goals we adopt as more actionable than they are likely to be,' observed Daniel Kahneman, the Nobel Prize winning psychologist.[82]

For example, the UK–US mining group English China Clays plc (ECC) had fallen on hard times by the mid-1990s. The chief executive launched a turnaround and transformation programme, but early conversations with local leaders in Cornwall and Devon (the main base of mining operations) revealed that they did not think the dire economic situation of the company merited such an effort: 'As the biggest employer in south-west England, we would never be allowed to fail.' A costly assumption – despite successes in improvement projects, the company shrank and eventually succumbed to a takeover.[83]

We are all selective about what we absorb and pass on – the famous Imperial College modelling that caused the UK government to lock down the population to avert the worst of the pandemic was widely portrayed as warning of up to 200,000 deaths, when the actual worst case was a figure of 500,000 hidden in the small print.[84]

Planning fallacy

Focusing on goals and working on the basis of WYSIATI ('what you see is all there is', i.e., excluding others' experiences) results in an illusion of control and overconfidence,[85] including focusing on activity rather than results, neglecting known unknowns (far less unknown unknowns), rejecting data when inconsistent with the goal and persevering irrationally with proposals.

When BMW first bought the Rover Group (producing Rover, Mini, Jaguar and Range Rover cars) from British Aerospace in 1994, it was a hands-off owner. By 1998, losses at Rover Group threatened the entire BMW group; senior BMW executives arrived in the UK to turn around the failing Rover Group and some assumed senior roles in charge of car assembly plants. BMW plant managers were shocked by the poor quality of Rover plant production and immediately applied BMW assembly and painting techniques and quality standards. They engaged in purposeful activity that would probably have worked in BMW factories but, at Rover, this was displacement activity and little better than crossing their fingers and hoping that the improved quality would improve Rover's financial results. The quality of Rover cars *did* improve – but costs went out of control and losses increased because a quality Rover cannot be sold at the high price achieved for a same-quality BMW. BMW sold the business in 2000, keeping only the new Mini brand and production plant.[86]

The pandemic crisis over the availability of protective equipment was another example of the 'planning fallacy' cognitive trap: a focus on well-meaning busyness rather than understanding how to engage a complex system. UK ministers felt under pressure from aggressive media questioning as to why front-line NHS and care staff did not have sufficient protective gowns, gloves and masks when the pandemic struck. They responded to the implied 'blame' with a deliberate focus on how much activity they were engaged in: x deliveries last week, y pieces of equipment supplied, the Army have been brought in to help etc. The reality was that a complex international supply chain was always going to take time to boost purchasing of raw material, manufacturing, shipping of finished equipment – and then it would take time to get the equipment distributed to hundreds of hospitals and tens of thousands of care homes. Given the initial under-preparedness in Italy, the UK and New York state, none of these governments could solve the problem quickly by activity and planning, no matter how rapid and well-meaning. Under more intense media attention as the shortages continued, UK ministers resorted to talking about individual shipments expected 'today' from Turkey – the planning fallacy reduced to absurdity. [87]

Optimism bias and the planning fallacy are encouraged by the myth of the heroic leader who has all the answers – and the idea that change can be reduced to a formula.[88] The heroic leader is a product of propaganda over at least 2,500 years going back to Exodus and Moses, through Caesar's image-building conquest of Gaul 2,000 years ago, Shakespeare's depiction of kingship in his historical tetralogy 500 years ago and Thomas Carlyle's great-man history *On Heroes, Hero-Worship and The Heroic in History* 180 years ago. There are certainly psychological drivers at work: the appeal of an authority figure, the willingness to adopt a parent-child conformance – especially in the context of threat or emergency or war.

We leap too readily to the crisis experience of wartime with its military analogies and wrongly assume that leadership is all about being good in a crisis. In fact, crisis is a fraction of the overall context of leadership. During the peak of the pandemic – in a time of real crisis – we saw most business leaders send the right signals: cutting pay for top management, reassuring their people.[89] However, that crisis was in many ways the easy bit – the challenge of leading organizations through the change and adjustment to the new normal is tougher. In the long aftermath of the pandemic, we have also seen most charitable and community leaders dig in for the long term: engaging with the front line, learning from what works, delegating tasks that people could cope with and building resilience in their workforce.

Perhaps it is the centuries-old individualistic success story of senior leaders that predisposes many to read across from an individualistic model of change to how an organization actually behaves. And therefore they are misled as to how the organization will react. Organizations are influential, they behave differently from the individuals who make up the organization – and we have underinvested in understanding them: 'All important social processes either have their origin in formal organizations or are strongly mediated by them.'[90] A major reason for failed change programmes is that leaders do not understand how to influence their organizations effectively and do not understand the limits to traditional power. The leadership style of 'having all the answers' can be dangerous – in fact, the leader and the organization are taking big risks.

LEADERSHIP DEPENDS ON THE SITUATION

If you google 'leadership styles', you will get 2,520,000 results in 0.36 seconds. Within the first pages of results, you will be offered '12 Leadership Styles for Success', '6 Leadership Styles', '9 Leadership Styles' – pick your number – 'the leadership styles of digital leaders' and all kinds of historical or maverick leaders. Similarly, a glance at the array of popular management literature in bookshops shows a profitable market and evident fascination with the topic of leadership styles. Clearly, leaders are still searching...

By the time they reach maturity, few people change their personal style. Leaders in organizations are even less likely to change, because their style is reinforced by success – why would they choose to switch away from a style that has got them to their senior role? As already discussed, the desperate time shortage faced by senior leaders results in too-quick defaulting to the leadership style and the heuristics that have worked for them in the past.

That default personal style worked fine when leaders were in middle-ranking roles and they spent the bulk of their days working with a relatively limited group of people. This limited group working directly and regularly with the leader had enough exposure to enable them to understand and adapt to the style of their leader – whatever that style was! Even if the leader's default style was not particularly effective with their subordinates, the availability of time to contact, revisit and learn how to respond compensated for the leader's lack of flexibility to adopt a more effective style. One of the major reasons that successful middle-ranking leaders fail to make the grade when they move up to senior levels is that they do not build the capability to switch styles quickly as they deal with the fragmentation of their time into brief exchanges with different groups who are not familiar with the leader's default style.

Effective senior leaders need to be able to deploy the right styles into the different contexts – to exercise 'situational leadership' – whether it is to adopt the style of 'boss' or 'chair' or 'commander' or 'manager' or 'coach' or 'expert'. So what style is the match for major change? In answering this, I draw on the work of Keith Grint,[91] who argues that failures in our framing of the problem and consequent approach to resolving it explain why most change initiatives fail. He suggests differentiating between Critical, Tame and Wicked problems and associating these with Command, Management and Leadership:

Critical problems	are crises where there is no uncertainty about what needs to be done and the situation demands a **'commander'** who gives the answer quickly and clearly – e.g., 'there is a fire, leave now and by this exit'.
Tame problems	are complicated but amenable to a routine, trainable **technical solution** and usually have been solved before and the situation demands a **'manager'** who lays out the process by which the problem can be solved if we tap into expertise – e.g., 'it will be complicated heart surgery, but the medical experts know the process, facilities and have the skills'.
Wicked problems	are complex, with unclear cause and effect, intractable and contested with no clear 'stopping point' when the problem has been solved. It is a mistake for 'a leader' to think they can 'solve' a wicked problem – they require **collective action** to address the problem. The situation demands a **'leader'** who asks the right questions, rather than provides answers, to make any progress. The classic examples of wicked problems in the public arena are tackling obesity or providing national healthcare.

Leadership actions during and after a crisis:	Example 1: Pandemic	Example 2: BP
	During the pandemic of 2020, we saw leaders stepping through phases:	When John Browne took over as chief executive of BP Exploration in 1989, he applied all three styles:[92]
Always require leaders to be able to ask the right questions in order to mobilize collective engagement and action – **the 'leader' role.**	Community leaders, businesses and governments asked people to change their behaviour, apply common sense and help others in their community. Leaders provided a frame for people to work out the right answer for them.	BP people needed to own the search for change and Browne and his team repeatedly convened the broader leadership to address the major issues and come up with radical options. The organization processed the challenges and generated options, tested experiments and evolved over 10–15 years.
Probably require elements of new technical solutions – **the 'manager' role.**	Businesses provided technology to enable people to work from home. Governments invested in developing a vaccine, treatment and tracing apps.	New technical solutions needed to be introduced to improve performance of major development projects at BP. They were largely delegated, implemented and yielded results through the 1990s.
Maybe require a response to an initial crisis that sparks the whole change movement – **the 'commander' role.**	Government compelled lockdown. Businesses adjusted to panic buying and choked supply chains within weeks. We were told what to do.	BP was in crisis initially, having cut its dividend, and launched immediate financial responses for 12 months, but it was clear that the crisis passed quickly.

MATCHING THE WRONG STYLE TO THE SITUATION WILL FAIL

If the problem you are trying to solve is relatively trivial, then matching the wrong leadership style to the situation may be just a matter of degree – i.e., things could have been better, but they will work out, it might just take a bit longer. However, most organizational changes are not trivial and a mismatch can result in a major setback. When organizational change is, by definition, principally a wicked problem, applying a technical or manager style – or a commander style – will become visible as under-delivery of change.

Illustration: New protocols to address the child abuse scandal in the Catholic Church

The Pope and the Catholic laity in the pews see the need for behaviour change, but the bishops and the central departments of the Vatican appear to have treated it as mainly a technical challenge – just a matter of technical adjustments to the rules and processes in order to manage the issues a bit better. In 2015 and 2016, Pope Francis emphasized the need for evidence and due process when moving against bishops who were implicated, alienating Church members, investigators and the media. He soon grasped his error and admitted 'I was part of the problem. I caused this, and I apologize to you' – an unprecedented admission for a pope but essential to demonstrate the scale of the behaviour change needed.[93] By 2020, the Pope had moved from applying a technical solution to an adaptive approach which involved behavioural and attitudinal change from the clergy and the laity, with senior cardinals being publicly dismissed for failures.

Illustration: Technical investments at the height of the pandemic crisis

The anxieties across the world during the initial outbreak caused a natural longing for a technical 'fix' – and politicians played into this longing by investing in the search for a vaccine, building emergency hospitals, moving in hospital ships and funding tracing apps. Although there may eventually be important technical breakthroughs, these manager-like

---

interventions were largely a sideshow to the leadership challenge of taking the population on a journey of behaviour change to combat the threat of the virus.

Illustration: Leadership during the crisis of wartime did not match post-war problems

Many people, especially in the English-speaking world, are currently comparing their political leaders with Winston Churchill as Prime Minister in 1940–45. The problem is that most people carry around myths of that period (they forget that Britons were panic buying then just as they were at the start of the pandemic), which contribute to the 'heroic leader' image. In reality, Churchill only behaved as a 'commander in a crisis' for 9–12 months in 1940–41. Indeed, the unrelieved string of military defeats eroded trust and he came under increasing criticism in Parliament in 1941–42. His style was largely adaptive, engaging with the military leadership and selecting the right generals campaign by campaign – and ultimately the United Nations prevailed. However, Churchill neglected the 'wicked problems' of poverty and inequality facing Britain and never engaged voters through a vision of the future that they would fight for – other than victory. He left the vision of post-war society to his Deputy Prime Minister, Clement Attlee, who promoted the Beveridge report *Full Employment in a Free Society*, won the 1945 General Election and built our modern state.

THE LEADER'S ROLES IN MAJOR CHANGE: PROGRAMMATIC *AND* ADAPTIVE

Major change is distinguished from routine process or management change by being more a *wicked* problem rather than a routine *tame* problem – it aspires to change the complex system of the organization, demanding collective action and changes in behaviour to address the problem. We have left behind the worn-out intellectual model of 'rational economic people' who respond mechanically to sticks and carrots. Our modern and more human model of 'behavioural science' means leaders are truly up against complexity. The role of the leader is to establish leadership at all levels – but not by telling them what to do! Instead, senior leaders should focus on:

- Defining the scope and ambition of change and engaging the leadership necessary across the organization.
- Choosing the appropriate leadership style – asking more questions than providing answers (questioning to explore, not to catch out) while providing the programmatic decisions to support progress, balancing optimism with realism.
- Bringing the external world into the organization to combat game-playing and stimulate new options for the organization. This is often about stepping back from the daily crises to focus on the big picture, identifying what people might be missing.
- Telling stories of change that resonate with the organization.

Between them, the General and his leadership team identified the need for both programmatic leadership and adaptive leadership – they needed the realization that it is *both/and* rather than *either/or*. In major change, leaders need to balance two sets of activities, drawing broadly on left-brained analytical thinking for programmatic action (keeping the programme on track) and drawing broadly on right-brained exploratory thinking for adaptive action (enabling the organization to adapt to the change in its context) to gain commitment and search for positive next steps.

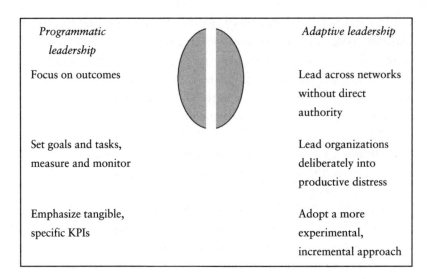

Programmatic leadership	Adaptive leadership
Focus on outcomes	Lead across networks without direct authority
Set goals and tasks, measure and monitor	Lead organizations deliberately into productive distress
Emphasize tangible, specific KPIs	Adopt a more experimental, incremental approach

In practice, leaders need to switch and mix programmatic and adaptive actions, as we saw during the pandemic and its aftermath:

> As part of their *adaptive* leadership, the government needed to voice optimism – 'We shall get through this' – and realism – 'People will die before their time' – simplifying sufficiently to enable people to grasp the need to adapt, then adding detail and challenge later as people absorbed the problem and sought clarity. The letter sent from the British Prime Minister, Boris Johnson, to every household in the UK stated 'one simple instruction – you **must** stay at home' and a direct warning: 'It's important for me to level with you – we know things will get worse before they get better'. Neither scientists nor politicians could judge how quickly the population would adapt – choosing to act (policing could never compel population-wide action or inaction), changing their daily behaviours and calibrating the guidance to their particular situation in a common-sense way. As people came to terms with the pandemic, new challenges – such as semi-permanent home-working and intensified infection control in the NHS, care homes, schools and workplaces – would prompt the population on to the next stage of the agenda for behaviour change.

As part of their *programmatic* leadership, the government needed to give some clarity and confidence to offset uncertainty and distress. Daily statistics and press conferences gave initial reassurance by tracking progress, while income-maintenance schemes staved off immediate financial distress for millions of families. Tools and phrases were introduced to give the population a language to use in describing complex ideas and some immediate steps to take – hand-washing, self-isolating, shielding and social distancing.

Effective leadership of change is about full and comprehensive use of the tools of leadership, not relying unduly on one subset of leadership tools – instruction and planning. While pushing leadership out to all levels of the organization, the hierarchy and authority of the organization can reinforce and encourage progress, but it cannot compel compliance. However, as is visible above, the greater weight of leadership of change falls on 'adaptive' rather than 'programmatic', especially for the long term.

Summary of the most influential writer on adaptive leadership

LEADERSHIP WITHOUT EASY ANSWERS by Ronald A. Heifetz (1994, The Belknap Press of Harvard University Press)

Heifetz's book does what the title promises: it defines the work of leadership in relation to followers and the book repays reflection after every chapter, because it asks difficult questions rather than providing pat answers. The subject matter is leadership, authority and the challenges of tackling very hard problems – especially the role of leadership in supporting followers facing challenges that require learning new ways.

Heifetz draws two key distinctions between:

- Technical and adaptive problems – routine problems versus those that demand innovation and learning. Problems are embedded in complicated and interactive systems.

- Leadership and authority – how people exercise leadership depends on whether they have authority or not – but all can exercise leadership, with the front line exercising creative deviance.

The roles of the leader are to:

- Identify the adaptive challenge and focus attention on the issues.
- Promote adaptive capacities – i.e., change in attitudes, behaviour and values in response to stress in the environment.
- Regulate the level of distress from confronting the issues by managing the pace, structure, resources, improvement and capabilities required.
- Provide followers with a holding environment, ensuring they are doing adaptive work and not engaging in work avoidance.
- Get up on the balcony and gain a perspective on the scene, spotting pitfalls, taking corrective action, changing the path or pace.

TELLING YOUR STORY OF ORGANIZATIONAL CHANGE

The General in our opening story failed to motivate his own leadership team and as a result they did not help in adapting the organization. The failure can be on both sides. Leaders may be habituated to 'having all the answers' but their organizations are often 'expecting all the answers' – and neither leaders nor managers are taking their responsibility to ask the right questions. Everyone needs to be on the journey – and the best way to demonstrate this is through effective storytelling.

Developing a new story or narrative is well established in the world of human therapy, 'facilitating experience of new stories – life narratives that are more empowering, more satisfying, and give hope for better futures'.[94] Conventional 'change management' with its definitive solutions is philosophically outdated and rests on traditional enlightenment modernism – i.e., that knowledge is objective. Consistent with the postmodernist world in which we live, realities are socially constructed, knowledge is constituted through language, and realities are organized and maintained through narrative.[95] The stories we tell add meaning to our lives, reminding us that actions have consequences,[96] all part of an approach to change that enables people to thrive, not merely survive.

In many organizations, I have seen leaders demonstrate that they are on the journey through structured storytelling:

- Beginning with a personal anecdote that demonstrates the case for change and their personal beliefs about an attractive future that is within reach.
- Explaining how they are choosing to lead, given the situation, balancing optimism with realism.
- Inviting others to share leadership and making clear that 'we all need to learn together'.

The storytelling process is not a speech – it is a conversation where, in the first round, senior leaders tell their story to their team, who then ask questions. Storytelling then cascades through the structure of the organization, team by team, recognizing the different leadership roles, asking the right questions *and* giving programmatic support – with everyone on the journey. This approach can mobilize the whole organization – generating leadership at all levels.

Illustration: The public focus on the manager in Premier League football – whereas the reality of the leader at the centre is all about relationships
Having spoken with the iconic managers of our era (Sir Alex Ferguson, José Mourinho, Arsène Wenger et al), Mike Carson's authoritative analysis identifies key mindsets and skills:
focusing on the key relationships with the owner and the team, communicating a shared vision, accepting that other parties are involved, and focusing on each relationship in turn.[97]

One big hint when drafting your story: don't start with an existential crisis. One phrase I would love to banish is 'burning platform', which conjures up images of danger and fear. Fear is not a great motivator other than in crisis. Fear doesn't last very long and it tends to stimulate a fight or flight response, instead of the careful reflection needed through major change. Psychology research and business experience show that people can much more easily be motivated and drawn to a positive image of their future. Usually people want identity and a sense of competence and achievement – and they look to their social group or the bigger organization or its noble purpose to provide these higher needs. I return to this in Section 8.

New technologies reinforce the need for leadership at all levels – social media enables rapid engagement and agile working relies on rapid, incremental work at the front line. Leaders actually have little choice but to engage in adaptive work – it is impossible to steer work from the centre in a modern, technology-enabled complex organization. We learned during the pandemic that the most centralized states, such as France and the UK, struggled with matching their actions to local needs. Trying to work as a 'commander' or 'manager' in leading change will be simply ineffective and disabling for the organization – adaptive leadership is required.

THE ZONE OF PRODUCTIVE DISTRESS

All organizations operate with a high degree of inertia – senior leaders may articulate the case for change but the complementary organizational structures, processes and capabilities will work together to accommodate that change with as little adjustment as possible. Fear-based change tends not to be sustainable and often it is simply not credible – organizations frequently underperform but are rarely in imminent danger of demise. Instead of 'if we don't change, we may not exist', the message should be 'if we keep muddling through, we won't achieve what we say we want'.

Most leaders need to guide their organization into this zone of 'productive distress' where the sense of dissatisfaction with the present state is maintained and held in front of people. This dissatisfaction or distress has to be enough to motivate and enable collective action that can make complementarity work for change, without spilling over into unproductive distress. Unproductive distress results in defensiveness, revolt, game-playing and escaping to better jobs elsewhere.

Productive distress was illustrated during the initial crisis phase of the pandemic.	Honesty and directness about the seriousness of the situation stimulated the population into lockdown and justified unparalleled government action and spending. Reassurance about how families would be helped to cope in the short term counteracted the natural reaction of panic. As it was, a sizeable proportion of the population reported a sense of panic and fear, while panic buying of household items rapidly stripped supermarket shelves.[98]
Unproductive distress was illustrated during the later phases of the pandemic.	Coming out of lockdown, the uncertainty and difficulty of the choices facing governments were obvious to everyone. However, government actions and statements became defensive and game-playing – 'we are led by the science' and 'now is not the time to make comparisons', even when mistakes were evident. Polling demonstrated erosion of trust in government statements and, more seriously, rejection of public health recommendations in favour of personal judgements of safety.

Leadership of change necessitates sensing the mood of the organization and resisting the calls of the organization for a quick fix that relieves the pain of a setback, but does not realize true long-term change. As Friedman says in his analysis of change in organizations and families, the leader needs to be 'well-differentiated' and capable of withstanding the herding instinct within organizations in order to lead others through discomfort toward change.[99]

This term 'productive distress' and the actions I describe are not the normal language of organizations and they call for capabilities that are not routine in complex organizations, where the system values continuity and constant management towards stability, routine and predictability.

To maintain this balance between productive and unproductive distress, leaders at all levels have to be capable of telling a highly persuasive story of change, one that challenges and supports people:

Senior leaders saying...	*Let's reframe our task... This is the context and where we need to get to...*
	What are all the options on the table? Who needs to be engaged? This is how we are going to test and challenge our ideas...
Front-line leaders saying...	*We shall work as a network... experimenting and developing options by...*
Management teams saying...	*We have a plan... to build some infrastructure and programme support... to identify potential threats... avoid making expensive commitments that will be hard to reverse.*

Summary   Change is a journey for the entire organization – and senior leaders need to be on the journey. They need to demonstrate that they are open to learning and changing their own views and behaviours.

Senior leaders need to match their leadership style to the context:

- Too often, senior leaders assume the 'commander' style of giving quick and clear instructions, but that style is only appropriate in rare, short-term 'crisis' contexts.
- The 'manager' style of providing technical solutions is appropriate when the organization faces 'tame' problems amenable to a known and trainable solution.
- The 'leader' style is appropriate for 'wicked' problems that require learning new behaviours and collective action to address the problem. The 'leader' style has to balance:
  - Programmatic leadership, when the leader provides a process and some first steps to start on the journey with confidence.
  - Adaptive leadership, when the leader asks questions, rather than providing answers, and maintains the organization in a state of 'productive distress'.

Leading organizations through change is not quick or direct. It is about engaging networks of people in a more experimental, incremental approach to the organization's search for answers.

Action   Provide initial programmatic leadership – the initial timing and design of the problem-solving approach, the process for engaging the organization and stakeholders, the goals.

Provide adaptive leadership through change by:

- Asking powerful questions that make people think.
- Telling your personal story of change.
- Reframing the task to enable people to connect with the problem.
- Encouraging options and experiments across the organization.

4

FINDING THE ANSWERS ON THE FRONT LINE: LEADERSHIP AT ALL LEVELS

THE STORY OF CHANGE ON THE FRONT LINE AT HMRC

The UK's HM Revenue and Customs (HMRC) was created in April 2005 from the merger of Inland Revenue and HM Customs and Excise. It was a huge organization with 90,000 staff and hundreds of locations around the UK. It inherited targets for cost reduction and customer service improvement, with the merger providing a catalyst for fresh thinking.

At that time, HMRC already had ambitious programmes for process redesign and rationalization of its estate, geared to reducing costs and improving service, but it was only beginning to consider the potential of 'lean' in its business. Lean originated in Japanese car manufacturing with the work of US Professor Deming, then spread to North America and Europe with the opening of overseas vehicle assembly plants by Nissan, Honda and Toyota. UK suppliers to Japanese-owned plants began working with lean in the 1990s, spreading rapidly to other manufacturing and service industries; then, by 2000, public sector organizations started to show interest.[100] Lean thinking and practices are all about improving quality and productivity *simultaneously* by listening to the voice of the customer and rationalizing waste in processes. Lean sparked well-known maxims such as 'just in time', 'continuous improvement' and 'right first time' and was synonymous with – and dependent upon – a highly engaged front-line workforce.

The new chairman of the merged HMRC sponsored a series of small-scale experiments with lean in various parts of HMRC's central services in London. Having been one of those advocating front-line HMRC experiments with lean, I was awarded what seemed then to be the short straw: 'If lean is so good, show us how it can turn around one of our least performing processing centres.' Rephrased for public consumption, we set out to demonstrate that the then new approach of 'lean' and local technology adaptation could revolutionize delivery at the sharp end of one of HMRC's largest and reputedly most unionized processing centres in the Lothians (a region of Scotland).

The first challenge was to persuade staff at the HMRC Lothians Centre to participate in a productivity and quality improvement exercise – because the changes could easily be interpreted as putting their jobs at risk. Lean is an approach that, by definition, cannot be driven from head office or by consultants; it had to be led by the front-line staff. As front-line leader, the Lothians centre manager, Kenny Carstairs, was critical to success, persuading his staff to engage and allowing them time and space to discover the issues, design the solution, test it, redesign it and struggle through to success. The Lothians HMRC lean team had minimal levels of consulting support, just one full-time experienced lean practitioner.

After all the juggling of organizational politics to get going, the real work of leaning the processing of income tax self-assessment forms was almost an anticlimax, although it was an intense working experience for the Lothians people. Front-line HMRC staff walked us[101] through the 'current state' of processing:

- The self-assessment forms arrived by post from taxpayers or were printed out and were stacked in boxes. The boxes then went on an 11-kilometre journey around the building that took an average of 35 working days.
- The journey took that long because the boxes stopped at a dozen locations, where staff executed *one* element of the processing on each form before they were

re-boxed and journeyed on. The boxes of forms then sat somewhere else in the building where the next element was performed by someone else – and so on.

- The HMRC staff performing this repetitive solitary processing unintentionally introduced errors into more than half of the forms they processed.
- Because the whole process took so long, there was a parallel tracking process (which needed its own staff and IT) so that when taxpayers called to ask what had happened to their tax refund claims, their form could be retrieved.

The most striking comments from HMRC staff in the Lothians processing centre were 'Of course this is crazy, but we can't change it' and 'We know exactly how it should be done'. After a month of discovering and debating solutions, the first version of a lean process and local technological fixes was piloted as the 'future state':

- The forms ceased their travels.
- The entire processing was handled by a small team sitting together, who pointed out errors to colleagues as they went and managed their own work, bringing the process duration down to 1.5 days per form.
- Within a fortnight, the locally developed quality-tracking showed that the right-first-time rate increased from 50 per cent to 98 per cent – and that the sickness absence rate went down almost to zero.
- The entire apparatus of tracking slow-moving forms through the system could be discarded and, in time, productivity doubled across the processing centre. As taxpayers got their decisions and refunds within a week of sending them in, complaints and enquiries to the call centre plummeted.
- Technology was an enabler but the context was crucial – simply deploying new technology will not deliver results without the front line engaging in experimentation.

At this point, the story appears poised for a happy ending: the successful lean approach was piloted and proven on the front line with immediate measurable and substantial benefits. However, HMRC failed to realize the same benefits when it was rolled out across the UK processing centres – how come a successful pilot in the large Lothians Centre did not turn into a successful roll-out across the UK?[102]

Now we come to the paradox: lean processing and the learning from the Lothians pilot went to the top of HMRC to discuss full implementation across the whole organization of 90,000 people. The executive committee mandated its adoption across all processing centres – normally a moment of triumph, for the pilot manager, the national manager and the consultant. In fact, it was a setback for HMRC. The mandate focused on the technology, the specific process and technical fixes developed in the Lothians. It disregarded the specific context of the Lothians and the month that their staff had spent in discovery and experimentation. The language of 'roll-out' and 'buy-in' betrays the challenge of selling something to people who had no input to the mandated solution.

HMRC did get there eventually – just years later. The problem was not ill intent – it was the typical short-circuiting of leading change due to a well-intended desire to speed up its adoption across the organization. It was too much 'programmatic leadership' when the moment called for more 'adaptive leadership' to leave the space for front-line leaders to discover and share the questions. To me, it is a powerful story of senior leaders trying to do others' jobs for them rather than focusing on what only they can do.[103]

LIMITS TO FRONT-LINE CHANGE CAPACITY AND READINESS

When Shell gave me my first 'real job' as regional sales manager in New Zealand, I was delusional about what it would entail. After business school and staff roles, I looked forward to introducing new strategies and change in the business. I did no such thing.

The constant operational issues and the ringing phone meant I had virtually no time to pursue anything remotely 'strategic'. It took a few months for me to twig that *my job was to be there to answer the phone and manage the daily issues* – for our customers, the Shell sales people and the transport supervisor who could fix individual deliveries to customers. In time, I realized that a few hours' change-thinking per week was both as much as was needed and as much as our people in sales and distribution could handle. In a sense, I discovered Mintzberg's analysis of the nature of managerial work 10 years before I read the book[104] – fragmented, minimal thinking time, big issues disposed of quickly, relationships crucial.

Once my delusions were dispelled, the scope for change on the front line, how it happened, its limits and the effort required for change to work emerged:

- There was a steady flow of initiatives from Head Office. Our reactions locally were usually a mix of polite surprise, compliance and visible support – but a suppressed disappointment that we had not had a chance to shape the initiative before it took final form and was being 'rolled out' to us in the field.
- New technology was a particularly fraught experience as management of the transition from old to new systems surfaced only when the (usually long-delayed) final system arrived for implementation, the project team having operated at a distance, both organizationally and geographically.
- When we took the initiative ourselves and prioritized themes of change locally, it seemed to take forever to find the time but, once started, was almost bound to succeed.

In the previous section, we observed failed central initiatives during the pandemic, in contrast to the power of local successes in communities, schools and businesses. But this should not be interpreted as an undiluted paean to front-line leaders and an attack on all centrally driven changes. It is a plea to recognize the systematic strengths and weaknesses in the *experiences* of front-line leaders and senior leaders:

Repeated experience – producing, selling, engineering updates	Front-line management's core role is constant attention to keeping the system stable for customers and producers, while interventions from the centre that threaten stability are complied with. Front-line management draw on the skill and expertise acquired through *repeated experience* – familiarity enables them to recognize the issue and apply the solution quickly. The front line have many of the answers and putting them at the centre of major change might take more time but will always pay off in terms of both better answers and real engagement rather than compliance. This plays into the philosophy and common sense of 'do what only you can do'.
New experience – crisis, irregular events, long gaps between action and feedback	Where front-line leaders' experiences can mislead their judgements is when the experience is *insufficiently repeated*. This can happen in a crisis or accident that renders previous experience irrelevant, when the environment is insufficiently regular to be predictable or when there is a long gap between action and feedback. These *new experiences* are rarely one-offs – they are frequently experienced as technology-enabled change or regulation-driven change.

When front-line experience is blunted by change, the answer is to work across organizational boundaries; it is not about imposing a view from the centre or outside. One of the unprecedented effects of the pandemic illustrates this: the death toll in many care homes was horrific as carers struggled to deal with a situation they had never seen before, had not been trained for and were not

101

equipped for. One care home in Northern Ireland was infected by the virus but more residents recovered and the spread of the virus was limited. Their success was due to the front-line carers discovering that they could adopt techniques of infection control, equipment and testing from their acute partners.[105]

CHALLENGES OF TECHNOLOGY-ENABLED CHANGE AND THE ROLE OF FRONT-LINE LEADERS

Technology is a double-edged sword – huge potential for customer service, but also for disruption. When it comes to 'who leads technology-enabled change?', the challenge is that it frequently straddles the experience continuum. It can be a 'new experience' that has to be in the hands of a separate project team for development, but then risks stumbling on transition to the complex system of 'repeated experience' field operations.

The rapid adoption of smart mobile devices gives the opportunity to revive trust in major technology-enabled change, as old-style 'waterfall' approaches give way to 'agile' approaches:

Flavour 1 of technology-enabled change: The waterfall approach	New or replacement enterprise-wide systems are traditionally developed in 'waterfall' approaches of conventional project management in a linear, top-down approach: agree goals and constraints upfront, write the code in a project team, then implement on the front line.
	Examples abound of failed projects – from 'core process re-engineering' to TSB's replacement of its old Lloyds operating platform with the Sabadell platform in 2018.
	The complexity, inflexibility and the standardization built into these change programmes almost immediately condemns them to failure. In particular, the combination of long-delayed implementation with apparently trivial parameters

agreed upfront (and long forgotten) ends up alienating the front line when it limits the flexibility and workability of the system when it is rolled out. The word 'roll-out' tells you all you need to know – stand in front of it and ask for flexibility and you will be steamrollered.

Flavour 2 of technology-enabled change: The agile approach Contemporary 'agile'-development projects appear to avoid many of the challenges of the enterprise-wide new systems, given the 'customer view' driving the project and the rapid phasing of 'scrum' development, so prototypes are tested constantly and improved.

The principles of agile system development are:

- Speed and focus on the customer – engaging the customer in design, testing and learning.
- Breaking the development process into small steps.
- Generating 'minimum viable product' with rapid prototyping.
- Testing with users, recycling feedback and iterating.

Agile-developed change offers huge opportunities, given its front-line customer focus, but it has its own challenges:

either when it is applied faddishly;

or when it is integrated with complex back-office systems;

or when the front-line engagement is limited and ineffective.

Agile as fad

Agile delivery methods for introducing new technology are capable of reducing the risk of major change by closing the gap between senior leaders (who set direction and provide funding) and front-line leaders (who shape solutions and adopt change). Sometimes 'agile' is misapplied as a label, but not really adopted – in which case it can cause more harm than good when, culturally and operationally, a new exclusive language is created around agile.

Agile plus complexity

There is huge pressure for established organizations to move from waterfall to agile approaches. Commercially, we can see laggards in online marketing literally going under financially. Government has committed to 'digital by default' and has hugely ambitious programmes running with Universal Credit, borders-immigration-customs and many more. The NHS is acutely aware that if it lags in exploiting its patient data, the global technology firms will move in and exploit the data commercially, as already illustrated by agreements to share anonymized NHS data. However, they all face the technical challenges of ambitious front ends bolted on to fragile ageing infrastructure – which implies all the same issues as any change in a complex system. Agile is not a 'get out of jail free' card; the hard work on organization change is still needed for success.

Agile under-scoped

The really big difference with new technology and the widespread adoption of smart devices is that it enables the front line to experiment much more and therefore change can be speeded up through agile working. In the NHS, a network of 2,000 quality improvement leaders are supported by NHS Improvement. To be clear, the key is not the technology, it is how front-line leaders work to experiment and apply the technology in their own context. This implies significant investment in capability-building to run the new systems in a customer-oriented intent. It also means that typical project management – isolating agile teams from established operations – risks late transition and collision with front-line reality.

CHANGE DEPENDS ON EVERY SET OF LEADERS DOING WHAT ONLY THEY CAN DO – IN A DYNAMIC INTERACTION

Technology is an enormous enabler of change, because it gives the front line access to much more information and to more app-based tools, and enables a tailored approach to customer needs, enrolling the customer in the process – rather than the standardization implied by past systematization. How should leaders act to realize these opportunities while steering around the challenges?

We have to avoid falling into multiple traps: presuming senior leaders have all the answers, or leaving the front line to deliver everything even outside their experience, or assuming resources and capabilities will redeploy themselves behind the change. In particular, small-scale pilots and demonstrations can give misleadingly positive results: demonstrations are often not tested on a large enough scale to give a valid sample. Pilots benefit from a lot of extra management attention and therefore typically respond more positively (the Hawthorne effect[106]). So a successful local initiative needs to be assessed before the organization invests longer-term with all the necessary support. Leaders at all levels have to do what only they can do well:

Only front-line leaders can...	...provide the flow of experiments and options that test new technologies and customer initiatives. Somewhere 'out there' are the positive deviants who have discovered improvements. Take advantage of the fact that there is no single way of 'doing'.
Only the **management teams** across the organization can...	...build the skills, culture and processes to execute change and optimize the organization behind the strategy.

Only **senior leaders** can…	…select the few front-line initiatives to invest behind;
	…grant the time, space and flexibility for the organization to explore;
	…commit the organization to a new direction and communicate it across the organization.

It should be evident that the interaction of all levels of leadership is dynamic – we have left behind the static models of change management. If we recognize the complexity of organizational systems and the potential of utilizing leadership at all levels, then the organization cannot go through defined phases of direction-setting, redesign and implementation. Instead, successful change has innovation, direction-setting, system design and implementation all happening in parallel and feeding off one another. This is where management teams play a crucial role: keeping balance and reinforcing success, while avoiding tipping into chaos.

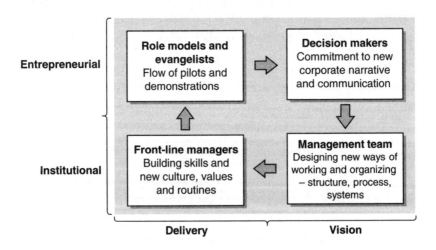

It is when leadership is operating at all levels – front-line experimentation, senior direction and functional-regional-industry management teams building the organizational capabilities – that major change succeeds and one can begin talking about the holy grail of many senior leaders' ambitions: culture change, a thriving organization and thriving people realizing their potential.

SOMEONE OUT THERE HAS THE ANSWER

We have already explored the challenges of working in complex systems and described the crucial role played by front-line management in making trade-offs and ensuring stability in the system. We have also explored how organizations tend to live in their internal siloed world and that the 'real world' has to be brought in to restore balance. A real world that is all too rarely visited by some leaders is their own front line with its experimentation and options.

The pandemic and its aftermath provide many case studies in front-line innovation and the challenge of disseminating and preserving learning:[107]

- Front-line leaders reorganized themselves to meet the challenge.
  West Suffolk NHS Foundation Trust reorganized its intensive care team (including my son) in anticipation of the crisis with bigger teams and shorter shifts and introduced a virtual appointments guide for patients – what to expect and how to prepare. North Bristol NHS Trust took a similar approach with mega-teams.

- Recovery rates in some care homes were much higher than average.
  Rosemount Care Home in Portadown achieved 86 per cent recovery rate among elderly residents who were infected due to insistence on early testing and strong support of an acute team from the local hospital – in

stark contrast to the toll in care homes across Northern Ireland.[108]

- Technology enabled decentralized front-line working. Zoom, Attend Anywhere and Teams became ubiquitous. The Royal Wolverhampton NHS Trust launched the #nogoingback campaign, including reorganizing district nurses and working remotely, empowering people to make changes. Like many trusts, they produced videos and introduced remote therapy for patients unable to attend rehab sessions due to the COVID-19 pandemic.

- Connection and belonging took deliberate action. Addenbrooke's Hospital and – separately – Deloitte introduced 'RCTs' (not the gold standard preferred proof of treatment 'randomized controlled trials') or Randomized Coffee Trials, connecting people in the organization who wouldn't normally meet, helping staff to keep in touch and avoid feeling isolated. The Mental Health Foundation had a daily online 'stretch' for all staff, among many other well-being measures. WhatsApp groups sprang up to enable informal interaction when face-to-face became dangerous.

- Stresses were addressed.
  Many NHS family liaison teams coped with the isolation on COVID wards, using iPads and FaceTime to help patients keep in touch with relatives and providing a postbox for letters and emails, operationally hosted by chaplaincy teams. Mental health support was provided for doctors and nurses having difficult conversations with relatives and working with deteriorating patients. Bradford Teaching Hospitals NHS Foundation Trust introduced 'wobble rooms' – a place to go for a few minutes to share worries, have a shout-out-loud, a

little weep or just be quiet. Scotland's First Minister admitted that she 'shed a few tears' at the impact of her decisions.[109]

- Kindness reached a billion.
  At the Mental Health Foundation, we changed the theme of Mental Health Awareness Week in May 2020 to 'kindness', because of its singular ability to unlock our shared humanity. The theme reached 1 billion online users, while almost 1 million people read our web pages. Kindness is defined by doing something towards yourself and others, motivated by genuine desire to make a positive difference. We know from the research that kindness and our mental health are deeply connected, with kindness acting as an antidote to isolation and creating a sense of belonging.[110] Donated Easter eggs were distributed to NHS staff in many hospitals. Cheshire and Mersey Specialist Perinatal Service created 'Be kind to yourself' for women self-isolating with babies or young children, to support them in establishing a routine, enhance their well-being and engagement in activities, while self-isolating.[111]

LEARNING HOW TO MAKE IT EASIER TO CHANGE BEHAVIOUR

CHANGE OR DIE by Alan Deutschman
(2005, Fast Company 52)[112]

People won't change their behaviour to (literally) save their lives. Cardiac patients could avoid surgery and improve their quality of life by changing behaviours in relation to diet and exercise. However, most do not. So why would we believe that people will change their behaviour for the benefit of their organization?

The key insight is that, to influence people's behaviour, leaders need to appeal to emotions as well as thinking and facts:

- Framing change: facts need to fit into a frame that enables people to make sense of them. It is the job of leaders to provide that positive narrative.
- Radical change: big changes are easier than small ones because they quickly yield benefits.
- Supporting change: processes, systems and other critical inputs have to be aligned and coherent.
- How our brains work: we can keep learning throughout our lives.

Mobile technology and agile working are changing our definition of the front line and how we organize for change. Technology firms and technology functions within organizations work as self-organizing multidisciplinary teams that are part or all of their 'front-line' contact with customers.

Technology and the exploitation of near universal smart mobile devices is the current focus of businesses and government. It can enable fundamental and profitable change in service for customers and organizational direction, profitability and sustainability. It presents challenges to leaders of major change programmes:

We know that, to be effective, technology relies on front-line experimentation...

...but shortage of technology skills and instinct to focus on the big opportunities results in central project teams driving the programme...

...resulting in functional-regional-industry management teams being unable to build the organizational capabilities required...

...unless senior leaders insist on finding solutions on the front line, where we know most innovation, whether planned or piloted or inadvertent or hidden, takes place.

Senior leaders

For senior leaders, this is not about *giving* leadership to the front line or *pushing* innovation to the front line – leadership is already being exercised at all levels and 'positive deviants' somewhere 'out there' are already successfully innovating. Senior leaders have to push other leaders to find them, listen to them and encourage more experimentation.[113]

Senior leaders can ask better questions of their front-line leaders, such as: 'In the outside world, things can be done very differently – what would be your version of this?' For example, management at Powergen reached out to the highest-performing power stations in the US as part of a 'global best practice' benchmarking exercise. They visited the lowest-cost power stations known globally, but the point of the exercise was not to lift ideas directly from the US and apply them in the UK. The point was to take the UK power station managers out of the comfortable world they knew and to stimulate new thinking, enabling them to see from the experience elsewhere that things could be done quite differently back home in their stations.

Front-line leaders

Mobile technology is transforming organizations' potential relationships with their customers, making the front line even more important. The cost of experimentation has declined dramatically with cheap mobile technology and the Cloud. Front-line leaders need to build the capabilities for a blossoming of front-line experiments and pilots that offer better-developed options from which senior leaders can select. Even in the apparently most sensitive and advanced of arenas, nuclear submarines, crew are encouraged to apply shop-bought technology to communicate and track events.

Management teams

Agile working and the impact of mobile technology need to underpin the organization's approach to change. However, the real costs and risks for established organizations come when agile-developed front ends need to be coupled to traditional large-scale systems that underpin the entire organization. This applies especially in institutions with huge stores of sensitive data – the banks, the tax authorities, welfare provision etc. Making a simple customer-facing app actually work and work securely requires infrastructure and scale of resources. This is a key task of the management teams that set priorities, allocate resources and encourage new ways of working across the organization.

Leadership at all levels

Senior leaders saying…	*My questions for you are…* *Where are we already doing things differently?* *What would it take to…* *Could you test how we could accomplish…*
Front-line leaders saying…	*Our current experiments and pilots are…* *We can try doing…* *We can keep the system stable while changing x and y if we reinforce a and b…*
Management teams saying…	*We have a plan… to build the organization and improve capability in…* *We have a realistic and affordable plan for technology*

Summary

Successful change in organizations depends on senior leaders, front-line leaders and management teams doing what only they can do – and it is usually the roles of the front line that are overlooked.

Only front-line leaders can provide the flow of options that test new ideas, while only the management teams across the organization can build the capabilities and infrastructure to optimize the organization behind the strategy – and only the senior leaders can select the few front-line initiatives to fund and commit the organization to a new direction.

Front-line leaders need to discover and shape the change solution for themselves. 'Selling' a solution or achieving 'buy-in' after the decision is taken will:

- *Frequently under-deliver and often fail outright due to unforeseen issues, lack of understanding and reluctant front-line adoption.*
- *Ignore the 'positive deviants' in the organization who have already discovered answers and could share their learning.*

Technology-enabled change should make it easier to experiment on the front line with agile pilots and easy access to technology.

Action

Do what only you can do. Ask others to do what they do best. Don't tell them how to do it – ask why they do it and what they could do differently.

Work proactively across senior leaders, front-line leaders and management teams to design and deliver change in the organization:

- *Stimulate new thinking on the front line by bringing in the external world.*
- *Listen to front-line leaders and find the positive deviants.*
- *Manage the costs and risks of coupling agile-developed front-end to conventional organizational systems.*

5

TEAMS THAT WORK: GETTING THE REAL WORK DONE

THE STORY OF THE FTSE-50 MANAGEMENT TEAM

The chief executive of one of the most successful international gas companies wanted to improve the performance of the executive committee – six senior directors and him.[114] He was convinced that the executive committee wasn't working well as a team and, on the other hand, the six senior directors were convinced that the chief executive was unwilling to tolerate alternative points of view. At a routine executive committee meeting, everyone agreed to hold a series of off-site workshops to work together to improve how they worked. This was the first milestone on the journey: everyone had agreed to work on their effectiveness, and there would be open debate, legitimizing different points of view.

Then came the first disruption: the initial off-site workshop never got going. As everyone gathered for coffee before the starting time, the chief executive took one director aside and fired him on the spot, explaining that he could not face a day's discussion of 'team performance' including someone he thought was not behaving as 'a proper team player'. This shocked the remaining directors, and for an hour they debated: was it 'stop' or 'go' for trying again to work on their effectiveness? The issues had not gone away – but was it too dangerous to open up the issues? Would the executive committee break apart at a real cost to the organization? Everyone agreed to try again...

Then came the second disruption: The rescheduled off-site workshop a few weeks later blew up.

The chief executive and five senior directors had begun by going through an exercise to test alignment on strategic priorities, with each of them putting on Post-its their top four priorities for the company. When the Post-its were clustered and displayed, it seemed that they were all over the place – apart from two issues in common, everyone had prioritized different things. This pattern of diverse expressions of priorities within senior leadership is common to many organizations, but the chief executive was furious and could not understand how this could be, given that he had stated the company's priorities again and again. In his view, this showed that the executive committee had failed. The workshop paused – was it 'stop' or 'go' for continuing work on their effectiveness?

After a short break, they picked up the discussion – identifying the key issues for the company that needed to be resolved. But by then, the workshop format of round-the-table discussions with all six participants had grown wearisome. It was agreed to stop having off-site workshops and switch to a format of working together in pairs, with each pair working on one of the agreed priorities for the company. Over the next few weeks, all of the members of the executive committee worked in pairs on their agreed priority. The quality of the discussion and the enthusiasm improved markedly at subsequent meetings of the full executive committee. By doing the detailed work together to explore the issues and potential actions in pairs, the full executive committee was better equipped to debate the options, and approval for the actions came more easily with already supportive allies around the table. The difference in effective working was noticeable and gave the chief executive and five senior directors the confidence to talk about and reflect on the action-oriented 'real work' that had made them more effective as a team, as well as what made for less effective discussions.

This is not an unusual story. The elements that repeat for all kinds of teams in all kinds of organizations are: dissatisfaction with team effectiveness, pivotal role of the leader, misalignment on priorities, doing real work together – and thereafter reflecting on what makes the team more effective.

DOING REAL WORK IN TEAMS

Organizations are littered with teams of all shapes and sizes, with different tasks and capabilities – and often working suboptimally. The reason that teams emerge is in the nature of organizations. Both theory and observation suggest that once organizational units grow beyond 150, it becomes impossible for the leader to know everyone in the group and exert personal leadership – structures and delegated teams have to be inserted and distance grows between the leaders and the led.[115]

Is this a team?

'Team' is one of the universal management words that has been so overused it has lost most of its meaning – like 'project', 'change' and 'culture'. My former colleague Jon Katzenbach defined a true team (as distinct from a mere working group) in terms of its common purpose, complementary skills and mutual accountability.[116] However, most groups, committees and meetings are routinely labelled teams without much thought.

'Teams are greater than the sum of their parts' is perhaps the best-known aphorism about teams, but many so-called teams are actually less than the sum of their parts. Talented individuals manage somehow not to deploy their talents, hold back, are unclear on why they are there, and engage in competition within their fellow team members. Most management teams are at best partially successful – unconsciously mediocre because they are not doing real work together.

Is this real work?

If a team is not doing real work together, then it is unlikely to be an effective team. Sadly, much of what is labelled as 'team building' – from outward-bound exercises to evening drinking sessions – is not real work, but work avoidance.

- *Real work* is engaging with a significant issue, exploring its implications, generating options, testing them out and taking responsibility for implementation, revision and bringing resources to bear. It is about making progress on difficult issues, by deliberately bringing them to the team that has the resources and authority to resolve them.
- *Work avoidance* is engaging in pastimes that substitute for real engagement with the issues, including critiquing PowerPoint presentations, pushing personal ambitions and pet projects, outward-bound activities, or attending seminars at a golf resort hotel or a business school. So-called team-building events can actually depress morale if ill thought-through and they fail to address the issues that require serious solutions.[117]

Outright *work sabotage* is fortunately rare, but examples include undermining and delaying tactics in and around meetings. It is not surprising that the CIA's wartime manual for sabotage, which covers all the expected techniques for damaging property and gathering intelligence, also lists tried-and-tested organizational techniques such as delaying and encouraging uncooperative attitudes. The CIA recommended these techniques as key tools for long-term agents working within organizations in occupied Europe, because of their negative impact on productivity while remaining above suspicion.[118]

Do I have to like them?

A successful team is judged by whether its members engage fully in the work that it is charged with. It is not about harmony within the team – conflict is good if it is productive – but trust is needed. Trust at work is quite specific: it is about doing as you say and giving honest and open input. Management teams are watched closely by their people – and the visible style matters as much as the results. Like parents using bad language or bad behaviour in front of the family, it will be copied and come back to haunt you.

When working on team performance, I was accustomed to saying 'You don't have to love one another', but when we used that line with the Church of Scotland, a participant quietly pointed out 'Actually, I think we do'. So now I say: 'Team dynamics can vary from stormy to collegial as long as there is trust – it is up to you to decide as a team the style needed to deliver results in line with your values.'

INVESTING IN TEAMS THAT WORK

Teams can perform effectively, or they can work at a slow pace – or they can play games, just as leaders and organizations play games. One of the most productive investments that leaders can make is to invest to improve team performance. The actual investment is a little time and willingness to learn from three well-tried principles, set out below. The pay-off is effectiveness, faster change and effective delegation – taking pressure off time-bereft leaders. The most productive team-improvement investments are in:

- *The team around the top leader*
  The 'top team' merits investment simply because of the need for visible shared direction. The senior team can fight like cats in a bag behind closed doors as long as they like, but they must be credibly in the same space (not necessarily word-perfect identical) when they deal with the wider organization.

- *The management teams across the organization*
  The key decision-making teams made up of the functional leaders and the regional leaders and the customer/industry leaders across the organization

merit investment, but are frequently ignored. They are essential for building the skills, culture and processes to execute change and optimize the organization behind the strategy, the classic 'glue' within the organization. They bring together overall direction and front-line needs, resolving trade-offs of time, resources and performance.

After watching some senior leaders work again and again on their teams' performance as they moved through senior roles in different organizations over the years, I concluded that it is easier to change the behaviour of a team than it is to change the behaviour of an individual senior leader.

One senior leader struggled with his team at an Australian bank, made progress, was promoted to a UK bank – and promptly struggled with his team there. In both cases, this senior leader never really addressed the weaknesses in his own style – people rarely change after decades of success – but he did get his teams to perform better. The teams worked on the basics and their improved work was reinforced by success in the business. Having worked with many dysfunctional management teams in companies, government and charities, I observed that universally they lifted their performance following simple principles:[119]

- Doing real work together
- Cycling through action and reflection
- Aligning direction

Doing real work together

Senior groups labelled 'teams' – often 'the senior management team' or 'the leadership team' or 'the executive' – frequently do not do much real work. They engage in work avoidance: commenting on presentations or asking detailed questions on monthly performance reports are two of the favourite work avoidance tactics. Usually it takes the senior leader in the group to feel overwhelmed or frustrated with a lack of progress before work avoidance is called out. The remedy is to:

- *Manage the agenda*
  Identify the one (or at most two) big business issues that will be tackled at a team meeting and make sure they are taken first on the agenda, allowing them to take at least half the meeting time.

- *Keep the work within the team*
  The problem-solving has to be done by the team, not delegated to junior staff to prepare options. By keeping the debate and follow-up within the team, who are best suited to resolve the issue, success is more likely.

The result of doing real work together is better answers for business problems and greater confidence in the team. Over time, practising real work will build a common language for business problem-solving and a focus on real-world issues rather than game-playing.

Cycling through action and reflection

Most teams enjoy action and feeling like they make things happen. Conversely, they feel awkward when asked to pause and share impressions of how they or their teams are doing – 'What if I say the wrong thing?', 'What if I offend someone?', 'Isn't it a strange thing for senior people to be playing psychology?' Often the excuse of 'we have a full agenda, we can't afford time navel-gazing' is deployed to shut down discussions on 'how are we doing as a team?' There are two simple steps to demystifying the essential 'reflection' component of improving team-working:

- *Building in time to check in*
  If a team is spending time on a critical business issue, then agree in advance what success will look like,

then check in for 5–10 minutes on 'how are we doing on what we set out to achieve?' This is not amateur psychology – you, the team, said what you wanted to achieve. Now you take responsibility for stating whether you are on track and, if not, why not. The check-in might only be at the end of the meeting (if it is short) or at the end of each section (if a half- or full-day meeting).

- *Increase the odds of a real exchange of views during the check-in*
  Do not just invite comments from the group – ask everyone to take two minutes to think in silence and note their points, then invite the discussion. This will dramatically improve the quality of discussion and avoid the work avoidance tactics of groupthink or waiting to hear what the senior person says before venturing an opinion.

A little reflection will go a long way for a team that has prided itself on action – and will not embarrass anyone or risk becoming 'touchy-feely'. The result of getting into a regular cycle of action and reflection is a more efficient approach in getting to better answers for business problems and more open discussions. Over time, it will encourage people to take responsibility and exercise leadership within the team.

Aligning direction

One of the most dramatic illustrations of the need for reflection to balance action in senior teams is to ask how aligned the team is on direction – as we saw in the initial story of the senior team at the international gas company. Many leaders express frustration with their team: 'Why are we agreeing within the team at the meeting, but then doing different things outside the room? I thought we were very clear about what was agreed.' Some individuals might indeed be cynically saying one thing while doing another. However, the explanation is more often that it is very easy to agree in a meeting to a *general* direction of travel, but then say and do very different things outside the room, because people draw very different *detailed* implications from a general statement.

Tackling this common misalignment is a matter of testing and exploring priorities:

- *Test for alignment*
  I ask the members of a senior team (who have recently concluded a strategy review or something similar) to write down the top three priorities of the organization, each on a separate Post-it, so a team of six generate 18 Post-its. Then we cluster the priorities on a flip chart so everyone can see them. A perfectly aligned team will have only three clusters, but I have never seen that team, so far. A typical team might broadly agree on four priorities with a long tail of others – illustrating the challenge.

- *Explore the consequences*
  Let's explore that typical senior team, who have been confronted with evidence that they are broadly aligned on only a few priorities. After the initial reaction (which is usually silence and expletives and surprise), the team needs to counter its rush to action. The team will need to invest much more time in exploring the consequences and implementation of its agreed actions – it needs to keep acting, but to take the time to ensure direction is actually aligned.

The result of doing real work together, reflecting on how the team is doing and checking for alignment will be better answers for business problems and growing confidence in the team – both in the quality of discussions and in the behaviours outside the room. Over time, the wider organization notices the difference in terms of leaders speaking the same language and this encourages staff and stakeholders to exercise leadership themselves with greater confidence.

This trickle-down effect on the wider organization is critical, especially when key pressure points for change can be identified. In financial services, one pressure point is critical: the investment guidelines. These are the parameters that govern what loans/ investments can be made, the rates of return required, who may receive them, etc. – they are the bibles that set the boundaries for what happens on the front line:

- *Lloyds Banking Group*
  Building social investment is a key part of the bank's sustainability strategy. Alignment of the senior team was a precondition to enable a different approach to financial returns plus social impact, rather than just the rate of return. Just having an agreed strategy was insufficient – a key management team had to write the necessary words into the formula before the front line could move on from focusing solely on financial returns and lend the money.

- *Big Society Capital*
  The social investment wholesaler and market-builder had the opposite challenge when it began work in 2012 to create a sustainable social investment market. Lending to charities and social enterprises had been all about grants and soft loans rather than financial returns. In order to attract mainstream investors, Big Society Capital had to do more than articulate a general strategy to earn acceptable returns; they had to be perfectly aligned around specific target returns and publish their investment policies.

SHARE STORIES TO BUILD COMMON PURPOSE IN CHANGE

So far, there has been little about psychology, self-disclosure or other emotional adventures that people often expect in team-building. It is true that there is much that leaders can learn from psychology and therapy, including narrative therapy – i.e., the stories we tell about our lives. Similarly, in organizations, the stories that people tell also play an important part in shaping the culture – as we explore further in Section 9. The pandemic and its aftermath are the most widely shared experiences that we now share through our stories.

Did your team have a good pandemic?

Placing aside the fact that the pandemic was universally regarded as a tragic catastrophe, some businesses had a relatively 'good pandemic' – some were in the right place at the right time to pick up customers suddenly working from home. There are obvious examples from Internet-based delivery of telecoms through shopping but, less obviously, most businesses dealing with government, the NHS and public services also did well. Procurements that normally were competitive and lengthy were suddenly awarded without competition.[120] It remains to be seen whether health and social care services come out of the pandemic's aftermath fundamentally stronger – we return to this topic in Sections 8–10. During the crisis, when they were isolated from customers and suppliers, some businesses had to go into a hibernation from which not all would wake after the pandemic eased. Other businesses developed powerful new habits of rapid decision-making, team-working and decentralization that need to be retained.

Many businesses were like Mental Health At Work Community Interest Company (CIC)[121] and went through a cycle of crisis management, change and settling into 'the new normal'. Mental Health At Work is a social enterprise focused on selling mental health training and development to companies, enabling their managers to have the essential conversations with all employees to support their mental health. It is a growing market as companies take on responsibility for their people's health and realize the benefits of a mentally healthy workplace – a topic we return to in Section 10. But the pandemic was a turning point for us:

'Crisis' for a month	Mental Health At Work delivered facilitated workshops face-to-face. The lockdown postponed all work. Revenue went to zero and the sales pipeline vanished. Leadership assured all staff and contractors that their personal income was safe. Staff and contractors developed, tested and launched a virtual product with nine-person groups on facilitated video conference.
'Accelerate' for a quarter	Having negotiated all current customer contracts over to the new virtual product, staff and contractors worked to reinforce the quality and economic viability of virtual delivery. The business development team made the first sales of the virtual product.
'Pace' for the long term	At this stage the team were tired, elated and needing to draw breath after delivering a new model for the business in a few months – rather than the few years that had featured in the business plan. Sustainable change dictated that people begin to pace themselves for the longer term, rather than risk burnout.[122]

You may or may not have powerful stories about your organization's experience of the pandemic. I recommend that you actively shape the stories that you and your team tell about what matters to you – it is a powerful approach to creating team identity and purpose. If you don't shape together the stories told within the organization, then you will live with what other people tell as stories, because organizations tend to seek out stories to tell – good or bad.

What's your story?

Storytelling is a powerful way into sharing experiences and needs within a team, particularly when building capability to lead change. It appeals to the human desire to see life through a story and builds the team's shared identity and purpose – as explored further in Section 8:

Writing the story	Most leaders sit at their kitchen table one Saturday morning and write a story that begins with a personal anecdote that illustrates the need for change, connecting it with the intended direction, then closes with what the leader will do differently – and what they need others to do differently.
Telling the story	The story is told, without props or slides or paper, to a small group, who listen without interruption. The group spend 1–2 minutes silently noting down their questions, then taking turns to ask a question and listen to the answer until all the questions have been asked.
Cascading storytelling	After the senior leader's story, each member of the team will go through the same story-writing and storytelling with their team.

Effective storytelling will communicate the direction of the organization more memorably than any strategy document and will also create a human connection among the group who listen and engage with the story. Over time, people and the wider organization will start using more of the same language, look for their own real examples and thrive through engaging in the real work.

Of course, this is not a magic wand. A substantial divergence between the leader's story and the current state will increase the investment and time lag needed to bring them into alignment. Leaders will want to work with the grain of the organization and build on established organizational stories as far as possible. They will need to think hard about how to give people confidence in the realism and sustainability of a story that departs radically from the *status quo*. New experiences and memories have to be laid down by doing real work together in teams and telling stories of success.

WHAT BEHAVIOURAL SCIENCE TELLS US ABOUT COMMUNICATING FOR IMPACT

HARNESSING THE SCIENCE OF PERSUASION by Robert Cialdini (*Harvard Business Review*, October 2001)

Behavioural science enables us to understand and appeal to deeply rooted human needs. When questioning the performance of your team and looking to build shared identity and purpose, you will need to influence people to consider your point of view, or adopt your opinion. When approaching a discussion to win one or more people over, the six scientific principles of influencing people are:

1 Liking: to influence people, win friends.
2 Reciprocity: give what you want to receive.
3 Social proof: use peer power.
4 Consistency: make others' commitments active, public and voluntary.
5 Authority: don't assume your expertise is self-evident.
6 Scarcity: use exclusive information to persuade.

LEADING THROUGH YOUR TEAM GIVES YOU BACK TIME

Leaders' time is hopelessly crammed and fragmented – they have little time for reflection and preparation and fall back on default ideas, practices and behaviours that have worked for them in the past. In the context of leading change, one of the biggest pay-off investments that the organization can make is to improve the working of the management teams that set priorities and allocate resources across the organization. Leaders do not need to indulge in the expensive or exposing techniques advocated by some team-builders. Practical steps and support can result in a greater focus on the real work, create a much more common language and prompt leadership behaviours across the organization:

Senior leaders saying...	*I shall prioritize spending my time on...* *You should remind me and feed back when you see...* *My story is...*
Front-line leaders saying...	*Our jobs are about making trade-offs, deciding what is needed right now to keep things moving. So, let's make the trade-offs explicit, learn from them, ask...*
Management teams saying...	*We are doing the real work together... to build capability and hold the organization together.* *We share our stories of change...*

Summary   *Successful change in organizations depends on the management teams across the organization being effective. They bring together the overall direction articulated by the senior leaders and front-line needs, resolving trade-offs of time, resources and performance. The key decision-making teams made up of the functional leaders and the regional leaders and the customer/industry leaders are essential for building the skills, culture and processes to implement sustained change.*

The team around the top leader and the management teams across the organization repay investment in their effectiveness.

Improving management team performance is only accomplished by doing real work together – real work being team problem-solving on core business challenges.

Action   *Leading through your team gives you back time – the steps to getting teams to work effectively are straightforward:*

- *Do real work as a team, in cycles of action and reflection, and align priorities.*
- *Challenge your team to really align on direction, rather than settling for lowest common denominator.*
- *Share stories to build common purpose.*
- *Exercise situational leadership.*

PART FOUR

'WHAT DO I DO WHEN WE MEET BUMPS IN THE ROAD?'

Change in organizations is challenging due to the inherent complexity of organizations and the time pressures on leaders that can lead to over-reliance on past experience. However, 'challenging' does not mean 'impossible'. There are bound to be occasional failures and adjustments while on the journey, but these are just the bumps in the road:

- *There will be mistakes along the way* Many commercial, public sector and voluntary organizations conceal leadership failures and consequently they – and we – miss the opportunity to learn from many of them. Perhaps more importantly, when the cover-up is found out, then trust is lost.
- *There will also be adjustments in strategy along the way* This is inevitable with complex organizations navigating a changing world – akin to sailing a boat, you have to tack regularly to make progress against the wind. One leadership mistake can be avoided by making these 'tacking' choices clear, both in advance where possible, and certainly when they happen.

The common theme for successful navigation of mistakes and changes is to equip yourself with an effective language to deal with it. Don't look to management consultants or popular business texts for that effective language – conventional 'change management' language of 'transformation plans' and 'project management' implies a static, controlled and sequenced view of change. Improving the chances of successful change needs a more dynamic language and conversation, reflecting the complexity of the organization and engagement of leaders at all levels. In a sense, 'change management' is dead.

Senior leaders, front-line leaders and management teams each have to do what only they can do to lead change in the organization – but they do have to perform in concert. Collaboration across the leadership within the organization is essential in order to avoid disjointed conversations and frustrated leaders. Collaboration is not all about shared performance indicators and reporting, although you may need *some* of that apparatus of control. It is about learning together and being on the journey together – and to do that implies:

- *Bringing the real world inside the organization*
  Organizations defend the status quo by focusing on their
  internal world and conforming to established wisdom,
  limiting change until there is a visible disaster. Mistakes
  need to be learned from, not obfuscated. Designing
  change that brings the 'real world' into the organization
  enables leaders to inject both optimism and realism by
  providing evidence of real-world change and experience.
  This reduces risk by learning from others, especially
  from the 'positive deviants' within the organization, who
  are already finding better ways of working.

- *Creating a shared language of change*
  Shakespeare conceded that 'indeed words are very
  rascals … words are grown so false, I am loath to prove
  reason with them'.[123] However, words are a key currency

of leadership and that currency is typically debased in management-speak. I am not suggesting that you need to develop the great oratory abilities of Mandela – everyday language may suffice – but it will become loaded with the meaning that matters to you and your leaders. Delivering change requires 'learning and creating a new common language' and 'stories of change' that enable organizations to focus on what really matters and avoid obfuscation.

- *Holding the vision and building capabilities through waves of change*
  No single project can deliver everything. It may not yet be apparent what the ultimate goal is. Given the complexity of organizations and continually changing environments, it is clear that transforming an organization is never a one-shot-deal. One of the tasks that only senior leaders can perform is to articulate the long-term vision (in so far as they can see it) while a wave of change delivers – pivoting and shifting short-term focus periodically, while building the capabilities that are required for the next wave of change.

This does not mean that the senior leader is controlling or directing everything. It means that teams need to be aligned, that leaders are learning together and the capabilities being built for technology-enabled change. Leaders can prepare to turn 'bumps in the road' into 'take-off ramps' as set out in the following sections:

6 **Learning from leaders and mistakes**
  Creating a forum for shared learning across the leadership of the organization is frequently very powerful – in improved outcomes, demonstrating shared values and building support for change. Shared learning can take many forms – from a top-class

formal programme to a series of structured 'open
house' meetings. The key features of whatever forum is
chosen are:

- Signalling that every leader within the organization
  has to learn and change.
- Acknowledging mistakes when they happen and
  learning from them.
- Engaging the leadership across the organization in
  creating a community with a common language of
  change.
- Enabling leaders to tell new stories – a vital step,
  given the impact of stories that shape behaviours
  across organizations.

7 **Tacking through waves of change**
Time pressures and expectations of quick results
lead senior leaders to focus on rapid change in their
organizations. The reality is that successful change takes
time and leaders cannot move in one step to a radically
different organization. Time is needed for waves of
activity that work indirectly towards the ultimate goal,
building the capability of the organization, including
maintaining the stability of day-to-day operations.
Leaders' language will reflect elements of:

- The long term: where we are aiming for ultimately.
  Perhaps not visionary or specific, but this is the goal
  and its characteristics.
- The journey: the roads we need to travel and the
  intermediate achievements that will be necessary for
  us to be fit to get to our goal.
- The short term: what we need to do now – and when
  we may need to adjust direction like a boat tacking
  across the wind to reach its destination.

6

LEARNING FROM LEADERS AND MISTAKES: CREATING COMMON LANGUAGE AND A COMMUNITY OF PEERS

STORIES OF MISTAKES – WHO KNEW? THE INSIDERS KNEW

Failure is commonplace in leadership, but you would never know that from a quick glance at the 'Heathrow Business School' (after business travellers' predilection for 'how to' manuals), which displays prominently the books from celebrity leaders on 'how I triumphed singlehandedly'. Even official investigations of big corporate and public service failures provide little insight. Against this backdrop of 'not talking about failure', I want to focus on a niche: the stories of insiders who knew how and why failure was imminent, while regulators-investors-media and (sometimes) senior leaders were unaware or turning a blind eye.[124] The stories encompass financial failure by companies, public service failures and projects failing to deliver:

Enron   *The 2002 collapse of the global energy giant amid fraud*
Enron was, for a decade, one of the most lauded corporate
success stories. A group of investment bankers and management
consultants took over a dull gas pipeline company, acquired other
power and gas utilities and, applying the trading instruments
developed on financial markets, turned the slow world of utilities
into a high-value, fast-moving business. Eventually, it all came to
an ignominious end when accounting fraud and cash shortages
emerged, Enron went bust and took the accounting firm
Andersen with it. Years later, senior Enron leaders went to prison.

For me, one of the most interesting points about this failure was that the power industry ceased trading with Enron a year *before* the collapse. While the Enron share price was still rising and before regulators noticed Enron's fragility, the power industry insiders were aware that Enron was not generating cash and might drag other trading partners down too. Insiders could see that Enron was doing unusual trades in the market that betrayed an unstable financial situation.[125]

Baby P   *The 2007 tragic death of a two-year-old boy known to be at risk by the child protection services in Haringey, a local authority in London*
English local authorities' children's services deliver, for the most part, high-quality child protection services in a complex environment calling for highly resourceful leadership.[126] When quality slips and a child dies, there is naturally public outrage and a private tragedy. Following the review in 2007 of the death of Baby P, the government dismissed the responsible Director of Children's Services (DCS) and launched a development programme for all DCSs in England to improve their capabilities and performance.[127] The DCS programme explored how professionals could work together to support colleagues and their local authorities – to improve both those at risk of failing to meet delivery standards and those performing strongly.

DCSs – like medical or care workers – may find themselves subject to conflicting demands: as *professionals* they have a duty of candour when they see harm or poor judgements by colleagues; as *leaders* they will form judgements as to which local authorities or hospitals or care homes are in danger of failing to deliver good care; as *participants in the regulatory system* they know that the mere suspicion or voicing of concerns may be enough to cause a catastrophic loss of faith and a media storm that will cost colleagues their jobs. In conversations, it was clear that DCSs knew precisely which authorities were about to fail and why.[128] For the best of reasons, insiders are sensitive to the risks of sharing their knowledge about which local authorities are likely to fail next.[129]

Boeing 737
MAX and
the FAA

The emergence of the unsafe safety engineering of the Boeing 737 MAX

The 737 MAX was a major departure from the older 737, with an extended fuselage to increase passenger capacity and range to match the Airbus competitor that was capturing airline sales. It was not classified as 'a new aircraft' and therefore avoided the thorough testing that the Federal Aviation Administration (FAA) would have required if it had been treated as 'new'. However, radically modifying an old design introduced additional complexity. More powerful engines matched the greater size and weight of the aircraft, but they were fitted to the wings in the same position as the older design. The greater power caused the nose to rise and a new system called MCAS (manoeuvring characteristics augmentation system) was added to the aircraft's software to prevent stalling – and resist pilots' commands even if they are flying manually.

Following two major crashes in 2018 and 2019, it emerged that insiders at Boeing had known about risks – additional 'optional' safety devices and pilot training were offered to certain airlines. The FAA had waived the normal scrutiny and relied on Boeing assurances, but internal Boeing communications revealed that in 2016 Boeing employees misled the FAA in withholding information about MCAS so that it would not be included in the pilot manual for the 737 MAX.[130]

Crossrail

The 2018 'surprise' of the London railway cost overrun and delay

Crossrail was the poster child for UK government projects. The new railway line running under London was trumpeted as 'the largest engineering project in Europe' with a carefully structured project bringing together tunnelling firms, rolling-stock manufacturers, signalling installers and the London Underground operator. It was repeatedly promised to be on time and on budget for opening in December 2018 by the Queen, who would then rename Crossrail as the Elizabeth Line. However, in September 2018, the government quietly released an update that Crossrail would be a year late and well over budget, because 'further testing and safety work on software' was needed – now being investigated by the parliamentary spending watchdog.

For insiders, the delay and overrun were not surprises – the surprise was that the setbacks only became public so late in the day and then debate focused on who knew and when they knew. Many people within the companies involved with Crossrail knew that the separate software systems on the trains and signals and track did not talk to one another, and privately commented that Crossrail could not operate as planned by 2018. The problem was that no one within Crossrail or the subcontracting companies was prepared to put the problem on the table – and take the opprobrium of 'causing the problem' – until it came so close to the opening that the problem had to be admitted.[131]

Oxfam	*Abuse of vulnerable people in disaster zones*
	The charity sector is not immune to bad behaviour, regardless of the organization's noble purpose and the altruism of most of its people. Disaster zones attracted individuals who exploited power imbalances and, although insiders knew, whistle-blowers were not listened to.[132]
Hanford in the US, Ozersk in the USSR and Windscale in the UK	*Concealing mismanagement and huge risks during the Cold War*[133]
	These three sites were the locations that manufactured plutonium for nuclear weapons in the first decades of the Cold War. The political environments may have been very different, but the leadership was uncannily similar. Insiders deliberately hid the truth from regulators, the public and front-line staff who literally absorbed the risk.
	Mismanagement of the programme – sacrificing safety and the physical environment to the dictates of production targets, lack of records and poor materials massively increasing clean-up costs for centuries.
	Concealment and falsification of records – health impacts on the workforce and emissions to air and water supplies impacting the general public.

This phenomenon of 'insiders know about the mistakes' illustrates the opportunity for learning and dealing with mistakes. If insiders usually know about impending failures long before anyone else, then that implies we miss opportunities to intervene before crisis hits – when active peer input and challenge could avert mistakes.

Leaders who fall from grace are particularly vilified – media moguls, actors, bishops, politicians, corporate leaders who were once feted as heroic leaders. Media and regulators play out 'the vengeance game' – first, condemnation in the press and parliament, then a formal review with public *mea culpas* in front of a parliamentary select committee or public inquiry, and finally the full report that condemns the failures of leadership and promises 'lessons will be learned'. The idea of learning lessons is intriguing, because it implies that we should have known better – and that we need to do some learning. However, the initial scapegoating of the senior leader seems merely a classic case of hindsight bias at work and is highly likely to breed defensiveness and dysfunctional behaviours, such as cover-ups.

After decades of failing corporate leaders and public services leaders who are condemned publicly, there has been little apparent progress in remedying leadership and reducing the frequency of leadership failures. It is hard to address leadership shortfalls – and we opt for easier ways out:

Easy way out 1: *1 bad apple*	Media and public inquiries focus on human error rather than system error. It is easier and more satisfying to find a specific individual to blame, rather than an anonymous and diffuse system. The '1 bad apple' theory of blame enables everyone to declare the problem 'solved', it deflects blame from the system leaders, and the media and regulatory circus move on. Pressure for harder work or change comes off the system.
Easy way out 2: *More process*	Regulators and reviewers in their countless reports and inquiries begin by diagnosing the latest public disaster as 'a failure of leadership'. When one turns to the recommendations there is actually little on improving leadership but lots more complex

	governance and reporting. It is easier to focus on tangible processes for selection and decisions than to address how one might build leadership capabilities.
Easy way out 3: *More training*	'Improving leadership' is frequently confused with improving individual leaders and tends to focus on the individuals at the top. This confusion explains why, despite the vast amount invested in learning and development (approximately £3 billion per annum in the UK), senior executives typically report dissatisfaction with its impact on the quality of leadership demonstrated. To paraphrase David Ogilvy's comment on advertising, half of the spend is wasted, but we don't know which half.[134]

THE CHALLENGE OF GROWING NEW LEADERSHIP CAPABILITIES

It is not surprising that mistakes happen during change, because leading major change demands leadership capabilities that are not routine in organizations, where the system values continuity and constant management towards stability. Therefore, learning *new* leadership capabilities is essential for successful change. The gap between demand and supply of this 'major change leadership' capability is universally wide because, in order to deliver leadership at all levels, it has to be *home-grown*. By definition, major change is about:

- *Giving the work to the leaders across the organization* Engaging leaders across the organization at different levels reduces the risk that the new tasks and responsibilities will threaten the stability and day-to-day delivery of the system. This means that a large number

140

of leaders have to learn how to change as an individual, as a group and as an organization.

- *Bringing new experiences and capabilities into the existing leadership*
  To avoid 'just more of the same', a large number of leaders have to be exposed to outside perspectives and ideas. It is essential to engage broadly and develop future capabilities organically, so they live on within the organization's culture and the language of the organization.

Bringing in new leadership capabilities and expecting the existing leaders just to adopt them simply won't happen. Even for the best-intentioned participants, it will induce a sense of threat. For the more troubled and siloed organizations, it will invite opposition – active and passive. Silo behaviour is alive and well regardless of easier communication and adoption of smart technology. Silos focus on their internal world, blinding organizations to market realities, discounting the views of other organizational actors, blocking information that does not fit the established view, maintaining secrecy and minimizing collaborative working.

This is a point of genuine crisis for senior leaders, one that too many rush through. There is bound to be a degree of organizational distress in the change journey – either deliberately induced by senior leaders to enable a shift in collective working, or as the accepted result of trying to deliver major change. Senior leaders need to create a 'breakthrough moment' when they engage with their people:

How shall we articulate the new direction and the case for change in language that people will get?

What is the vehicle to engage all these leaders across the organization and build the capability to deliver this new direction?

Whether it is called 'management conferences' or 'leadership academy' or 'programme learning' does not matter, but the breakthrough moment for leadership of change is the point where *leaders begin to learn from other leaders.*

THE BREAKTHROUGH MOMENT: LEADERS LEARNING FROM LEADERS

Leaders of major change have to create the capabilities within their organization by bringing the reality of the outside world into the organization, encouraging the creation of a common language of change that works for the organization, and creating a community of leadership at all levels that learns and deploys new capabilities – and regulates the distress of change across the organization.

Formal training programmes have a bad rap. Technical training has gone online. In the sphere of leadership and behaviour, training programmes suffer from the 'Monday morning' or 'aquarium' effect. While a single leader may acquire skills and commitment away on a programme, come Monday morning, back at the office, few of his/her colleagues will notice a difference. This is context and complementarity at work – an isolated individual will struggle to change an organization, even a small one. The aquarium effect makes the point that, when the fish in a tank are looking sick, one can take individual fish out and clean them up, but returning them to the aquarium will result in continuing sickness – because it is actually the water that needs changing and the tank cleaning, whereupon the fish will thrive.[135]

The kind of learning that works for leaders is:

Not 'training' but 'sharing'	It is about sharing leadership experiences in a format that builds collective commitment to action, less about acquiring technical skills.[136]

Not 'fault-finding' *but 'debriefing'*	It is about peer learning and challenge, like in aviation, psychology and medicine, where a professional reviews a case before a peer panel.
Not 'development' *but 'capability'*	It is for the leaders who are probably doing the biggest job of their career and who bring unparalleled experience and capability to make things happen.

Case study of the gold standard in learning

MAJOR PROJECTS LEADERSHIP ACADEMY
Cabinet Office[137]

The MPLA was established to build a cadre of world-class major project leaders to deliver the 300+ £1 billion-plus projects in the UK government's major projects portfolio. The MPLA complements standards, review panels, metrics, approval processes and training programmes provided by the Cabinet Office. It has catalysed improvements in project performance, returning its investment costs many times over and changing the culture in government project delivery.

The MPLA is delivered by Oxford Saïd Business School and consists of:

- A 15-month programme for a cohort of 24–36 project leaders, with 20 cohorts launched 2012–18.
- Building competencies in leadership of self, major projects, technical and commercial leadership.
- Residential, action learning, masterclasses, reading, mentoring, assignments, evaluation elements.
- Sessions led by senior civil servants, private sector leaders, academic thought-leaders and – increasingly – programme participants.

The impact of MPLA has been through:

- Improved knowledge, skills and experiences of major project leaders.
- Bringing the reality of commercial project experience, market constraints, international projects into the programme.
- Creating a common language around major projects.
- Building leadership at multiple levels in the Civil Service.
- Building a community of major project leaders.
- Peer support and challenge.

The implication of what we know about how leaders learn is that everyone needs to be on the journey, as with change itself. The leadership capability-building is required at least as much for motivation and community-building as it is for skill acquisition. Behaviour change is less daunting with peers. The 'programme' has to emphasize face-to-face interaction while allowing for different learning styles through providing a range of learning formats – small group, online, reading etc. Finally, the learning programme has to engage all significant leaders – the senior leaders have to be visibly on the journey with the leadership at all levels. Leaders (and most adults) do not enjoy or gain much from 'schooling' – we know that:

- *Adults learn when they need to*
  Leaders will be interested in listening and acquiring learning only 'just in time' as they need to apply it – and will retain it only if its value is demonstrated quickly.

- *Leaders learn from leaders*
  Although an outside expert may bring the reputation to obtain a hearing, leaders get the motivation to apply learning from their peers – first, because of their street

credibility and, second, because of peer pressure cum reassurance. 'If they can do it, so can I.'

- *Everyone has a different preferred learning style*
  Although everyone needs to be on the journey, one size will not fit all – and technology gives us many new options that will be blended in, not cheap replacements to enable a 'sheep dip' of learning for leaders.

Formal learning/sharing programmes have a big role to play in change programmes. This does not mean days of events off-site. It does mean regular events, attended by all members of a business or function, at all levels of seniority. Motivation to learn is critical, because a lot of 'skill' issues in changing behaviours are really 'will' issues – and a lot of 'will' issues are in reality about confidence. Formal learning/sharing signals 'changing all of us' and forgives past failures: 'If we are all saying we have learned something new, then I can admit that what I used to do wasn't right either.' A formal programme will help leaders overcome the psychological barriers to acknowledging mistakes and avoid some of the consequent extreme lengths that people go to in order to justify their mistakes – missing the opportunity to learn from experience.[138]

Organizations have taken many different approaches to learning and sharing among their leadership – from the top-end Major Projects Leadership Academy led by Oxford Saïd Business School for the Cabinet Office's Infrastructure and Projects Authority, through knowledge retreats at McKinsey to 'Tuesday night briefing and curry' at Powergen – or discussing at work what female staff have learned from their AllBright online reading.[139] The critical factor is not how much money you spend, but the impact delivered in terms of bringing the real world inside, creating a common language and mobilizing a community. When it comes to curriculum and format for a learning programme, regardless of industry or change ambition, I have observed a surprising degree of commonality regardless of industry or size of organization:

Highly focused and limited external or expert input	Stimulating thinking and the ability to ask a better class of questions, rather than giving the answers.
Series of events for cohorts of 20–40 participants over a 3–18 month period	Building a supportive community of peers, creating a common language and (crucially) building confidence to challenge top managers.
Learning from the group – and learning as a group	Starting with a common curriculum, but increasingly the cohort takes charge of the curriculum and calls on peers for expert input.
Expanding horizons to encompass the real world	Covering the economics of the business from an external perspective, strategy/policy dilemmas, leadership skills, personal resilience, approaches for managing risk, technology, change.
Providing multiple learning formats	Ranging through small groups, online, action learning, classroom, reading, coaching, assessment tools – ensuring that everyone finds an approach that works for them and (crucially) getting away from senior leader broadcasts.
Valuing the 'white space' of the programme as much as the 'black print'	Recognizing the value of bringing leaders together to spend time in discussion.

The visible outputs of the 'leaders programme' have always been the common language that enables leadership at all levels to work together and erode organizational silos – created by the supportive group of peers on the learning programme that becomes a network across the organization, solving problems.

Learning together establishes shared values and creates a sense of belonging, and the fact that senior leaders turn up creates a degree of intimacy that generates commitment and performance – football manager Kevin Keegan built his legendary relationships with his teams on 'being there'.[140] Change is about learning and renewal – and leadership has to model learning.

BRINGING THE REALITY OF THE OUTSIDE WORLD INTO THE ORGANIZATION

Everything that already exists in an organization came into being for a reason, even if we have now forgotten why. I talk pejoratively about 'silos' but they exist because organizations always have to balance efficiency and effectiveness. Focused tasks and dedicated resources were chronicled by Adam Smith in the first chapter of *The Wealth of Nations 1776*, where he describes the pin factory and the effect of task specialization.[141] Most organizations exploit task specialization until they become suboptimal – creating silos that block effective cross-organization working and building up a sense of community that isolates from 'the other'.

Senior leaders often grow impatient at slow progress of change in their organizations and some decide to shortcut the process by isolating change in a big (often IT-enabled) project that sits outside the line organization. Progress seems rapid until two crises hit at the point when the programme transitions from 'project team' to 'front-line implementation' – first, the project lacks input from the front line and may not fit customer needs and, second, the project is not 'owned' by the front line and they are not motivated to implement it. As described in earlier chapters, senior leaders can be misled by the cognitive traps of 'optimism bias' and the 'planning fallacy'[142] when organizations:

- Assume WYSIATI – 'what you see is all there is' – blindness to experiences other than your own.
- Neglect known unknowns – far less unknown unknowns.

- Reject data when inconsistent with the project and persevere irrationally with proposals.
- Test proposals against 'best-case' scenarios rather than realistic 'reference cases'.

Examples are plentiful:

- *Commercial businesses*
  The insouciance of UK–US mining group English China Clays in its decline and the arrogance of BMW when it acquired Rover, as described in earlier sections.

- *Government projects*
  Audit reports on the Scottish Parliament building and on Universal Credit, and the tendency of companies to overbid to win contracts then rely on add-ons to retrieve losses.[143]

- *Pandemic planning*
  Governments do plenty of planning for pandemics – the challenge is for the plans to lead to any action. It is difficult to persuade paymasters to fund any kind of preventive work, whether pandemic or child abuse or crime, because the harm is always distant in time while the expense and effort is here and now. The conclusions of pandemic exercises, whether the Cygnus Review in 2016 or the regular scenario exercises I and colleagues led with public servants, were always too big and terrifying for leaders to accept. Finally, organizational jealousies prevented rational strategies, such as engaging the private sector in readiness for ramping up testing capacity to cope with a pandemic.[144]

Bringing in the outside view or the 'real world' is essential. It comes in many sources, perspectives and formats that can be mixed and tailored for the learning programme:

From *internal* sources …in informal conversation, workshops or sitting in on actual customer service	Front-line people can bring a perspective on what works – and what will not work. They may be innovating and delivering in ways not visible to senior leaders.
From *business* sources …in facility visits, service reviews, planning meetings or workshops	Customers, suppliers and partners can challenge preconceptions and stimulate innovation. They may also offer comparisons with competitors and perspectives on regulators.
From *external observers and experts* …in learning events, workshops, leadership conferences, or benchmarking	Industry experts, researchers and journalists can introduce new perspectives and potentially disruptive trends. They may prompt radically different thinking.

Change means bringing the real world into what are almost always inward-focused organizations. Introducing a learning programme builds habits of 'real-world testing' in three ways:

- *External experts' views – a little goes a long way!* Exposing leaders to the best thinking and experience is important, but the real work is for the participants, thinking about what the external world perspective means. There is a limit to what can be received from experts; people need to discover for themselves. In addition, there is an illusion of expertise that can lead to overconfidence in a complex system.[145]

- *Doing real work together on the programme* Projects and action learning establish the habit of bringing different points of view and experiences to bear on the real issues facing participants. Unchallenged projects can go adrift – although few as awry as the Spanish submarine that was too heavy to resurface after diving, then too long for its home port.[146]

- *Learning from participants as the programme moves into co-creation*
  It is fine to lay out the curriculum for the first few weeks as participants find their feet but, increasingly as leaders identify their learning needs, they should develop their skills and motivation to share in the answers from co-participants, learning 'as a group' not just 'in a group'.

CREATING A COMMON LANGUAGE OF CHANGE THAT WORKS FOR THE ORGANIZATION

Organizations use language to convey in a few words complex concepts loaded with meaning for the insiders – this 'organizational vocabulary' is critical to informal organizational behavioural norms and to efficient debate. A few institutions have been around for long enough to create literally their own language: 'Jackspeak'[147] in the Royal Navy has filled a moderate dictionary with naval equivalents of mundane daily items (e.g., 'gash' for rubbish or garbage) but also terms that have entered our language (e.g. 'brass monkeys') and terms that convey complex concepts of control in the naval context.

There is a world of difference between a coherent common language and a mash-up of the current management-speak transplanted from other organizations without full adaptation to work in a new situation. A current example is the widespread adoption of 'agile' (the philosophy and methodology applied in most Internet-based IT development and process redesign) into every management process. Applying an 'agile' sticker inappropriately misses the preconditions for success with agile methodology, notably boundaries to existing processes and systems. It also fails because the real needs of the organization are being sidelined by a solution that sounds fashionable, reinforcing prejudices to *comply with but not commit to* 'the latest change initiative'.

Most organizations' common language of change is only a few words, but these few words encapsulate complex concepts or convey common terms or shared values to colleagues. When mobilizing the whole organization, a signal of progress is the emergence of the three or four phrases that encapsulate the change or the key vehicles of change. Examples include:

- 'Performance' and 'agreement' at BP encompasses a contract, performance indicators, review processes and peer group support – a whole set of structures, processes and capabilities.
- 'Major project' in government encompasses structures, processes, reviews, the Major Projects Leadership Academy and 'thinking like the chief executive of a temporary organization'.

The senior leader can shape some of this language – but it is the leadership of the community who will create it and deploy it. For many senior leaders, this will come as a relief – it reduces the burden on the senior leadership to expand 'the vision thing'. Many senior leaders will find it more practical and motivating to move on from overall direction to engaging with colleagues in creating the common language of change in a dialogue – rather than endless PowerPoint.

BUILDING A COMMUNITY OF PEERS ACROSS THE ORGANIZATION

Leaders can make the single most tangible investment in successful major change by building in learning for a community of leaders. The characteristics of this investment are:

Encouraging cohorts of leaders through the programme, building the community of leaders.

Building in learning pays off as major change is effectively delivered by capable leadership at all levels. The learning programme is part of the solution because it accelerates change in comparison with letting learning bubble up from informal sharing of experience. By simply existing, a learning programme signals that 'we all need to learn new ways of working'. The focus on learning will build capability to test options through experiments/pilots and others' experiences – rather than relying on individuals' hunches or experiences elsewhere.

Asking powerful questions – questions that demand people think before answering and open up new options.

My favourite powerful questions include:

'Who are our allies in making this happen?'

'What has kept this system accident-free until now?'

'Who has already solved this problem?'

'What is the potential value if we can do this?'

'How many options can we create?'

'If we relax this constraint, what could we do?'

Working alongside leaders across the organization, creating a common language of change with them.

Investing in learning also has another counter-intuitive benefit for the top leaders: it helps set up a barrier to the universal temptation that besets leaders. The temptation is to grow impatient with progress and decide to short-circuit change by 'just telling'. Having to show up for the learning programme also keeps senior leaders honest as they debate with participants the mix of adaptive and programmatic change needed in the organization. It pushes senior leaders *back* into their adaptive role and pushes participants *forward* into their leadership role, committing them to change as part of group norms:

Senior leaders saying...	*What is the reference case (not the best-case scenario)? How would others see this? Whose experience can we learn from? Let me tell you my story... What are the few core ideas that we are setting out to accomplish?*
Front-line leaders saying...	*What this language means to us and to operations is... Our reality test is... We want to hear from...*
Management teams saying...	*This is a coherent story. We can see how we shall fill gaps and dispel illusions. This is what we are doing – and what we are not doing. What are we not hearing? What are we not facing up to?*

Summary   *Insiders always know the truth about leadership mistakes and failure, usually long before it becomes public knowledge. When failures of leadership become known to regulators or investors, ever more complex governance processes are added rather than learning lessons and building leadership.*

Learning is a critical enabler of change, because new leadership capabilities will be required for success.

In order to deliver leadership at all levels, leadership capabilities have to be home-grown – they cannot be imported or reside in a few senior leaders.

Leaders learn from leaders who share real-world experiences. Organizations should tailor their own learning forum and approach – it does not need to be ornate or expensive or lengthy. Shared learning among leaders is:

* *Signalling that everyone has to learn and change, realizing human potential rather than just surviving change.*

	• *Creating a common language of change that works for the organization.* • *Building a community of peers.*
Action	*Give leaders a regular forum to hear, practise and tell stories – and create a community of peers to support and drive change across the organization:* • *Sharing, not training.* • *Evolving the curriculum as the organization goes through waves of change.* • *Bringing the reality of the outside world into the organization.*

7

TACKING THROUGH WAVES OF CHANGE: AMBITION, PACE AND CAPABILITY

'Tacking: making a series of changes of course while sailing'
(Oxford dictionaries)

WISDOM OF LONG-TERM THINKING – OR A CORRECTION AFTER GETTING IT WRONG?

National Power and Powergen faced critical challenges when the UK created the world's first competitive electricity market in 1989. The huge state-owned Central Electricity Generating Board (CEGB) monopoly was split up by the Electricity Act 1989 into these two commercial power generators plus a number of other companies, some remaining in state ownership initially. National Power and Powergen had to learn how to make the new markets work and literally keep the lights on – no one had done this before in a commercial environment. Each company had inherited from the CEGB a mixed portfolio of coal-, oil- and gas-fired power-generating stations of varying vintage and efficiency and their share of the technically expert CEGB workforce, albeit with a non-commercial mindset. The new companies had to operate in 'the pool' (the world's first wholesale market for power) and customers could choose among competing suppliers for the first time.[148] Powergen's strategy for the first years was clear and dramatized by the 'good crisis' of privatization and nascent competition:

- Setting up each power station as a business unit, each responsible for driving up its availability and its thermal and operating efficiency, against world-class benchmarks. It was a mindset of 'survival of the most efficient'.
- Responding quickly to half-hourly commercial opportunities in the electricity 'pool' and performing in newly competitive customer markets. Initially, National Power and Powergen operated a duopoly that maintained prices and profits.
- Exploiting the availability of North Sea gas and turnkey combined cycle gas turbine technology to invest in new gas-fired power stations, while closing the less efficient coal- and oil-fired stations.

After a decade, the ruthlessly Darwinian Powergen strategy of 'driving efficiency' of the UK power stations was switched to one of 'working as one', optimizing spend across the network and standardizing processes. *Individual power stations* had had the freedom to adopt the resourcing, maintenance and operating measures that kept them at the top of the efficiency rankings – and therefore surviving when others closed. Now the *portfolio of power stations as a whole* operated common processes for maintenance and central procurement and the inefficiencies of treating each station as a separate business (or 'playing shop', as it was labelled) disappeared.

By the 2000s, National Power and Powergen were substantial companies and attractive acquisition targets: National Power was acquired by RWE, while Powergen was acquired by Eon in 2002 and Scottish Power and other players were acquired by French and Spanish electricity companies.[149] In 2019 Eon and Innogy completed an asset swap that saw Npower rationalized into Eon, so the waves of change continue.

156

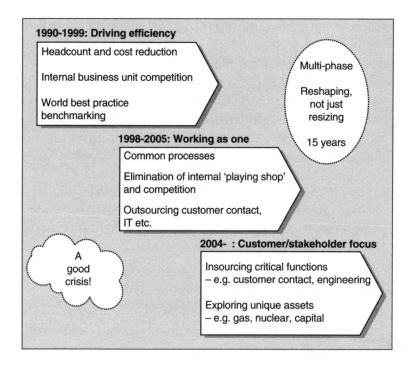

The impression may be that the UK moved smoothly and coherently over 30 years towards cleaner, more competitive power, financed by investors rather than taxpayers. In fact, there was never a plan for the transformation that transpired. The industry tacked through waves of change: privatization; entry by US companies, exit by US companies, entry by European companies; monopoly followed by duopoly followed by oligopoly followed by concentration; vertical and horizontal disintegration followed by reintegration; the 'dash for gas' in power generation funded by investors, followed by consumers' subsidization of renewables; the erosion and closure of nuclear capacity, recently revived through government-guaranteed funding; opening up to competition, then increased regulation and limiting of competition.[150]

So, was the strategy of the first decade wrong and had Powergen/Eon now switched to a better strategy? Was short-term leadership merely reacting to the latest events? In the case of the UK electricity market, it can be argued that the long-term transformation of

Powergen required the absorption of a performance culture before the optimization strategy would have a chance of success. In due course, the transformation moved into a third wave of change, 'customer/stakeholder focus', including taking back in-house critical functions that had been outsourced in 'working as one'. Even if never deliberately designed in that way, each successive set of changes yielded short-term gains and built on previous waves for long-term transformation. The lessons for leadership are:

- *The vision may hold, but plans have to change*
  Leaders articulate a lasting – albeit evolving – definition for long-term success. A broader vision or purpose needs to last, when short-term plans are overtaken by events.

- *The model of thinking in 'waves of change' is more helpful than 'that was wrong, this is right'*
  Organizations cannot flit from one plan to another unconnected plan; they have to build on their capabilities and current position. 'Tacking' or 'pivoting' are more accurate descriptions than 'now for a new strategy'.

How scientific thinking develops as waves of change

THE STRUCTURE OF SCIENTIFIC REVOLUTIONS by Thomas S. Kuhn (1962, University of Chicago Press)

Kuhn's seminal work laid out how knowledge actually advances in science and how we develop our understanding of the world. Transformative ideas do not arise from experimentation and data, but from revolutions. Breakthrough ideas disrupt 'normal science' and offer new ideas and a new 'paradigm' (language that Kuhn was first to put into widespread currency):

1 Normal science works on an established paradigm, with adherents dedicated to solving puzzles remaining within the paradigm.
2 Serious anomalies (more than just discrepancies between theory and data) lead to a crisis and competing articulations.

---

3 Resolution of the crisis by a new paradigm replacing the old.

The new paradigm is not chosen because it is true but more because of a change in world view and a move away from inadequate interactions with the world. He cites classical and modern examples of new paradigms, including Newtonian and quantum mechanics and the discovery of oxygen and X-rays. He highlights the criticisms made of revolutionaries – even Lord Kelvin, when President of the Royal Society, said X-rays will prove to be an elaborate hoax. Scientific knowledge advanced through a revolution in thinking, rather than a linear or cumulative progress to the truth.

Kuhn would have interpreted the debate around climate change as a classic example of a scientific revolution in thinking, with expert scientists taking sides and battling for different theories and citing their evidence in support. He documents the role of scientists as providing leadership in waves of change and his work has been applied in complex settings of legal and political thinking and military strategy.[151]

Kuhn's thinking is related to that of Joseph Schumpeter in *Capitalism, Socialism and Democracy*, published in 1942, which developed the concept of creative destruction as capitalism brought new businesses into being at the expense of old ideas. It is in stark contrast to the logically pure approaches of:

- Karl Popper in *The Open Society and its Enemies* (1945), which suggests that knowledge develops by putting forward hypotheses and subjecting them to testing through falsification attempts – i.e., through a strictly logical approach in pursuit of truth, in an open society, generating new thinking free from totalitarian authority.
- Friedrich Hayek in *Law, Legislation and Liberty* (1973), which suggests that laws and knowledge emerge incrementally through expert discernment and most democratically in a society that diffuses political and economic power in a free market.

HOW MUCH AND HOW FAST?

A typical corporate change programme will arrive for many people by clicking on 'Message from the chief executive' in the inbox of their work email:

Dear colleagues

The management team have launched the next project in our transformation plan. Project Advance will deliver the new processes and systems to underpin our new model of interacting with our users and suppliers. Project Advance is set up with:

Management team sponsorship – we shall review progress, taking advantage of management team experience with similar projects in other organizations.

Front-line input – I have asked leaders of four of our processing centres to provide guidance and ensure implementation.

Dedicated project leadership – Jo will be full-time Project Leader. Her perspective in strategy and policy and stakeholder expectations will keep the project focused.

Professional support – we shall retain a consulting firm recognized in the field and technical resources to ensure we follow best practice.

Jo will be in touch shortly with the timeline and details of your engagement in Project Advance. It is a top priority for the organization and for me personally – I look forward to your contribution to full delivery within 18 months.

Frank

What goes through your mind on reading this launch email? A typical change initiative... logical project structure and clear top-level commitment... but is it realistic in its goals and calendar? Will it succeed, does it have support from front-line leaders, will management teams prioritize it over other initiatives? And how do you feel? Excited? Weary? How will you survive?

'How much?' and 'How fast?' are the two critical upfront scoping issues in designing a 'transformation' or a major change programme. Leaders announcing 'transformation' need to answer questions as to:

Ambition	What are the boundaries of change? How radical? What are the areas excluded from change? How much of the ambition is cost reduction?
Decisions	Who are the decision-makers? What have they signed off already? Who will have to be won round? What timetable has been committed?
Capabilities	What dedicated resource is committed to the programme? What are the IT enablers and how do they play into the programme? What new capabilities need to be built?
Legacy	What has been learned from past programmes? How successful were they? What does the organization typically struggle with? What are the expectations?

Clearly all of these sceptic's questions matter, but it is the last category, 'legacy', that needs most exploration. Organizations are not completely prisoners of their history, but they are heavily conditioned by their experience. Therefore, when making these critical upfront scoping decisions about how much their organization should take on in one go, it turns out that senior leaders tend to rely on their personal experience of what worked during their earlier careers, rather than drawing upon the breadth and history of the organization's experience. The success of every change initiative can usually be predicted by where the organization is coming *from*, more than where it is going *to*.

CONTEXT AND COMPLEMENTARITY DRIVE CHANGE

When leaders speak about 'our context and why we are changing', they typically refer to specific issues or challenges

161

in their environment – e.g., the economy, new regulation, new competitors or demand/cost pressure. Understanding organizations as complex systems means we need to take account of a much broader 'context' that constrains change:

- *Organizations' internal contexts* include structures, processes, systems, identity, behavioural norms, espoused values, capabilities. Add in more complexity if they are part of a larger system that exerts its norms over the specific organization – e.g., a public body that is influenced by the Civil Service or a broker that is influenced by the City or the BBC influenced by government threats around its periodic charter renewal.
- *Organizations' external contexts* include owners, regulation, customers, suppliers, competitors etc. as per Porter's Five Forces model, which determines the competitive intensity of the industry based on competitive rivalry, the bargaining power of suppliers and customers and the threats of new entrants and substitute products.[152]

All of these contextual elements are 'complementary' – i.e., they reinforce one another because they evolved together over time and each individual element will adjust to accommodate the others. Complementarity is a positive strategy to boost organizational performance by ensuring all elements are coherent, aligned and boost the overall performance – mixing and matching simply does not work.[153] However, unintendedly, this makes the overall system highly resistant to change. The implication is that, if a leader chooses to change only one element – say, organization structure – then all the other elements will effectively dampen and perhaps negate the change that was intended. In other words, change will automatically be stifled and its impact minimized. This is the definition of inertia.

Now, that may be fine if only minor adjustment was intended by changing one element in the system. However, if major change is intended, then a sufficient *number* of the contextual elements have to change by a sufficient *degree* in order to force the necessary readjustment of all the other elements. In my observation, multiple elements in the system have to change in order to move on from the status quo and shift the balance from inertia to change.[154]

Although they may receive plenty of advice, ultimately only senior leaders can take responsibility to define the scope of major change 'just right' to get complementarity to work positively for effective change, without overwhelming the organization. If the ambition is to 'change everything', then the risk is organizational chaos. If the scope is limited or a series of 'isolated projects', then the risk is of only delivering minimal impact. And if people act independently when flooded with data, then they risk system failure.

1. Change everything

One of my consulting colleagues used to joke that his more unrealistic clients were 'with one leap changing from a crocodile to a gazelle'. Although trivial, the joke highlighted real risks. More measured examples include:

Defence Infrastructure Organisation (DIO)	The DIO was created 2010–14, bringing into one organization all of the Ministry of Defence's property management, housing and new facilities.[155] This mammoth organization inherited long-standing underinvestment and deeply unhappy customers in the armed services. It embarked on a transformation programme that simultaneously changed the DIO structure and processes around new ways of working, enabled by new IT systems – all to be implemented in a diverse and geographically distributed workforce who had never worked together before.[156] And, just to complete the

picture, this multifaceted programme was to create an interim organization that would shortly thereafter be replaced by an outsourced arrangement with a private sector consortium. Although there were other contributing factors to the eventual collapse of the transformation programme, this was an upfront scoping decision that simply tried to do too much, too quickly and was assessed by the National Audit Office to have failed to deliver.[157]

Marconi plc and ICI plc   Activist investors succeeded in demerging conglomerates to realize stock market revaluations of attractive businesses, but often left the remaining business as an unattractive 'rump' and so the chief executive embarked on a 'transforming acquisition'.

Marconi plc remained after General Electric Company plc sold its defence businesses, made a series of ill-judged acquisitions, proclaimed itself a technology company in 1996 – and collapsed in 2001 after failing to deliver results.[158]

ICI plc remained after the Zeneca pharmaceutical business was spun out, made an overpriced purchase from Unilever, proclaimed itself a speciality-chemical company – and was acquired cheaply in 2008 after failing to deliver results.[159]

Reform of healthcare   Both the US and the UK launched significant top-down legislative reforms of their healthcare systems 2010–2014. The Patient Protection and Affordable Care Act of 2010 or 'Obamacare' was the most comprehensive reorganization of US healthcare in a century and the Health and Social Care Act 2012 was the most extensive reorganization of the National Health Service in England in over 60 years. In both cases, apart from the continuing controversy, the ambition was partially reversed in subsequent years as it proved difficult to realize the gains through structural reform, which were hugely disruptive, and costs were significantly higher than expected.

BMW's acquisition of Rover

Acquisitions can also be too big a mouthful or their difficulties underestimated. As mentioned in earlier chapters, BMW's acquisition of Rover in 1994 was unloaded in 2000 after huge losses and two failed integration strategies – first overly hands-off then followed by excessive micromanagement.[160]

F-35 Joint Strike Fighter

The Joint Strike Fighter programme was conceived in the 1990s as the most ambitious aircraft development effort in the history of the US Department of Defense. One company would oversee design and production of three different versions of an aircraft that could be operated by the United States Air Force, Navy and Marine Corps as well as America's allies, who would help offset the development costs. The project would result in a technologically superior plane that would be manufactured in such large quantities that the F-35 would cost no more than the older planes it would replace. The project has suffered long delays, escalating costs and performance problems continue due to its all-encompassing but isolated execution:

- Design specifications demanded by one branch of the military would adversely impact the F-35's performance in another area.

- Serious problems resulted from starting
  production while the aircraft was still
  under development. The strategy was meant
  to allow the services to begin flying their
  F-35s sooner. Instead, F-35s started rolling
  off the production line with unresolved
  technical problems, forcing the Pentagon to
  continually retrofit even newly built jets.
- Because the F-35 was intended to replace
  so many legacy fighter jets, military leaders
  essentially had no choice but to keep going.
- Lockheed produces not only the F-35
  itself but also the training gear for
  pilots and maintenance technicians, the
  aircraft's logistics system and its support
  equipment. Lockheed also manages the
  supply chain and is responsible for much
  of the maintenance for the plane. This gave
  Lockheed significant power over almost
  every part of the F-35 enterprise. Because
  Lockheed was not required to report its
  financials in detail, the programme office
  itself did not have a clear picture of exactly
  how much an F-35 truly cost and how the
  money was being used.[161]

2. Isolated projects

The ambitions of senior leaders can be equally undermined by
a high-profile project that simply does not touch most of the
organization and what people actually do. Examples include:

Defence Equipment and Support	In another part of the Ministry of Defence in the same period, the Defence Procurement Agency and the Defence Logistics Organisation were merged under one chief into Defence Equipment

166

and Support. This may have affected the top of
the hierarchy in the organization but, as a purely
structural initiative, it had minimal impact on
most people in the organization and this upfront,
apparently radical scoping was too little to deliver
real change in the absence of complementary
changes in processes and behaviours.[162]

English   The UK–US mining group English China Clays
China   plc had fallen on hard times. It launched a
Clays plc   turnaround and transformation programme with
a series of highly successful projects focused on
specific problem/opportunity areas in the business
in south-west England. Despite the short-term
financial success of the projects, the company
struggled to deliver sustained change across the
organization, because a series of projects did
not add up to the complementary programme of
reinforced change in structure, processes, systems
and rewards that was needed.[163]

3. Infodemic in the system

One of the challenges of the Internet era is that data is much
more freely and rapidly available. During the pandemic there
was a great opportunity and risk of us all becoming armchair
epidemiologists. More seriously, the extent of the pandemic
meant that people in leadership roles had to make judgements
from fragmentary information derived from a blizzard of data
that they were ill-equipped to interpret. Labelled the 'infodemic',
leadership actions in complex systems have had unintended
consequences. Examples include:

Schools as   Reopening schools after lockdown was presented
part of the   as 'it is safe for children to go to school'.[164]
system   However, operating a school is a complex system
with multiple adult populations including

167

parents, cleaners, admin staff, food providers and contractors in addition to the teaching staff. Opening schools has wider system effects.

The care home/ hospital system

Setting a target for NHS acute hospitals to empty beds of medically dischargeable patients ahead of the expected wave of COVID-19 patients made sense when looked at as an NHS capacity issue. However, when the scope is expanded to consider hospitals and care homes as one system, it looked much less sensible to seed potentially COVID-positive patients into the most vulnerable settings.[165]

CREATING WAVES OF CHANGE

To work across the organization without creating confusion requires a single view of the future – not a prescriptive detailed plan (that is the task of the many individual leaders across the organization), but a clear direction that channels the collective energy that is being mobilized. When an isolated project is insufficient and changing everything is too risky, the answer lies in timing and scoping that tackles organizational inertia. What will increase the organization's willingness to change – and therefore reduce the 'shock treatment' needed to overcome inertia?

Exploit or create catalytic events – or even a 'good crisis'

Privatization was the catalyst for change in the electricity industry. Catalysts are not always negative – and the term 'burning platform' should be avoided because fear is only a short-term motivator. Privatization alone did not guarantee change, but it provided a focal critical point and the expectation of change within the organization – 'things are now different, we cannot continue as we were'. Rahm Emanuel (Barack Obama's first chief of staff and later Mayor of Chicago) coined the saying about 'never letting a good crisis go to waste' – and there are ways of creating non-harmful catalytic events that inspire action rather than spread fear:

- Create a new unit focused on the task, while guarding against project isolation. The creation of Big Society Capital in 2012 catalysed funding large-scale social enterprise in the UK.
- Create a 'year zero' by putting businesses/functions/ teams through a (say) 12-week process to reorient, set goals and build capabilities – then those who 'graduate' successfully move to a new status or unit within the organization with greater autonomy.

Dividing up the long term into a series of short terms

Transformation may take 15 years, but the strategy has to yield results during the first five years. Leaders can break down the task, making the most of early evidence of progress to motivate the organization, and also linking tangible progress in daily operations (costs, sales, customers) to the change objectives.

Delivering short-term will absorb most of the organization's energy – so that has to be the foundation of the change programme. Breaking down the tasks and linking them to operational indicators is more likely to connect with front-line leadership.

Accept reality and plan for multiple waves of change, 'tacking' towards the ultimate goal

Constraints on organizational capabilities make transformation slower than ideal. Like a sailing boat tacking to windward, organizations often cannot go directly into the wind; instead, the navigator needs to 'aim off' and deliver in stages. This is similar to John Kay's concept of 'obliquity' – that all our goals are best achieved when we approach them indirectly, that complex problems are rarely susceptible to frontal attack and that we need to go through a gradual process of risk-taking and discovery.[166]

Build capability every step of the way and at every level – to enable the next wave

In the case of Powergen, the first wave of change built a cadre of managers who became world-class individual plant operators, learning from global best practice power stations in the US, then strategic operators across the network. This approach is the antithesis of relying on one heroic individual leader and instead it recognizes the transformational role of high-performing front-line people – it needs organization-wide leadership.

We began with the simple questions of 'How much?' and 'How fast?' but the effective senior leader adds 'Where to for now?' as the key question to make sense of the initial scoping judgements. Many metaphors of change and leadership unnecessarily reinforce the idea of the heroic leader, setting direction and going directly from where we are to the ultimate destination. The highest-level design of the change programme is indeed the task of the leader – but maybe not as a metaphorical captain of the ship, rather as the 'navigator' of an expedition that relies on rough-and-ready maps and instruments with a crew who need to train and work together in an unfamiliar boat. The organization needs to stay the course despite the conflicting pressures of wind, tide and current and – of course – it cannot steer directly upwind, it has to zigzag or tack. In this metaphor, we would hear more of:

Senior leaders saying…	*This is the ultimate goal… how far can we get in this phase?* *What foundations need to be laid for the next phase?* *What we need to deliver short term is…*
Front-line leaders saying…	*What works for us is… how we operate to deliver this phase.*
Management teams saying…	*Our understanding of the ultimate goal is…* *We have a plan… to build capability through this phase and into the likely next phases.*

Summary   *Transforming an organization in a single programme is
unrealistic. Fundamental change takes time – it may
take years of advance, adjustment, reaction to events,
renewed advance – and will build on capabilities
acquired and developed during the transformation
itself. That implies an approach of successive waves of
change.*

*Clearly, no senior leader has the forecasting ability to
detail waves of change years into the future. Senior
leaders need to articulate the long-term vision of
transformation, while adjusting direction wave by wave.*

*Judging how much to change and how fast depends
on how much the organization can cope with and
deliver in each wave. Each organization's context will
indicate constraints on how much it can do and how
fast. But it will also set the pace needed to overcome
complementary forces that hold the organization in
equilibrium – and resisting change.*

*Designing a successful programme needs to avoid
extremes:*

- *Change everything simultaneously – can overwhelm
an organization and end up slowing overall
progress.*
- *Isolated projects – can absorb attention and energy
without achieving critical mass of organization-
wide change.*
- *Infodemic or overload of data – can spark system
failure.*

Action   *Articulate the vision for transformation over time and...
plan for waves of change, building the capabilities of
the organization in successive waves.*

Design the programme to:

- *Exploit or create catalytic events.*
- *Divide up the long term into a series of short terms.*
- *Accept reality and plan for multiple waves of
change, 'tacking' towards the ultimate goal.*
- *Build capability every step of the way – to enable
the next wave.*

PART FIVE

'HOW DO I BUILD PURPOSE, BELONGING AND MENTAL HEALTH?'

Past generations' lives were shaped, for better and for worse, by the social and economic experiences of depression and war. The inequitable consequences of depression for a large part of the population and the shared endeavour of the war effort contributed to a consensus for political, economic and social change. Political events, even as dramatic as the fall of the Berlin Wall and 9/11, did not prompt reactions on such a scale, in part because they did not catalyse a sense of inequity nor shared effort. Although the parallels should not be drawn too tightly, the expectations of current generations are being shaped by the experiences of the financial crash of 2008 and the COVID-19 pandemic of 2020. They have not been uniform experiences, but the lessons are being drawn in businesses, public services and community groups for how we organize, lead and participate.

It would be easy to focus on the dramatic negatives flowing from 2008 and 2020.

The gap between the 'haves' and the 'have-nots' has widened. The lockdown hit the most disadvantaged in society hardest – women and children not safe in violent homes, the disabled, those in care, ethnic minorities, the poorly housed, migrant families, the mentally unwell. Polling on the mental health impact of the pandemic indicates rising levels of anxiety and trauma across the population. Attempts to redress economic distress had the unintended consequence of reinforcing privilege, as cheap money boosted asset prices (housing and stock markets) after both crises.

But there are also many – less dramatic – positives from our reactions to 2008 and 2020.

Positives include an upsurge in community activity, realization of who are our key workers, appreciation of the importance of extended families, prominence of rights to mental health as much as physical health, appreciation of improved air quality and green spaces, wider access to technology, more flexible ways of working, upturn in cycling, encouragement of local leadership, knowing our neighbours. However, it is still unclear how long we shall sustain these positives.

This is not to assert that everything changed following the crises. The collective will for change will ebb and flow and some initially attractive options will fall by the wayside, but history and people's experiences do not go away. Leaders in organizations have been pursuing three of the emerging positive priorities over the past decade or more – and they are clearly being sustained:

- *Organizational purpose rather than individual and economic alienation*
  Greater overall prosperity during recent decades has frequently been at the expense of alienation. At the individual level, people were better paid but may have worn a 'psychological mask' to survive; they were present at work but productive neither for the organization nor for themselves as human beings. At the level of the globalizing economy, anonymous firms channelled flows of capital to wherever it earned the highest return.
  Leaders of organizations are increasingly recognizing that purpose and belonging are vital to attracting and retaining their people. Investors are increasingly

looking for both financial returns and social impact, as demonstrated by the trends towards social investment, impact investing and profit-with-a-purpose.

· *Cultural inclusion rather than power plays and resistance to change*
The failure of many change programmes has often been attributed to 'cultural rejection' of change, usually reinforced by influential peer groups frustrating senior leaders' desired change. Reacting to this frustration by launching a 'culture change' programme tends to be ineffective and a substitute for real work.
Leaders of organizations are increasingly prioritizing real inclusion. Rather than protecting the interests of existing exclusive and influential groups, leaders are supporting the emergence of new stories of change and new peer groups shaping the organization's culture.

· *Supporting mental health rather than accepting the burden and cost of mental ill health for individuals and organizations*
An epidemic of mental ill health afflicts all sectors – corporate, government, public services and voluntary sectors. Individuals and organizations are stressed financially since the 2008 crash, by the erosion of social capital, and prospectively by a 'future of work' shaped by artificial intelligence, mobile technology and the gig economy. There is no such thing as 'good stress' or 'an acceptable level of stress'. Stress is about frustration, overreaction, powerlessness and alienation and can lead to ill health.
Leaders of organizations are increasingly recognizing the potential for stresses and act to protect their organization and people – and themselves. This is not only a moral obligation on leaders – it is an economic necessity, a legal duty and frequently an intense personal challenge.

For businesses and public services, the experiences of the last decade have prompted increasingly radical departures from traditional organizational life – but these are not new to many community organizations, faith groups, start-ups and charities. What it means is that we can tell stories of leaders and organizations already on this path, as set out in the following sections:

8 **Thriving and belonging: individual psychology and organizational purpose**
To thrive as individuals and organizations, leaders need to be constantly nurturing organizational purpose and belonging. Change will succeed only when people within the organization commit their discretionary effort and engage with change, which depends on leadership actions to:
- Reinforce real-world purpose and ethos.
- Ensure everyone has a say and invite alternative perspectives.
- Build leadership capabilities through apprenticeship and modelling psychological safety at work.

9 **Culture that includes everyone: changing the powerful and invisible**
Cultures are informal organizational behavioural norms that influence people's behaviours and prospects in an organization. Culture can be a significant barrier to change and can alienate individuals. Nudging the culture into new behaviours and inclusivity takes leaders who:
- Provide new assumptions for use by leaders when trading off priorities and choices.
- Tell new stories about what matters in the organization.
- Invest in new cohorts, new affiliations and influential peer groups.

10 **Promoting mental health: the leadership opportunity**
Work – and change at work – can be productive and
positive for mental health. Leaders need to move from
awareness to action:
- Build personal resilience and peer support for
  yourself.
- Equip line managers to talk mental health with their
  people.
- Engage in the real work of difficult choices.
- Provide the basics of a mentally healthy workplace
  and tackle bad behaviours.

8

Thriving and Belonging: Individual Psychology and Organizational Purpose

STORIES OF ORGANIZATIONS WITH PURPOSE

Volunteering is a powerful impulse in humanity – the 22,000 volunteers in Samaritans are there 24/7 for people who need someone to listen. In our experiences of the pandemic, stories of altruistic hard work in local communities inspire us and illustrate the powerful human need to work for a bigger purpose. For example, the Chair of Feeding Bristol reported that:

> 'The response has been amazing: In the past two weeks alone, foodbanks have seen referrals of residents struggling to make ends meet tripling; FareShare South West have doubled the volume of food coming into their warehouse, distributing food to over 100 projects across the city; four new emergency foodbanks have opened to add to the seven already in place; the FOOD Club network has grown from five to 16, all supporting 50 families each; pop-up food distributors run by closed pubs and restaurants, and volunteers from businesses and community organizations, are all adding to Bristol's food response.'[167]

Across the UK, 750,000 people signed up as volunteers to support the NHS and local needs at the start of the COVID-19 crisis, although many were ultimately left idle.[168] Ten million volunteered during lockdown for all kinds of community action, with thousands of spontaneous mutual aid groups emerging to support the most vulnerable people in society with shopping, collecting medicines, companionship, financial stress – demonstrating the wider potential of community power.[169]

Purpose and national interest have been the driving forces behind most state-owned enterprises and public services, even if some of them periodically revert to behaving like any big business. Leadership behaviours have blurred between the private and public sectors for 40+ years. Management of public services has become more business-like and most business leaders work in a system of *stakeholder*-capitalism rather than merely shareholder-capitalism – i.e., they are legitimately accountable to deliver for a broad range of stakeholders (especially their employees and host communities), not just their financial owners. The growth in corporate social responsibility (CSR) is based on voluntary benevolent 'giving back' or compensation for harm done in pursuit of profit. In addition, over the last 20 years, a new movement has emerged for financially sustainable returns and social impact labelled 'social investment'.

In 2012, Big Society Capital was set up to build the social investment market and to deliver social impact. The UK government allocated £600 million from dormant bank accounts and the four major banks (Barclays, HSBC, Lloyds and RBS) added £200 million, which has been used to create a social investment marketplace almost from scratch. Using their knowledge and capital, BSC collaborate and invest with entities such as fund managers and specialist banks who also want to create a better, sustainable future. These entities then invest in charities and social enterprises, and together they create the social impact. BSC recruited highly motivated staff with a good understanding of finance as well as a genuine desire for impact and immense motivation grounded in BSC's purpose. Their drive can come over as evangelical and sometimes 'only our way will do', but they are generous with their time and supportive of others who are interested in growing their organizations. BSC shares globally and other countries have introduced variations on the

BSC model, including Japan, Portugal, South Korea, Canada and Italy. By 2020, Big Society Capital had built a new marketplace and boosted investment in UK charities and social enterprises, transforming their ability to scale and innovate:[170]

- *Stories of human impact* – speaking with social enterprises such as St Mungo's and Hull Women's Network, it is inspiring to hear stories of people rebuilding their lives, providing volunteering opportunities, accessing safe and affordable housing – with the scale of the human impact magnified by investors' capital.
- *A new social investment marketplace* – with 35 venture impact funds, 18 UK retail impact funds, 70 outcomes contracts and four funds specializing in financing outcomes contracts, over 67,400 community share investors, over 85 Social Investment Tax Relief (SITR) deals, a UK social property market of £2 billion+, a UK charity bond market of £369 million.
- *Huge social impact* – £78 million committed to social enterprises and charities through 109 investments in communities, £34 million committed through 203 investments in employment and education, £37 million committed through 34 investments in income and financial inclusion, £22 million committed through 51 investments in families, £52 million committed through 209 investments in health and well-being – and others.

Despite these visible successes, social investment is not suited to addressing many social issues; BSC has its challenges going forward[171] and it is not the only player in the returns-with-impact space. Community Interest Companies (CICs) were introduced in 2005 for small enterprises using profit and assets for public good. The term 'impact investing' was coined in 2007 and the Global Impact Investing Network (GIIN) was founded in 2010, linking social impact to financial return, and

Environmental and Sustainability Governance (ESG) stimulated corporate and public policy focus on sustainability. Although social enterprises and philanthropic investors are a key element in the marketplace, the thinking is now spreading rapidly among purpose-driven organizations.[172] 'Doing well and doing good at the same time' is getting attention on both sides of the Atlantic, beyond CSR.

At the American Business Roundtable, 181 CEOs signed a new *Statement on the Purpose of a Corporation*, committing to lead for the benefit of all stakeholders – customers, employees, suppliers, communities and shareholders. The British Academy issued a new report on the future of the corporation entitled *Principles for Purposeful Business*, proposing that the role of corporations should be 'to profitably solve problems of people and planet, and not profit from causing problems'. Deloitte commented that the consensus today is that purpose and profits march hand in hand[173] and introduced 'people and purpose leaders' across its organization, while Ernst & Young opine that 'Organizations will have to make their transformation projects work harder and be more attractive to an increasingly purpose-driven workforce'.[174] Accounting principles and corporate reporting requirements are changing to require companies to account for and comment on their impact on the environment and society. It might be churlish to question all this purposeful activity, but it remains to be seen how business organizations and their financers deal with trade-offs in hard times.

MEETING OUR NEEDS FOR BELONGING AND PURPOSE AT WORK

No one ever got out of bed to deliver an efficiency saving or to create value for shareholders (unless they were themselves a shareholder or partner in the business), but they do get out of bed to control their own destiny or to deliver a public good. People spend a third of their life at work and they want to get something out of it. Now, it may just be pay – there's a reason it's called compensation. But usually people want some degree of fulfilment, a sense of identity and of achievement – and they look to their social group or their organization to provide these higher needs:

- Identity that can come in many forms – status, role, companionship, trust and especially *belonging*.
- Achievement that also comes in many forms – delivering results, building competence, demonstrating allegiance, kindness and especially *purpose*.

Pursuing a bigger purpose leads many organizations to thrive, as do individuals belonging to these organizations, and families and communities connected with them. If you belong to a faith group, as I do, they provide purpose and connection. During the pandemic and its aftermath, many of us rediscovered the importance of family, neighbours, local shops and community activity for our sense of who we are and what we do. Leaders should be drawing lessons from this about purpose, belonging and trust – they can tap into their people's psychological needs or they can make a few superficial gestures and lose their trust.

Purpose, connection and belonging are fundamental to human organizations – and especially to the up-and-coming generation, who have limited tolerance for organizations and leaders whose behaviours do not show respect and inclusion of individuals – or where change is imposed to defend share prices or top management pay. Younger people are often more visibly critical of traditional leadership styles because they dare to speak out, act up or leave. Disenchantment among this younger generation should worry organizational leaders in advanced economies that are increasingly oriented to services industries. Demographics indicate that advanced economies are desperately short of people and especially people with the skills and experience of applying new technologies.

Many senior leaders appear to launch change programmes with a 'mechanical' model of the organization that assumes that people within the organization will simply obey if the leader just pulls the right levers. This may be grounded in their personal experience of coming into the workforce and taking up their first leadership roles during the decades of the late-20th century, which were dominated by the baby-boom generation. Baby Boomers are characterized by attachment to large institutions, secure careers and trust in leaders. It is commonplace that younger people coming into the workplace do not share this automatic organizational belonging and trust in leaders – it has to be earned and continually reinforced.

So it will be vital to build organizational belonging among the emerging generation of future leaders but, vital as that pending demographic crisis is, there is a pre-existing endemic threat. The bigger challenge for leaders of organizational change are the people who remain within the organization but keep silent, appear to comply and wait for this wave of change to wash over and dissipate. Traditionally, organizations have looked at staff turnover and sickness absence as telling indicators of healthy change. This is one half of the equation – *losing* people with potential and experience is not going to help. The other half of the equation is that the people who are *staying* will have much more influence – positive and negative – on delivery of change. These people may assert that they identify with the roots of the organization, but if they do not identify with or support the change pursued by senior leaders, then they will not apply their discretionary energy to ensure change succeeds. 'Discretionary energy' is the extra effort, the 'going the extra mile', the local initiatives and the bright ideas that make the real difference between change that succeeds and change that fizzles out.

FORCING THE PACE OF CHANGE WILL ERODE TRUST

The 'war for talent' management buzzword appeared in the 1990s and, 25 years on, organizations know that they will suffer if they fail to match best practice in the battery of HR/people strategies – flexible career options, rewarding performance, individual development, diverse workplaces etc. However, these conventional elements are not enough to ensure organizational belonging through a major change. What changes with change?

- *Change is positive for some individuals*
  Many aspects of change have positive potential: some will be promoted into new roles, some will have more stimulating work and will enjoy new colleagues, and for others simply shaking things up and having a bit of excitement makes work more engaging. The most sustainable positive impact is when the organization becomes a place to belong, aligning individual and organizational purpose and working in better ways for its people.

- *Change is negative for other individuals*
  For some, a changing organization is no longer the one they joined (or thought they joined) and they perceive deterioration in ways of working. The way people are treated as a result of change is always especially sensitive – it is a mistake to think that exits go unnoticed across the organization. Those who remain after the change may note that they will receive the same treatment if they become surplus to requirements. Finally – and critically – failed change and consequent disappointment can be even more alienating than not changing at all.

- *Leaders can exercise power*
  Leaders can be tempted to take an instrumental view of people and try to force the pace of change by exercising power, although often benignly paraphrased as 'let's give people an incentive to do what we want them to do' or 'go on a war footing'. Increased reporting or supervision or KPIs or incentives or sanctions or new processes can increase short-term compliance, but can accentuate negative aspects of change for individuals, because it plays into feelings of powerlessness.

The COVID-19 pandemic gave us actual masks, but leaders who 'force the pace' will also force individuals to decide whether to don a psychological 'mask' to survive change. Masks come in many forms: acceptance of goals or ethos or style or characteristics that do not fit the individual. But, whatever the mask, leaders are reinforcing individuals' reluctance to fully commit their energies to an organization and the tendency to not 'bring themselves fully to work' – and diminishing the prospect of individuals 'going the extra mile'. Organizational belonging and a shared sense of organizational purpose is critical – successful leadership of change requires that people put in the discretionary effort and engage.

People want to believe in their leaders during a crisis, but trust in any one individual leader is a fragile thing. When times are good for the organization, people will be willing to extend some extra tolerance because everyone benefits from success, even if some benefit more than others. When leaders ask for extra effort just to stand still or, worse still, actual sacrifices from people, then trust becomes highly conditional:

During a crisis, trust depends on being visibly 'all in this together'
During the Second World War, rationing was mainly about visible shared sacrifice at all levels of society – other policies would have been as effective and less disruptive, but would have undercut the sense of common purpose.

During the financial crash of 2008, the taxpayer bailed out the failures of financial institutions, regulators and governments. However, trust eroded rapidly when it became clear that inequalities of wealth and opportunity widened as consequences of economic and social policies.

During the lockdown of 2020, the rules stipulated that people not travel to their second homes, even if dispersing people from cities made sense from a public health perspective. Breaches of this rule were condemned as undermining equality of sacrifice during the crisis and, similarly, business leaders who did not quickly share the pain of financial losses were shamed into pay cuts.

After a crisis, the leader has to earn trust afresh

After the Second World War, gratitude to Winston Churchill was evident on VE Day, but six weeks later he was out of power because his opponents had the credible vision for post-war Britain that Churchill had neglected during the war.

After the financial crash of 2008, unprecedented taxpayer interventions prevented a 1930s-style depression, but the electoral results of 2016 across Europe and the US showed how voters felt left behind.

After the lockdown of 2020, voters re-evaluated national leaders based on their handling of the crisis and its aftermath, with some losing voter trust and others being rated higher. Interestingly, three women received generally positive comment for their leadership during the initial crisis during the first half of 2020 – Jacinda Ardern, Prime Minister of New Zealand, Angela Merkel, Chancellor of Germany and Nicola Sturgeon, First Minister of Scotland.[175]

Trusted leadership is being inclusive, showing appreciation, drawing in those who don't feel part of the culture – as we explore further in Section 9. It is also about providing the right balance of organizational excitement and calm – encouraging those who might self-stress through perfectionism and workaholic patterns to adopt healthier thinking and practices.

POWER-BASED LEADERSHIP IS A TEMPTING SHORT-TERM FIX – IT *WILL* COME UNSTUCK

Tolstoy wrote: 'Every happy family is the same; every unhappy family is unhappy in its own way.' [176] A few leaders dispense with trust and exercise power, resulting in many different types of dysfunctional organization. A selection of power-based behaviours includes:

- *Making clear that they are the sole arbiter* – using fear rather than authority.

- *Demeaning people* – criticizing individuals or categories of people, refusing to share credit for success.
- *Challenging individuals publicly or crudely* – bullying, pursuing scapegoats.
- *Dismissing alternative ideas or experiences* – refusing to look to others for input, dodging the question.

Most leaders would never contemplate the outright-toxic behaviours listed, but we see numerous examples where leaders edge away from trust-based to more power-based behaviours. Even during the pandemic, it is noteworthy that political and health leaders struggled to speak directly, taking refuge in language like 'we have been very clear' and preferring to focus on activity and numbers rather than connecting with people's concerns and admitting shortfalls. Organizations that engage in downsizing are implicitly or explicitly treating people as disposable, losing their work community, and being placed in social isolation is the same – stress and potential anxiety and depression. In feedback to Samaritans, 40 per cent of men said that talking to others helped with concerns and worries during the pandemic.[177]

Power-based leadership has inevitable consequences – wasted energy while individuals invest in protecting themselves, insufficient challenge to the leader,[178] poor behaviours spread across the organization as they are role-modelled with impunity, and disenchantment with the organization, which suppresses contributions to change.

BUSINESS IS CHANGING – HOW WILL SOCIETY CHANGE?

Economic impacts of the pandemic are driving rapid business change

The effects of the downturn and fear of recurring health crises will play out over the long term: reduced economic activity, mistrust of globalized supply chains, more pressure on government spending, growing requirements for resilience as well as efficiency, more distributed working – and higher national, corporate and household debt.

Businesses were supported by unprecedented taxpayer interventions during the peak of the crisis: about a third of the UK's 33-million workforce were being supported by the government, through the Coronavirus Job Retention Scheme, the Self-Employment Income Support Scheme, the Coronavirus Business Interruption Loan Scheme, the Bounce Back Loan Scheme or Universal Credit; a further third were working from home and a final third were at work. Business growth was limited to health and social care, grocery and online retail – in a four-week period, 7.9 million UK households ordered groceries online, up from 4.8 million in 2019.[179] Retail, education, entertainment and healthcare businesses adapted rapidly in order to continue operating. After years of hesitation, GP telephone consultations became the norm. US employees working remotely quadrupled to 50 per cent of the workforce.[180] Some businesses prospered – like the small players providing technology-based solutions that had their moment. However, corporate giants were forced to cut dividends, some large players closed their doors permanently, supply chains withered and many sole traders and micro-operators vanished. The distribution of economic pain accentuated pre-existing inequalities: people under 30 or over 60, in part-time work or on low pay or from Black, Asian and Minority Ethnic groups were the most likely to have been furloughed or made redundant – and Samaritans research found less-well-off men did not receive the support they needed.[181] Conversely, those aged 35 to 59, on higher pay or in full-time work or from white ethnic groups were the most likely to be working from home and to have remained in employment.[182]

While the lockdown was still in its early days, corporate leaders and consultants and think tanks were already shipping out new strategies, ideas, warnings and buzzwords on a daily basis.[183] The survival instinct and the nose for an opportunity are the normal evolutionary responses of corporate animals to changes in their ecosystem: 'Coronavirus is an opportunity to move to the future faster,' said Ginni Rometty, Executive Chair of IBM, eyeing faster adoption of new technology.[184]

Social impacts of the COVID-19 pandemic pose big questions

The effects on society will also play out over the long term and the jury will remain out for some time: will society reorder its priorities in a way that was not done after 2008? Even a few brief questions illustrate the scale of the task:[185]

- *Who is priority? Recognizing the people we really depend upon.*
  Reallocating rewards to the redefined key workers within society, welcoming the migrant workforce that underpins public services.

- *How do we work as a society? Entrenching local decisions and resources.*
  Decentralizing government to enable local action and responsiveness, bringing kindness to bear as an explicit value in public policy, supporting charities and social enterprises to match the hidden subsidies to commercial businesses and the City of London.

- *What inequities do we need to fix? Striking a new deal across the generations.*
  Discriminating in favour of those who currently have least access to resources and opportunities, integrating health and social care, driving down property values, investing in mental health, mitigating and adapting to climate change.

189

Why might we see society reorder its priorities this time? We have the social consensus of a shared experience during the pandemic and its aftermath and we have demonstrated the potential to mobilize community resources and to work in radically different ways – we know we can lead and change our organizations. We can align organizational purpose and individual belonging at the level of social micro-enterprise or tech start-up as well as at the level of a corporate behemoth such as JP Morgan, whose chief executive, Jamie Dimon, called the pandemic 'a wake-up call ... for business and government to think, act and invest for the common good'.[186]

THE HEART AROUSED – Poetry and the Preservation of the Soul in Corporate America by David Whyte
(1994, Currency Doubleday)

David Whyte is a writer of lyric verse who has worked with those who have chosen to live out their lives as managers and employees of organizations, and who struggle to keep their humanity in the process. Organizations now desperately need the powers historically associated with the poetic imagination not only to see their way through the present whirligig of change, but also, because poetry asks for accountability to a human community, for rootedness and responsibility even as the community changes.[187]

'If work is all about doing, then the soul is all about being: the indiscriminate enjoyer of everything that comes our way. If work is the world, then the soul is our home...' explores the possibility of being at home in the world, melding soul life with work life, the inner ocean of longing and belonging with the outer ground of strategy and organizational control. The time seems right for this cross-fertilization. It seems that all the overripe hierarchies of the world, from corporations to nation-states, are in trouble and are calling, however reluctantly, on their people for more creativity, commitment and innovation.[188]

190

Whyte explores these human and organizational needs through poetry including Beowulf, Dante, Coleridge, modern poets and his own work:

The complexity trap for leaders

Trying to run complex companies, big or small, by imperial command, from the top down, may be *the* single most unnecessary burden carried by any organizational manager. Attempting something that is doomed to fail, they produce a manual of required responses covering all eventualities. Doing this, the system they are forced to employ becomes Byzantine and cumbersome. It also carries an implicit lack of trust in the essential elements of the system – people. Not only that, but hierarchical systems based solely on power emanating from the top cannot plan for the wild efflorescence of impossible events we call daily life. They are continually immobilized by the changing nature of reality.[189]

The change trap for individuals

Organizations ask us for commitment and dedication and then go their own way, shifting its goals in order to prosper and survive, and devil, it seems, take the hindmost. We stop working at the edge between creativity and failure and start managing change in the best way we know – by attempting to diminish its occurrence. Finally, we learn how to keep our heads down and endure, hoping the CEO's finger of death will not point to our department as things go slowly but irrevocably wrong.[190]

The need for real-world connection – individual and organizational belonging

A great deal of the exhaustion that comes from work can be attributed to losing sight of the very world we are serving. There is tremendous natural 'beauty' in an organization that allows people to bloom and grow, to be excited, to be proud of their work, and to understand the connection of the work to a greater ecology than the organization alone.[191]

SURVIVING CHANGE – OR THRIVING WITH CHANGE?

Building a sense of identity and belonging is about the bigger purpose of the organization – what one firm called 'WHAT we do when we are at our best' – and also the ethos and ways of working in the organization – 'HOW we work'. Both matter equally in helping people thrive.

Of course, none of this is new, even if it is achieving greater prominence in the aftermath of the crises of 2008 and 2020. The father of economics from my home town of Kirkcaldy, Adam Smith, described in *The Theory of Moral Sentiments* of 1759 how people act to benefit others even at economic cost to themselves. Smith warned of the danger for society of dissociating work from a meaningful purpose, although this was overshadowed by his more famous *Wealth of Nations* of 1776, which analysed the effects of self-interest and task specialization across the economy.

Whether people are surviving or thriving will have a huge impact on organizational performance over time and the successful delivery of change in particular:

- If people are merely *surviving change*, then the probability of successful change diminishes – as well as the well-being of the individuals deteriorating.
- If people are *thriving with change*, then the organization and change benefits from people's willingness to give their discretionary effort – and their greater well-being.

Leaders' behaviours drive the cycle of individual and organizational 'surviving' or 'thriving' because individuals react rationally – whether withholding or contributing to change – which, in turn, has inevitable consequences for energy and innovation at work. This direct connection from leaders' actions through individuals' reactions to organizational performance is not a matter of emotion or communication or personal idiosyncrasy. It is rational acting and logical consequences.

Surviving change	Thriving with change
Leaders act: • Incentivize their priorities • Force the pace • Transmit stress	*Leaders act:* • Invite challenge • Demonstrate inclusive behaviour • Absorb stress, modulate what they transmit
Individuals react rationally: • Dig deep: do more when tired or stressed • Assume 'the mask': consent and comply • Question whether they belong	*Individuals react rationally:* • Provide discretionary effort and ideas • Bring all of themselves to work • Aspire to and identify with being a leader here
As a consequence... *Organizational stresses:* • Increased turnover • Increased presenteeism and work avoidance • Reduced learning and improvement	**As a consequence...** *Organizational potential:* • Energy and innovation • Inclusive, retention, cohesion • Performance management
Individual stresses: • Powerlessness • Leaders say they have solved my problem for me	*Individual potential:* • Self-development and challenge • Learn and improve

This comparison is starkly simplifying between 'surviving' and 'thriving'. The reality is of course that different individuals survive and thrive in various combinations and subtleties.

Individuals can and will react psychologically and rationally to change with consequent higher or lower sense of organizational belonging

Most individuals acquire the ability to mask their actual reactions within the organization when they are called upon to demonstrate compliance and consent. There will be a few mavericks who have the courage (or insensitivity) to speak their minds, but they tend to be discounted or manoeuvred around. Most people need the organization to provide the psychological safety to encourage different views – 'When people have psychological safety at work, they feel comfortable sharing concerns and mistakes without fear of embarrassment or retribution … crucial source of value creation in organizations operating in a complex, changing environment.'[192] But, even in organizations that espouse psychological safety and realize it in most of their units, some parts of organizations are not just psychologically unsafe – they can be made toxic by bullying leaders.

The sense of organizational belonging drives individuals' choice of how much discretionary effort they invest in change

Inclusion is a sure route to innovating and improving performance, through generating ideas and options for change, and guarding against unintended consequences. The probability of successful change increases with inclusive leadership because individuals feel greater organizational belonging and put in discretionary effort. Think how exhausting it is for those who have to 'wear the mask' to work in their organization and have to restrain their personal identity in order to 'fit in' with the leadership behaviours and appearances of the organization. Many of us have experienced 'wearing the mask'; it doesn't have to be a racial or gender or religious or health characteristic – it can simply be a more entrepreneurial approach or a less traditional schooling or more modern pastime that is simply not the norm in the organization.

Leaders' behaviours are a powerful factor in shaping individuals' reactions

Encouraging that discretionary effort from individuals who feel they belong within the organization takes leaders who:

- Use language that draws people in, telling stories that people relate to and that illustrate people taking the risk of sharing and being accepted.

- Ensure everyone has a say, inviting alternative perspectives and acting as an ally to role model psychological safety at work.
- Develop their people as leaders through apprenticeship – modelling and supporting and encouraging healthy boundaries.

'DO AS I DO' AUTHENTICITY: DEVELOPING LEADERS THROUGH APPRENTICESHIP

The basics of talent and leadership development include psychometric profiling, development programmes and – most important of all – mentoring and coaching in the day-to-day working environment. Building individuals' leadership capabilities is one of the surest routes to reinforcing organizational belonging and individual thriving. That is one of the reasons that senior leaders and HR functions keep investing in organization-wide leadership programmes, but the problem is that these central programmatic elements are the easy bit and the lowest pay-off elements.

Mentoring and coaching of every person in the day-to-day working environment cannot be delivered or measured easily. It requires leaders to adopt a mindset that seems a little old-fashioned now in the era of automation: that of the apprentice working to a craftsman. The apprenticeship model is not about telling people what to do or following a central programme. It is about a relationship with the apprentice that is:

- *Demonstrating leadership* – role-modelling values and effectiveness.
- *Stepping back to let the apprentice try out new skills* – learning without fear of blame.
- *Providing the flow of work so the apprentice can perform* – focusing on the task without distraction by sales or generating work.

- *Providing psychological security* – openness to criticism and improvement.
- *Sharing learning* – demonstrating that we are all on the journey together.
- *Inviting perspective* – making inclusion happen.
- *Encouraging healthy boundaries* – protecting mental health through good practice.

Leaders' language is the first step in building organizational belonging:

Senior leaders saying...	*What we are really here for is... Our purpose – and reason for coming to work – is... Our contribution to the big questions in society is...* *What's your perspective?* *Let me tell the story of how I first dared to voice an opinion...* *Let me show you – then you try...*
Front-line leaders saying...	*The way we want to work together is...* *What's your experience?* *I remember how this person came up with a different take on the problem – and that's how we changed our approach.* *Let me show you – then you try...*
Management teams saying...	*How can we make this happen?* *What are the key themes and contrasts across our staff surveys, upward feedback, exit interviews, retention trackers?* *How do our recent promotion decisions match our planned development paths and psychometric profiles?*

Summary   *Providing a sense of identity and achievement for people at work is vital to creating organizational purpose and belonging. Where it is absent, people with potential and experience may leave or choose not to 'go the extra mile' when needed. Leaders who 'force the pace' of change in organizations often play into negative aspects of change and feelings of powerlessness, forcing people to don a 'mask' to survive and eroding trust. Toxic leadership will come unstuck.*

The aftermath of the pandemic poses questions for business and for society, which require common purpose and trusted leadership. WHAT organizations do matters – as do HOW they work:

- *If people are merely surviving, the probability of successful change diminishes – as well as the well-being of the individuals deteriorating.*
- *If people are thriving, then the organization benefits from their discretionary energy – and their greater well-being.*

Leaders' behaviours are a powerful factor in shaping the common purpose and the trust needed for success:

- *Providing psychological security, inviting alternative perspectives.*
- *Developing leaders through apprenticeship.*
- *Using language that draws people in and inclusive behaviour that encourages discretionary effort and change.*

Action   *Reinforce real-world purpose and ethos.*

Build leadership capabilities through apprenticeship and modelling.

Tell stories that people relate to and illustrate the value of people taking the risk of sharing and being accepted.

Ensure everyone has a say; model psychological safety at work.

9

Culture that Includes Everyone: Changing the Powerful and Invisible

STORIES TOLD TO NEW JOINERS TO REINFORCE THE CULTURE

Establishing a corporate culture begins with induction of new joiners. The values that an organization believes about itself are apparent in the stories that people tell:

Shell	When I joined Shell from business school, I learned all the usual stuff about how the organization works – the roles and decision-making by different elements of the structure and the business planning process. I also heard stories – not officially, but passed on during the first weeks by many colleagues as they described 'what it is like to work in this organization'.
	Story 1: One of the fastest-growing businesses and a critical technology was Liquefied Natural Gas (LNG), the technology for compressing vast volumes of natural gas in order to ship it from the gas reservoirs (typically discovered in isolated regions of the world) to centres of population. Once the LNG arrived in Japan, the US and Europe, it would be re-gasified, injected into the national grids and consumed. Shell (rightly) took great pride in pioneering LNG in order to monetize its gas reserves in Brunei.

The story was that LNG technology had been invented by a group of engineers in Shell as a sideline to their real work, using leftover assets. Once the engineers had demonstrated that the idea worked on a tiny scale, Shell piled in with the huge capital investment to make it work at scale. One of Shell's biggest businesses would be known now as an original 'skunkworks' operation.

Story 2: I was introduced to the director of Shell's retail business in the Netherlands – a high-profile job in one of Shell's home countries.[193] It was explained to me that he had made his name early in his career when the IJseelmeer (the then open lake in the heart of the Netherlands) had frozen over to the extent that cars were driven across the ice, taking a huge shortcut from one side of the country to the other. When the IJseelmeer froze, he was then a local sales representative for a district nearby and he had built a tiny refuelling station in the middle of the ice, using a few drums, old pumps and a Shell sign. Very little petrol was actually sold but the station appeared on the TV news and his – and Shell's – reputation was made. Decades on, I am sure that different stories are now being shared in Shell about more recent heroic deeds!

Further probing cast doubt on key elements of the stories, but that was not the point. Everyone in Shell knew the stories and they were passed on to illustrate what the company wanted to believe about itself: that is, despite the size and complexity of the world's second-largest company, Shell people could make things happen. Honestly told as motivating legends, they also defended the status quo of bureaucratic power in the world's largest company.

McKinsey   In contrast, when I joined McKinsey 12 years later, stories about people in McKinsey were transmitted during formal induction and repeated by colleagues throughout the years. Partners told stories about how they had emulated the firm's founder, Marvin Bower, when they turned down profitable business because they doubted whether the project would deliver real value for the client. In his book, Bower insisted the firm 'maintain an independent position, being ready to differ with client managers and telling them the truth as we see it even though it may adversely affect Firm income or endanger continuance of the relationship'.[194]

Every McKinsey recruit could repeat mantras such as 'client first, firm second, self third' and 'the obligation to dissent' – the duty to speak up and challenge, despite the hierarchy. There were also unhelpful sayings: 'We don't learn from clients, we learn from one another' reflected the arrogance that came from success. 'We recruit insecure over-achievers and keep them insecure' reflected the tough personnel policies that were designed to keep people constantly at top performance, while sifting out people until 5% ultimately made it to partner in the firm. Bower would have deprecated those unprofessional attitudes and he would have been horrified by scandals around the 2008 crisis that led to McKinsey leaders being convicted of insider trading.

Again, it didn't matter that later experience demonstrated that the values illustrated by these stories were honoured in the breach as much as in the application. These passionately narrated anecdotes and mantras were what McKinsey people wanted to believe about their firm: that is, despite the pressures of winning clients and the constant need to grow in order to maintain partners' incomes, McKinsey is an organization of principled people pursuing higher goals.

200

Deloitte   Things were very different when I joined my
third firm, Deloitte, 13 years later. There were
no stories of mythical exploits; instead, everyone
introduced themselves as 'I'm from Andersen' or
'I was old Deloitte'. In 2002, after Enron went
into bankruptcy with criminal implications, their
auditor, Arthur Andersen, was convicted following
the destruction of documents in their Houston
and Chicago offices, and the global Andersen firm
was carved up and merged into different local
competitors. In the UK, following the near-death
experience of their firm, Andersen merged into
Deloitte in an acquisition/merger that created the
modern Deloitte. When I joined five years later,
people were still processing the trauma of the
collapse and the rescue – described by the then
senior partner as 'an ordeal'.[195]

Deloitte partners' initial positioning as either
'ex-Andersen' or 'old Deloitte' regularly led on to
discussion of 'how we did things differently/better
and what changed after the transaction'. Following
the crisis of 2001 and the US Sarbanes-Oxley Act
of 2002, Deloitte and the other 'Big Four' firms
shifted significantly from the collegial partner-led
culture to a corporate-style organization structure
and processes, accompanied by systems to minimize
future risks of an Enron/Andersen-style implosion.
Apparently a history story about conflicting
cultures, it both questioned and defended the
power of the corporate centres that cut across the
entrepreneurial drive of a partner-owned and led
business.

Every organization – even the youngest – quickly acquires myths,
caricature stories that encapsulate desired values, maybe entirely

inaccurate stories that amount to misleading propaganda. Accurate or not, these organizational myths and stories are powerful because they are not only 'ways of getting things done' – they are also 'ways of stopping things' and 'who has the power around here':

- *Culture can be a significant barrier to change.*
  Failed or underwhelming change programmes are frequently blamed on 'our culture' for lack of progress or frustrating desired change.

- *Culture can alienate individuals.*
  Especially when cultures are shaped by and around power groups within the organization, cultures can easily become an exclusionary force and undermine organizational belonging.

THE POWER OF CULTURE

Getting to grips with culture and influencing its effects is made harder by the fact that, like the words 'project' and 'team', 'culture' is frequently unhelpfully bandied around without clear definition.[196]

Sometimes culture is casually termed 'how we do things around here' and then the speaker moves on rapidly to more serious topics like structures and decision-making. That seemed to be the case when the chief executive of global aero-engine giant Rolls-Royce characterized recent announcements of significant restructuring as being explicitly about 'changing the slow and bureaucratic culture' of the company. However, the specific changes he announced were all about reducing the numbers of managers and the layers of management and decision-making rights.[197] Formal organization design can influence behaviours but the informal – usually invisible – organization matters at least as much. Senior leaders, especially external appointees, often reach for the 'reorganization lever' too quickly, adopting a slew of new KPIs or processes or structures – because those are the visible elements of the organization and apparently easier to influence. It is only with the benefit of time and study of organizations that have gone through decades of restructuring that one can see just how limited the impact of formal organizational restructuring can be – think of Barclays, BP, GM, Siemens, the NHS: notorious for (almost annual) reorganizations. This is deeply unfortunate for everyone because, as academics point out, rules govern about 20 per cent of behaviour within organizations – but culture about 80 per cent.[198]

This tendency to relegate culture as a topic is illustrated in the best-known models of organizations: Jay Galbraith's Star Model™[199] lists strategy, structure, processes, reward and 'people', while McKinsey's 7-S[200] are strategy, structure, systems, staff, skills, shared values and 'style'. Even writers who set out to describe culture specifically end up talking as much about strategy and structure: Ed Schein's model[201] defines culture as three layers – the formal structures (artefacts), the espoused strategy and values, and then the underlying assumptions with culture at the centre.

Instead of an all-encompassing view of strategy and organization, I focus on the unique aspects of culture as 'informal organizational behavioural norms' and their effect for and against change:

Informal	Clearly understood but uncodified.
Organizational	Followed by groups across the organization at scale.
Behavioural	Govern trade-offs made by leaders and what leaders pay attention to.
Norms	Exhibit power without authority.

When starting work with a new client, I always briefed my teams of consultants to 'Look for the invisible' and 'Listen for the dogs that are not barking'. It was a deliberate provocation of the responses from my consultants: 'Well, Keith, how do you expect us to *see* the invisible or *hear* silence?' Actually, it is not so hard. It takes time, an absence of ego, distance from the day-to-day, the ability to ask the right questions and observation of patterns in responses and non-responses. The clue for interviewers is to listen particularly hard when:

- Leaders do not understand why you are asking certain questions.
- Leaders think the answers are so obvious – in other words, the questions are naive to an insider.
- Leaders feel constrained from acting in line with logic or common sense or external standards.

Cultural norms are all about people – as we saw with Shell, McKinsey and Deloitte – and I could add examples from corporates, government, public services, churches and charities. Cultural norms govern what people treat as important, what gets discussed and what does not, the kind of people we recruit and promote, what it takes to be successful, how we behave when we get together – all unwritten rules that govern the daily experience of people within the organization. The power of organizational culture is that leaders simply take it for granted because it has always been present as far as they are concerned. Cultures, almost by definition, have been shaped by those who hold the power to shape many small decisions over a long period of time – particularly decisions about people and about the groups that matter. Cultures will, by definition, lag changes in the composition and behaviours of the workforce in the organization.

A common assumption is that senior leaders are generally empowered by organizational culture – while those further down the organization are disempowered. First, let's challenge senior leaders' automatic empowerment by organizational culture – and come back to disempowerment later in this section.

A NEW CULTURE CANNOT BE IMPOSED OR POLICED

In fact, senior leaders are frequently frustrated with culture, precisely because it is powerful, invisible and uncontrolled. If 'people are not doing as they are told' and the prevailing culture is being blamed, then a common response is to launch a culture-change programme, which is really all about making culture visible and controlled from the top.

Promulgating a new set of behaviours from the top, then policing/rewarding/punishing systematically – taking a formal approach to an informal phenomenon – is destined for failure. A programme of this type does not directly *engage* with the culture – it seeks to *substitute* formal strategy and organization design for the informal organizational behavioural norms of the culture. It *will* have an effect, but the impact and timing is unpredictable. It may result in a loss of trust because new processes are in effect sending the message: 'I insist you do this – and do it my way.' There are a number of flaws in this approach:

- Adopting the style of a 'commander' is effective only in crisis – so issuing commands is unlikely to be an effective response to a long-established organizational behaviour pattern that has been experienced positively by the power groups within the organization.
- Senior leaders are 'othering the problem' – they are defining the problem as other people within the organization rather than themselves. They often decline to accept how their behaviour contributes to the problems they want addressed.
- Reducing the values and culture of the organization to a set of rules, processes and financial incentives can erode trust in the organization and its leaders, leading to game-playing.
- Most leaders hesitate to invest in the essentials of change: common language, bringing in the outside world, and enabling leadership at all levels. Senior leaders are wary of giving up apparent control over the change process and worry that it will be delayed or cost more.

In most organizations it is better to appeal to unifying values already embedded, but in need of an update. Culture change programmes that seek to replace these norms usually fail because they are *either* so prescriptive that they cannot have broad application – *or* so general that they can be given lip service. The analogy with policing new laws across a community tells us:

- *Ultimately, policing is self-imposed*
  Police officers are largely invisible on our streets and we are largely unobserved, but most people obey the laws.
- *A minority can paralyse policing*
  Northern Ireland during 'the Troubles' illustrated that policing breaks down if only around 5 per cent of the population are non-supportive.
- *Policing complexity is difficult*
  As soon as the lockdown during the pandemic moved on from one simple rule: *Stay at Home*, the adoption of new rules became reliant on common sense and policing became near impossible.

The first psychologist to win the Nobel Prize in economics

THINKING, FAST AND SLOW by Daniel
Kahneman (2011, Allen Lane) Nobel Memorial Prize
in Economic Sciences 2002

Kahneman and Amos Tversky[202] advance our understanding of how we make judgements and choices, challenging rational economic theory that assumes we make orderly logical choices. They describe two thinking systems, which give different results for the same inputs:

System 1 is fast, automatic, unconscious, instinctive, emotional. System 1 is rarely neutral, jumps to conclusions and fits judgements to recognized patterns. It is vital to living at a reasonable pace – we do not have time to calculate every decision *ab initio*.

System 2 is slower, controlled, more deliberative, more logical, infrequent, conscious. System 2 is called in when System 1 is in difficulty, in part because System 2 is easily overloaded – consistent with the limited capacity of the prefrontal cortex.

The human mind works by fitting new information into old patterns or heuristics. We take many decisions based on beliefs concerning likelihood and uncertainty that sometimes yield reasonable results and sometimes severe error. Errors arise from excessive confidence in what we believe we know:

Anchoring – we can be primed to over- or underestimate uncertain events; we reach for solutions that are available and enable us to fit events into our experience.

Substitution – we tend to avoid a difficult question and replace it with an easier one – we are rarely without an opinion!

Optimism bias and the planning fallacy – illusions of experience and control give rise to WYSIATI (what you see is all there is). Problems are treated in isolation and judgements based on known knowns, with a focus on what is measurable.

Hindsight bias – once we know something, we think it must always have been known.

Framing – our decisions depend on how options are presented. We are loss-averse; dislike risk. In judging possible outcomes, we over-weight sure things and very improbable events relative to moderately probable events – in other words, we are typically poor judges of probability.

Sunk cost – we attach disproportionate value to what we own (endowment effect) and we are irrationally averse to cutting our losses.

Simulation – we constrain our thinking about cause and effect to our own actions.

System 1 is a powerful instinct for finding cause and effect – and creating narratives – reflecting that we do not take decisions based on a number (unlike the assumptions of rational economic theory), we need a story. Compared to our 'experiencing self', our 'remembering self' is selective because 'We think of life as a story and wish it to end well... we all care intensely for the narrative of our own life and very much want it to be a good story with a decent hero'.[203]

Within this growing school of behavioural economics, Richard Thaler won the Nobel Prize for his nudge theory of behaviour – that small interventions could encourage people to make different decisions – explaining why people make decisions that can appear to defy rationality.[204]

NUDGING THE CULTURE AND POWER GROUPS INTO CHANGE

Culture can be changed directly – although it takes time to be effective. It requires senior leaders not to give in to their stress over cultural obstacles by vainly attempting to control the process. There is no one formula but successful shifts in culture are likely to include some blend of these tangible, visible steps that nudge organizations into new patterns:

1 Changing the assumptions that leaders bring to their trade-offs......by providing new assumptions or new evidence to shape assumptions.
2 Changing the stories that people tell......by providing new stories from different leaders to stoke people's desire to (re)tell stories.
3 Changing the peer groups that leaders belong to or respond to......by investing in inclusive cohorts, establishing new affiliations and moving on from old power groups.

1. New assumptions or new evidence

Leaders and management consultants typically overinvest in building a rational analysis of well-understood problems, with the excuse that an accurate picture of the facts will set you free to adopt new behaviours. This does not reflect how people actually behave – they don't analyse what they do – they use 'rules of thumb' derived from past experience to get through their jobs and lives. If we analysed every action we take, we'd never get anything done. The challenge is how to change these 'rules of thumb' that are so important in driving behaviours – tackling behaviours one by one won't work. The scientific thinking in the run-up to the pandemic illustrates the danger of applying intellectual shortcuts: lots of pandemic planning and modelling had happened and been debated, but basing the thinking on past experience of influenza was flawed. Others took a more thoughtful approach to shifting their people's assumptions about the future:

- *Shell* cultivated the fame of its scenario approach to planning as a way to 'think the unthinkable'. Some Shell scenarios discussed possible crude oil price increases before the first OPEC-led price hikes shocked the world economy in 1973 and it was billed as 'only Shell foresaw the crisis'.[205] Even with that heritage, there were limits to how quickly Shell people could change their assumptions about the world. Any analysis of oil market fundamentals predicting substantial shifts in oil prices and margins would spark debate. Obviously the first question was: Is the analysis credible and will it stand rigorous challenge? If it passed that test, then the second less-obvious question was: What do we do with it? Simply sending an email to general managers of Shell companies risked it being dismissed as 'just another point of view', no matter the persuasiveness of the analysis. After all, uncertainty in oil pricing was very unwelcome, threatening new investments and plans held dear by Shell companies around the world. An under-stated but high-impact vehicle was the answer – the analysis and predicted price changes were issued in 'the premises' – a centrally issued document that set out the oil prices and margins to be used in the biennial planning process across all Shell companies. This might sound like a pretty dry and theoretical document, but it was one of the most influential leadership tasks for senior Shell leaders, setting the assumptions used by general managers and finance managers across the Shell world.

- *Lloyds Banking Group* – and presumably every large lender – worked out that announcing a change of strategy towards small businesses would not be sufficient to cause the desired changes in lending patterns that the banks had agreed with government. Yes, broad supportive statements by the chief executive would help. To get real traction, however, they had to change the assumptions and behaviours of the bank's lending officers, the people who approved or declined loans to businesses. Getting to the lending officers meant, in turn, focusing on the handful of people who drafted 'lending principles' – the bible that lending officers live by – to redefine for the bank what a good customer looks like.

Expanding the assumptions that people bring to judgements and choices is a way of expanding the options that leaders will even consider. It helps to counter the cognitive trap that many leaders fall into of only considering options that they are already familiar with and have followed repeatedly during their careers so far – what Kahneman dubbed WYSIATI, 'what you see is all there is'.[206]

2. New stories from different leaders

Old stories do not disappear overnight, they fade slowly. However, new stories can be established with experimentation and adjustment as people respond, reject and challenge. The result of effective storytelling will be to communicate the direction of the organization more memorably than any strategy document and will also create a human connection among the group who listen and engage with the story. Over time, the wider organization will start using more of the same language, look for their own real examples and engage in the real work. The stories can be heart-warming or poignant or energizing:

- *The Church of Scotland* had supported projects and missions around the world but, with limited resources, their impact ended up being low across the board. The leadership accepted the logic of changing to a more focused strategy, concentrating on fewer countries/ regions and limited to activities clearly aligned with the Gospel mission. The challenge was how to tell the story to staff and missions, when the new strategy would apparently breach trust and long-term commitments. The turning point came when one mission in a low-income country *misinterpreted* part of the new strategy. Instead of simply acknowledging that they would cease to *receive* financial support, they *sent* a sizeable contribution to be spent supporting others – because the Church clearly needed it! It all became part of a heart-warming story of the poorest finding the resources to help others.
- *The Grenfell Tower fire* in 2017 and the stories from victims shocked and shamed – an experience anyone could share, but almost exclusively families who were BAME (Black, Asian and Minority Ethnic) and low-income.
- *UK NHS and care staff* on the front line were constantly in the media during the chaotic first weeks of the COVID-19 pandemic, again predominantly BAME and underpaid. The stories of the inadequacy of protective equipment and testing capacity, combined with our reliance upon them, catalysed public and political outrage.

- *Black Lives Matter* captured the essence of decades of inadequate action and indifference over casual everyday racism in the aftermath of George Floyd's murder in the USA. The personal testimony of young people relayed through TV shifted public perceptions of the urgency for action, including the important symbolism of removing public monuments to slave-owners as a legitimate act of public protest.

3. Changing peer groups with new affiliations and moving on from existing power groups

By definition, culture is a shared construct – change the mix of people and you get a different construct. This is why bringing people together to learn is so powerful in terms of creating a language for change and a community of peers supporting change. Groupthink needs to be called out[207] and needs to be worked with by shaping new groups.

One of the best-documented examples is President Kennedy, who learned from his decisions around the botched Bay of Pigs invasion of Cuba in April 1961, when Cuban exiles were supported by the US in a failed attempt to overthrow Castro. In the run-up to the invasion, the President had sought input only from his military chiefs and, consequently, he had been offered only military options. When satellite surveillance identified Soviet missile launch sites under construction in Cuba in October 1962, the President took active steps to bring in thinking from outside the usual military-diplomatic circle. In the run-up to and during the Cuban Missile Crisis, the President was advised by what he called his 'executive committee', a group of freer-thinkers led by his brother Attorney-General Robert Kennedy. The committee worked in parallel to the official military and diplomatic advisers and promoted the ultimately successful strategy of quarantining Cuba and selectively replying to only the compromise messages from the Soviet leadership – who had also been under pressure from their military to respond only with force![208] More modern examples include:

212

- *Professional services firms* changed behaviours during the 1990s as women joined the partnership. Some visible and superficial behaviours changed around the organization, but what was really important was the difference in expressed opinions in closed-door partner meetings where decisions were made about junior people on their way to promotion to the partnership. When there were no women partners, the groups saw men and culturally consistent behaviours as evidence of them being 'one of us' and pushed their promotion, whereas women had to jump through every official hoop. After women became partners and shared in these decisions, these 'one of us' attitudes disappeared – without any explicit discussion. There had been a real power shift to the younger women partners.
- *BP Exploration* created groups of line managers that played specific, significant roles in challenging the performance of business units – their peers.[209] 'Peer challenge' and 'peer assist' entered BP Exploration's common language of change and there had been a real power shift away from the centre to the peers in the field.
- *The Project Delivery Profession* within the UK Civil Service was boosted by the cohorts graduating from the Major Projects Leadership Academy and the Project Leaders Programme[210]. These new groups of peers could demonstrate their value to public service, spoke the same language, agitated for greater recognition within the Civil Service and supported one another in delivering their major projects.

INCLUSIVE CULTURE ENCOURAGES DISCRETIONARY EFFORT AND CHANGE

A neglected consequence of cultures being shaped over long periods of time by those in positions of power over people is that cultures will, by definition, lag changes in the composition and behaviours of the workforce in the organization. A powerful culture will feel very enabling for those who fit the mould – but leave others feeling powerless, that they are present for now, but that they do not belong. Group identity and belonging translates directly into behaviour because most people are 'conditional co-operators' – i.e., they will sacrifice their preferences in favour of group preferences, but only if others in their group do so as well.

In several organizations, I observed a series of peer groups discussing challenging feedback from people who had voluntarily left their organization. Different peer groups reacted very differently to the audio stories of people who left because they struggled with some culturally common behaviours – critical banter, universal alcohol-fuelled socializing and intrusive comments. The older and more senior groups were bemused at why we were discussing this at all, while the younger and more diverse peer groups reacted with 'Yes, this is how it is – and it is a problem that undermines our organization'. As the senior partner at Deloitte commented: 'It was probably one of the most powerful things we did, because it caused people to realize that ... something some people would have thought was just banter could be offensive to the person hearing that banter.'[211]

'Banter' has been used in some organizations to condone the exclusive values and language of the dominant social group. 'Management-speak' and overuse of military and sporting analogies can be symptoms of lazy thinking because war and sports are usually unhelpful comparisons for organizations but, in addition, they can be symbols of non-inclusive organizational cultures – potentially unfriendly to women and to minority populations. Language really matters.[212]

'Equality, Diversity and Inclusion' or sometimes just 'D&I' is an established management acronym. People can play the numbers game with diversity reporting and, falsely, inclusion is often assumed to happen when the diversity numbers look good.[213] Meaningful inclusion is harder work and harder to measure, although a start can be made by measuring participation in key events and presence at all levels of the hierarchy. Importantly for change, inclusion is a sure route to innovating and improving performance, because individuals feel greater organizational belonging and put in discretionary effort. It takes leaders who:

- Use language that draws people in, telling stories that people relate to and that illustrate people taking the risk of sharing and being accepted.
- Ensure everyone has a say, inviting alternative perspectives, role-modelling psychological safety at work.
- Nudge the culture into change, forming peer groups that bring in new influencers.
- Focus on changing the assumptions about the organization.

Senior leaders saying...	*Let me share the economic realities with you...*
	This is how we are spending our time and money right now...
	My story is...
	I would like this group of people to spend time together to come up with solutions to...
	Here are examples of what we do well...
Front-line leaders saying...	*There are many ways we could do this...*
	I can help others with... I need help with...
	Here's my story of...
Management teams saying...	*We can pull together a new group of people to...*
	We can work better together on...

Summary   *Every organization has its myths and stories that people tell and, accurate or not, these stories matter as examples of culture at work. They tend to be all about people – 'how we work and how to get ahead' – and are shaped over time by power groupings within the organization.*

Culture can be a significant obstacle to leaders promoting change – frequently they blame 'the culture' for frustrating desired change. Equally important, culture can alienate individuals from the organization.

Culture is the set of informal organizational behavioural norms that influence and constrain leaders' judgements and choices. These norms are understood but uncodified, and govern trade-offs made by leaders across the organization.

When frustrated with these invisible norms, senior leaders may launch culture change programmes. However, culture cannot be imposed or policed.

You can change culture directly, but only by nudging it into new patterns of behaviour over time – and by displacing traditional power groups.

Action   *Shape the culture and inclusivity of your organization by:*

- *Providing new assumptions or new evidence to shape the assumptions used by leaders when trading off priorities and choices.*
- *Telling new stories or giving new examples to stoke people's desire to (re)tell stories about their belonging to the organization.*
- *Investing in new cohorts, establishing new affiliations and influential peer groups within the organization.*

10

PROMOTING MENTAL HEALTH: THE LEADERSHIP OPPORTUNITY

MAKING SENSE OF MENTAL HEALTH

People frequently ask what lies behind the statistics showing a dramatic increase in mental ill health and the much wider discussion of mental health in the media:

Is this the evidence of success in removing the stigma around talking about mental health?

Or, is there really an epidemic of mental ill health sweeping organizations?

The answer is 'yes' to both questions. We are more willing to talk about mental health without discarding the affected individuals – and our ways of living and working are really damaging our health. Once upon a time, we were told that 'mental illness is rare and inexplicable – it's all about chemical imbalances, heredity and physical changes in the brain'.[214] You might or might not have been reassured by that outdated thinking – it had the effect of 'medicalizing' and 'othering' those who were 'ill'. In recent years, we have come to understand that:

- We are all on a continuum of mental health, just as we are with physical health – more or less mentally fit and healthy from time to time.

- Our experiences and our environment are primary factors in our mental health every day, far outweighing the impact of heredity or biochemistry.

Opening our eyes to the *impact of daily experiences and environment on our mental health* is liberating – because it enables us to make sense of both the scale of the challenge and the opportunity for leadership:

Challenge *of mental health for organizations*	The next few pages illustrate the range of individual anecdotes, the epidemic of work-related mental ill health and the huge costs to individuals, organizational performance and the wider economy.
Opportunity *for leadership in mentally healthy organizations*	Leaders can apply their knowledge, skills and experience in strategy, investment and organization to shape their mentally healthy workplace – described in the later pages of this section.

THE CHALLENGE OF MENTAL HEALTH FOR ORGANIZATIONS

Mental health is an ever-present critical issue – in stories from leaders and organizations, in the statistics on its extent and costs to the economy, organizations and individuals and in the impossibility of treating our way out of the crisis.

Stories from leaders and organizations

Leaders at all levels in organizations in every sector of the economy are struggling with the personal impact of work-related stress and mental ill health:

218

António Horta-Osório, Lloyds Banking Group Chief Executive	Took extended temporary leave from November 2011 after five nights of stress-induced insomnia, making a managed return to work in January 2012.[215] He recently commented that firms that ignore mental health issues risk 'breaking employees' lives and families'.[216]
Paul Rawlinson, Baker McKenzie, Global Chair	Took temporary leave from October 2018 for medical treatment following exhaustion and tragically died suddenly in March 2019.[217]
Civil servants and public services	Many talk about the excitement of change – but are overwhelmed by the stress caused by poor behaviours, the influx of new staff and routinized distrust among colleagues.[218] Health and Safety Executive statistics show that 3,230 cases of stress, depression and anxiety per 100,000 workers were recorded in public services, the highest rate of any sector in the UK and 77% higher than the all-industry average.[219]
Clinicians, health professionals and senior managers	Demand for healthcare and ever-changing targets overwhelm staff who see resources failing to rise to match needs. Turnover in new nurses and health professionals runs at 20% per annum as work pressure becomes stress when bullying is endemic and staff vacancies exceed 10%. Chief executives face 'toxic pressures' and their median tenure is only three years.[220]
Teachers, police, probation, prison officers	New performance standards and ways of working are imposed, while resources decline. Turnover in new teachers was 50% in 2010–18 and with new prison officers 19% in 2016–18.[221] Rising incidence of self-harm and mental ill-health is linked to pressure on schoolchildren and students to perform.[222]

Unpaid volunteers and overworked professionals	Pressures to take on public services after cutbacks are stressing shoestring organizations with increasing funding constraints, regulatory demands and media criticism.[223] Despite the services and jobs they provide, charities and social enterprises received minimal support during the pandemic crisis compared to businesses.
Faith groups	The Bishop of Lincoln, Nebraska took leave of absence with anxiety and depression from dealing with priestly abuse – a comprehensive story of trauma.[224]

Endemic mental ill health in the workforce and its costs

Globally, around 1 billion people a year (15 per cent of the population) experience one or more episode of mental ill health, with anxiety being the most frequently reported. Given the known under-reporting and poor data coverage of mental health across most countries (but especially within lower-income nations), we may even consider this a minimum estimate.[225] Depression is the leading cause of disability worldwide. Depression and anxiety cost the global economy US$1 trillion in lost productivity each year.[226]

Across the **US** economy, severe and enduring mental ill health causes US$193.2 billion in lost earnings each year, with 47.6 million adults (19.1 per cent of the population) experiencing an episode of mental ill health in 2018.[227]

In **Canada**, by age 40, about 50 per cent of the population will have or have had an episode of mental ill health. Anxiety affects 5 per cent of the household population, causing mild to severe impairment. The economic cost of mental ill health in Canada was estimated to be at least C$14.2 billion in terms of care costs and absence from work.[228]

In **Australia**, it is estimated that 8.7 million people (45 per cent of the population) will experience an episode of mental ill health at some time in their life and that 3.9 million people (20 per cent of the population) had such an episode in 2017. Of these, anxiety was the most prevalent, afflicting 14.4 per cent of the population, followed by affective ill health such as depression at 6.2 per cent.[229]

For **Europe,** the total costs of mental ill health are estimated at more than 4 per cent of GDP – or over €600 billion – across the 28 EU countries and the UK. These costs include: €190 billion (1.3 per cent of GDP) on direct healthcare spending; €170 billion (1.2 per cent of GDP) on social security programmes including sick leave benefits, disability benefits and unemployment insurance benefits; and €240 billion (1.6 per cent of GDP) on indirect costs due to lower employment and productivity at work.[230]

In the **UK,** annual costs to the UK economy have been estimated at £26 billion per annum through absenteeism, employment insurance, excess recruitment and/or redundancy.[231] Forty per cent will experience some episode of poor mental health in any given year – usually some degree of anxiety or depression. Most painful and scandalous, numbers of suicides are increasing annually by about 10 per cent in the **UK & Ireland.** Men are three times as likely to die by suicide than women – with men aged 45–49 at highest risk – but deaths by suicide are increasing among young people, especially females under 25.

We cannot treat our way out of this crisis

Although vital to severely distressed people and their families, properly resourced mental health services are only part of the answer, because we cannot treat our way out of this crisis. In the UK, prescriptions of antidepressants have doubled over 10 years to 17 million prescriptions to 7 million people (out of a total population of 66 million), while another 0.5 million receive talking therapies – but the epidemic shows no sign of abating. Often, when people turn to mental health services for help, it is a long time coming. In the US, only 43 per cent of adults with mental illness are treated, with an average delay of 11 years between the onset of symptoms and treatment.[232] In Canada, 49 per cent of those suffering depression or anxiety have never seen a doctor.[233] And in the UK, the NHS is losing 2,000 professional mental health staff every month, most leaving employment in health altogether, and has 22,000 mental health vacancies.[234]

The reality for most people is that they need to rely more on their own resources and their peers. They need their leaders to accept the challenge of ensuring a mentally healthy organization.

THE PANDEMIC EXPOSES MENTAL HEALTH – AND INSPIRES THE WAY FORWARD

The COVID-19 pandemic is one of the few periods of real anxiety that we have all been through – it is uniquely universal. Like all of us, leaders went through isolation and real fear for self, fear for families and friends, and fear of failure.

Direct impacts on mental health

The fears and isolation engendered by the pandemic had direct impacts on mental health.[235] The initial lockdown period saw widespread fear, panic and anxiety,[236] reduced services for those struggling with health problems (and their carers), increased stress and mental ill health, and unsafe homes for women and children who are vulnerable to abuse and violence.[237] For everyone, isolation neutralized a main support of mental health – i.e. the influence of other people in our families, workplaces and communities. During the first three months of lockdown, Samaritans supported half a million callers, of whom 25 per cent were anxious and distressed about COVID-19 and cited isolation, mental ill-health or unemployment.

For some, it went beyond fear to trauma. Front-line healthcare workers faced the first chaotic weeks of the pandemic with dramatically increased levels of patient suffering and death, anxiety over risk from infection from inadequate protective equipment and anxiety about bringing the virus home with them.

222

The large numbers of patients who spent time in intensive care face a 20 per cent higher risk of developing post-traumatic stress disorder. Relatives were not allowed to visit loved ones in their final days and then were forced to grieve alone, with isolation accentuating the trauma of grief.

But it was not the same for everyone. Inequalities in the pandemic experience had clear effects, including greater susceptibility to the virus among the Black, Asian and Minority Ethnic (BAME) communities, who are over-represented in NHS and care workforces.[238] Statistics compiled prior to the pandemic show that BAME populations are more vulnerable to mental ill health, in part due to racial discrimination, which can be a direct cause of mental ill health, and in part due to health inequalities rooted in poverty and lack of access to resources in the form of housing, employment, education, health services etc. So far, the data post-pandemic shows that this BAME vulnerability to mental ill health has worsened. The backlog of undiagnosed and untreated health problems in the long aftermath of the pandemic is likely to cause widening health inequalities, because the wealthier segments of the population attract disproportionate attention and resources.

During lockdown, families that had access to company and resources (such as a garden, income and technology) had a quite different experience from families a mile away[239] that included, for example:

- Migrants, fearful of contact with authority, struggling with English, including 100,000 children in families whose visas stipulate they have no recourse to public money.
- Families with small children living in high-rise flats with a single broken lift.

Family experiences are at the heart of inequalities in mental health because it is adverse childhood experiences – abuse, violence, poverty, separation – that do the most long-term damage.[240]

Indirect impacts on mental health

Longer term indirect impacts of the pandemic and its aftermath on mental health are also much more unequal: loss of employment or income has most effect on those with least resources to call upon, as is the case with all health inequalities. Depression within a loving family with access to resources is a totally different experience compared to those without family and resources.[241]

Left to itself, our economy generates wealth remarkably efficiently, but it does a poor job of attending to long-term sustainability of common goods – our environment and our health being prime examples. The financial crash of 2008 and the pandemic of 2020 highlighted how some sections of society are left behind.[242] Although the pandemic exposed mental health and its challenges like never before, it also inspires the way forward – kindness, community action and recognition that we can prevent mental ill health.[243]

Policy responses need greater kindness and attention to inequalities

The policy response to the financial crash of 2008 included reduced spend on public services per head, pay reductions in the private sector and freezes in the public sector, and accepting inflating asset (housing) values as a consequence of quantitative easing to keep people in jobs. The formula is different following the COVID-19 pandemic, but the financial pressures are even greater than they were in 2008 – the obvious financial pressures on families in need, and the frequently quoted deficit pressures on government finances.

Generational needs

The impact of 'shielding' the over-70s and the consequent loneliness is well publicized. At the other end of the generational continuum, it is critical to look at impacts on children and young people, because 50 per cent of severe and enduring mental illness is established by the age of 15, and 75 per cent is established by the age of 25.[244]

Community support is essential for those stressed or unwell in the new normal

Revival of neighbourhood solidarity and activities has been a shared experience of the pandemic, with bodies like the National Lottery and Big Society Capital injecting funds to support community entities. Continuing this support is vital to offset the decline of the traditional nuclear family, the economic and social dislocation following the closure of traditional industries, racial discrimination, disability (including stigmatizing mental ill health) and lower religious adherence – all of which contribute to widening mental health inequalities.[245]

FROM HOSTAGE TO SELF-ISOLATION [UNPUBLISHED]

Paul Dieppe, Professor of Health and Wellbeing at the University of Exeter College of Medicine and Health and former Dean of the Medical School at the University of Bristol, applied his experience as a hostage to the pandemic lockdown and self-isolation:

I was held hostage in Kuwait and Iraq for five months in 1990, without any phone contact, internet, or social media to help. For the best part of three months I was held in a small bungalow with six other men, as part of Saddam Hussein's 'human shield'. Towards the end of our time in Iraq we were provided with advice on what to do, but we found the bungalow group had previously adopted most of the suggested strategies. And my wife and I are adopting most of them again now.

First – establish a routine. Split the day up into manageable, max two-hour slots, sit down for breakfast, coffee break, lunch, tea break, and dinner at set, agreed times. We did this even

---

when we had no food, it provided a timetable, not allowing anyone to be alone or without an 'anchor' for any length of time. And you can have things like games evenings, and film evenings built into your agreed routine – if Wednesday is film evening, for example, it provides you with another anchor in the long weeks.

Second – be imaginative with the spaces you have in your house and garden. For example, if you like going out to the pub some evenings, do just that, set up a corner of the house or garden that is now your new 'pub', visit it and sit and have a drink there, establishing it in your mind as the pub. Similarly, you can establish areas of sanctuary, places to meditate, to be alone, or whatever works for you.

Third – pursue some creative activity. When a hostage, I wrote a lot – fortunately there were pens and paper in the bungalow (much of what I wrote was nonsense!). Now I am taking up calligraphy and getting back to carving. Doing something creative is good for the soul.

Fourth – get some exercise each day if possible. This may just be climbing up and down the stairs a lot, or following a set routine of the sort available on the web, using an exercise bike (we have one on order), or doing a lot of gardening – whatever works for you.

Finally, and perhaps most importantly – share and talk with others about your anxieties and difficulties. Use the phone a lot. Keep talking to family and friends, do not rely on social media alone, you need human voice and contact. If you are with other people, talk openly together, share the fact that you are having a bad day, going through a period of increased anxiety, or whatever, we will all have bad days and bad periods of time.

But the days, the weeks, even the months will slip by OK, and normality will be restored.

THE OPPORTUNITY FOR LEADERSHIP IN MENTALLY HEALTHY ORGANIZATIONS

Work can and should be positive for mental health

Good work can be very beneficial to mental health – providing purpose, community and a sense of achievement. All of these positives are reinforced by effective:

Management of self – know and control one's own stressors, protect time focused on the real and inspiring purpose and community at work.

Line management – managing work well, talking about opportunities to move forward, accommodating home-work needs, rewarding management behaviours that de-stress tough situations.

Work can be negative for mental health

Stress at work, when it reaches anxiety-inducing levels, can result in presenteeism and/or absenteeism. It can be triggered by:

Self-stress – perfectionism, imposter syndrome.

Inefficient work practices – frequent unnecessary changes in tasks, goals, reviews; inadequate coverage for absences etc.

Conflict with line management – including unresolved issues about workload or daily pressure that is (or is close to) bullying.

Handling 'the s-word' in mental health discussions with leaders

This entire section on promoting mental health is from the perspective of a leader, not a health professional. Conversations among leaders frequently stumble when 'the s-word' comes up – stress. Stress is a difficult concept.

'Challenge' is appropriate – and may be an essential part of purpose, meaning and belonging at work

Work always comes with a challenge, even if it is just boredom – it wouldn't be work otherwise.

High achievers may deliberately seek out added challenge, either to 'get on' or because that is how they motivate themselves.

Some people know they perform best when they put themselves under pressure, with deadlines or isolation or short-term targets etc.

Organizations that work to a social purpose are usually dealing with some of the most challenging issues or populations.

A great team ethos can carry individuals to accomplish more than they knew they could do – or set out to do.

Stress is subjective

Stress is hard to measure, although some organizations do a good job of measuring stresses caused by inefficient work management – e.g., overtime, sick days, excessive meetings, quality failures.

Stress may not be visible – different individuals have different levels of tolerance for different types of stressor, some conceal their stress, some may be unconscious of it.

Managing stress can be damaging – some may try to manage stress through alcohol.

Some take it out on co-workers, on family or others through poor behaviour at work or at home or on the roads or elsewhere.

Stress is layered – the root cause may not be work-related (but shows up at work) and work stress may be overlaid on home and other stressors.

'Stress' should be reserved for harm – whether experienced by an individual or a team or the organization

'I am stressed' or 'I am stressed by...' are never positive statements – they are only about a cost being paid by an individual, whether imposed by another or self-imposed.

Many sources of stress – notably inefficient work management – are also lost productivity for the organization. Self-stress, such as perfectionism or workaholic patterns, can be equally as harmful for the organization as for the individual.

Leading change inevitably raises challenges – performance expectations, stepping up to the next level of leadership, developing personally, practising new leadership capabilities. Challenges all demand motivation and application, but they are all part of the work of leading change, as long as they are made clear and achievable. Individuals may only partially succeed in meeting these challenges or fail outright but, with proper support, they are an inevitable and appropriate expectation of successful leaders at all levels.

Stress, however, should be reserved for harm and leaders should not confuse themselves or others by talking about 'good stress' or 'an acceptable level of stress'. Stress is about frustration, overreaction, powerlessness and alienation and can lead to ill health. At its worst, people work under intense pressure with a consequent individual and organizational toll of anxiety and depression – largely ignored, constantly in fight or flight, worn down over time, overwhelmed, negotiating to ease the pressure.[246] Stress accounts for an average of 23.9 workdays lost for every person affected[247] and 40 per cent of total absence from work.[248] The Health and Safety Executive estimates 15.4 million days lost per annum due to mental ill health, accounting for 50 per cent of total absence from work.[249] In the public sector alone, civil servants took more than 300,000 days off in 2017 over mental ill health.[250] Women, young people, ethnic minorities and those in poverty are more likely to be affected.[251]

STRESS – ARE WE COPING?

Drawn from research by the Mental Health Foundation[252]

Stress is our body's response to pressures from a situation or life event – hormones trigger a 'fight or flight' response. What counts as a 'stressor' can vary hugely from person to person. When exposed to stressors too frequently or intensely, this pressure can make us feel overwhelmed or unable to cope and it can impact both physical and mental health.

74% of the population reported being so stressed at some point in the past years that they felt overwhelmed or unable to cope – with 51% of that 74% reporting feeling depressed and 61% of the 74% feeling anxious. 500,000 experienced work-related stress that resulted in an average of more than 20 workdays lost for every person affected.

Work-related stress is associated with imbalances in workload and reward, long hours, poor sleep, poor job design, job insecurity, lack of respect or being undervalued. Even before COVID-19, NHS staff reported particularly high levels of stress, anxiety and depression – in part reflecting that people who are attracted to the caring professions might be more vulnerable to mental ill health, and in part the stresses of working in the NHS itself.

Tackling stress at work should be a major priority, as should be creating a supportive workplace culture that promotes mental health and enables people to seek help safely, without risking adverse consequences. Organizational culture at work can be enhanced by offering effective leadership and line management training and workplace interventions to reduce stress and improve mental health at work.

So what is the opportunity for leaders in working around challenge and stress and achieving mental health at work?

It is not about...	Reducing the challenge of work, because that would diminish the value of work to good mental health. Becoming a therapist to your people, because that needs trained skills and professional calling. Avoiding the real work of leading change, because that ends up adding to stress as organizations play games of change instead.
It is about...	Becoming more productive and more flexible. Improving motivation and performance. Investing in resilience, support and equipping line managers. Grasping the nettle of unacceptable behaviour.

Achieving mental health at work is about strategy and leadership

It is a leadership task to ensure that strategies for growth, efficiency and customer service are sustainable along multiple dimensions – including the mental health of the organization. This is not about being touchy-feely – it is about taking smart, sustainable strategic decisions.

As we discovered during the pandemic, the 'future of work' has to be mentally healthy as well as more productive and more flexible

Most organizations are being forced to rethink what they mean by flexible working and what they will provide in technological support. The trends bunched together under the rubric 'future of work' are already impacting our lives at work – artificial intelligence, robotics, the gig economy and mobile technology are all increasing our reliance on technology at work rather than direct human interaction. One consequence of this is that we talk less, when we already know that screen time diminishes oxytocin, a hormone produced in the brain that plays a vital role in social bonding.[253] The pandemic experience gave us an accelerated taste of the 'future of work': better for the 'haves' and frequently bad for the 'have-nots'. Those who already had resources could work from home moderately well while the worse off were typically employed in settings vulnerable to infection and had few choices.[254]

Not all jobs can be high income, but low earners need the balance of greater security

Some employers used the lockdown to offer contractors advance earnings or interest-free loans to help them manage the short-term crisis, but also to build commitment from contractors whom they would need for the future economic recovery. This contrasts with the precarious employment usually associated with 'the gig economy', such as contracting-out and zero-hours contracts, which reduce predictability of earnings for those least likely to have savings available to smooth income fluctuations.

Long-term gains in productivity mean tackling time pressure and fragmented effort

Reducing fragmentation and consequent time pressures will simultaneously improve productivity and reduce stress at work. Many organizations have accumulated unnecessary tasks (waste, diversions, box-ticking and micromanaging) as we discussed in Section 2. This is not just the case in established organizations – starting up a business or a charity is an equally significant source of stress.[255] The 'daily grind' can erode mental health, where being expected to do more with less resource can result in individuals being repeatedly confronted with failure or disappointment. Only line managers and colleagues can help alleviate the widespread issue of languishing or suboptimal mental health at work that is due to overload and fragmented time.

Organizational capabilities, relationships and 'corporate memory' benefit from longer tenure

Allowing people to stay in post for longer, while still growing, is a well-known strategy for improved performance. Moving people on to their next job after only two to three years afflicts corporates (Shell and BP have been talking about it for decades) and public services, where rapid rotation means loss of knowledge, connection and commitment to long-term outcomes. The consequential reduced capability and 'loss of memory' slows down organizational response to change and increases frustration for employees.

Motivation and performance improves after tackling short-termism and bullying

Productivity improves when good management practice is visibly rewarded and poor management is not tolerated – even if it appears to give some quick wins. Recruiting firms commonly say that 'people leave bosses, not organizations', so the short-term gain from a harsh boss can erode very rapidly. Harsh line management can stray easily into bullying – and that is when 'A lot of line managers make the people they manage mentally ill'.[256] Large, hierarchical institutions are especially prone to bullying – in the UK's largest employer, 30 per cent of NHS staff report bullying behaviours by patients and their families, and 25 per cent of NHS staff report bullying by colleagues.[257]

Plain language is human and motivating – while management-speak alienates

Language – both words and body language – matter and are easily decoded by people. Leaders' words need to match honest and collegial intent. That means plain language and expressing empathy, especially in tough situations. In corporate life, a range of euphemisms are commonly deployed to cope with the brutality of organizational life. 'Performance management' deliberately applies increased stress on individuals. Personal insecurity is used to drive exceptional performance in elite firms, exacerbating the pressures felt by 'insecure over-achievers' who cannot be honest regarding the impact on their mental health.[258]

Investing in mental health at work pays off

Legally and morally, employers are already obligated to protect their employees' health and safety at work. No one would argue that leaders should not take seriously their impact on *physical* health at work and organizations are prosecuted for failures around physical health at work. But mental health also needs to be protected at work – and slowly the law is expanding into this area. For example, stigmatizing mental ill health can lead to lawsuits alleging discrimination on grounds of disability under the Equality Act.

Fending off the lawyers is one thing – leaders need to ask themselves: How different would our organization look if we applied the same right to *mental* health at work? There are two important pieces of good news to lighten this story:

1 **Mental ill health can be prevented – not just coped with.**
   The first piece of good news is that there is a body of evidence on effective prevention of mental ill health.[259] This analysis focuses on anxiety and depression – first, because they are by far the most prevalent forms of mental ill health and, second, because the role of line management is crucial in addressing them in the workplace. More severe and enduring illnesses (such as psychosis) need medical intervention, but line managers need to engage with their people who are dealing with stress-induced anxiety and depression in the workplace. It is an inescapable role for leaders at all levels, and is increasingly recognized by leading businesses[260] and public services.

2 **Investing in mental health pays off financially – as well as in human terms.**
The second piece of good news is that investing in mental health yields a positive financial return for employers, with a range of initiatives all showing a pay-off with an average return of £5 for every £1 spent[261] – but the best returns come from equipping line managers to talk with their people about anxiety and depression.

Tackling stress at work should be a major priority, as should be creating a supportive workplace culture that promotes mental health. Organizational culture can be enhanced by offering effective leadership and line management training and interventions to reduce stress and improve mental health at work. A mentally healthy workplace would:

- *Invest in personal resilience and peer support at the level of the individual.*
  There is a hunger for advice about techniques to manage anxiety and depression. This is more than one-size-fits-all 'well-being'[262] practices around good sleeping-eating-exercise patterns. What is needed is a series of tailored interventions for target populations, reflecting the challenges and stresses of their particular work situations. Peer support is vital – 49 per cent of employees surveyed would not discuss their mental health with their line manager.[263] In many workplaces, people are particularly susceptible to overworking and self-stressing – and peer support is essential to maintain balance.

- *Invest in equipping managers from front-line supervisory level to senior managers.*
  Line managers need practice in productive conversations to moderate the frequency and the severity of many of

the incidents of anxiety and depression that are the most frequent evidence of mental ill health in the workplace. They need to address the 51 per cent of employees willing to talk with their line manager and win over the 49 per cent currently unwilling.

- *Promote leaders as allies for mental health in the organization.*
  The power of personal example and apprenticeship is the most powerful signal of leadership commitment to 'what matters around here'. Instead of 'managing' people struggling with mental health, 'allies' invite people to contribute, share career goals, push to get people on projects, speak up when stereotypes are being invoked – and talk about them as fellow humans, not 'problems'.

- *Appraise the impact of senior leaders, front-line leaders and management teams.*
  Leaders need to think about the impact of their decisions on their organization's and people's mental health. They need to avoid game-playing and instead engage in real conversation with their people.

- *Grasp the nettle on short-termism or bullying or other forms of toxic leadership.*
  Coping with a toxic leader is challenging for individuals who have the misfortune to work with them. Individuals may feel compelled to continue working with them while protecting themselves by setting boundaries that limit work, building alliances against them, recording events and – ultimately – exiting, internally or externally. It is a primary test of senior leaders' integrity to reject toxic leaders *especially* where they make stellar individual contributions and *before* they become role models.

MEDIACOM'S STORY

MediaCom is the largest planning and buying agency in the UK, with a strongly established People First culture. In 2017 work began on their mental health programme, with a series of speakers, from campaigners and organizations including Mind and Stonewall, encouraging employees to be open about their mental health. MediaCom is a client-focused, creative organization with a young employee base, often living and working away from family and friends for the first time, which can put particular pressure on individuals.

MediaCom wanted to create a culture of openness around mental health:

- Recognizing that we all have mental health – which exists on a continuum and can change on a daily basis.
- Ensuring that everyone in the organization has someone that they can talk to – experts in listening, ready to signpost for support if needed.
- Noticing changes early and acting to potentially avoid a more serious issue or crisis and, with adjustments, keep someone in work.

The programme is sponsored by Josh Krichefski, EMEA Chief Executive and Global Chief Operating Officer of MediaCom. Josh speaks openly within the organization, with clients and across the industry about his support and passion for ensuring that everyone has someone in the workplace that they can speak openly to about a mental health concern.

MediaCom also developed a Mental Health Ally programme, with the support of Mental Health at Work CIC. These allies are a group of 50 volunteer employees available for any employee with a mental health concern to speak to. Their role is to listen without offering advice, to signpost the employee to resources for further support such as the Employee Assistance Programme and (if needed) to help safeguard whilst clinical expertise is sought. MediaCom embedded the Allies' vital roles with workshops for line managers across the organization, enabling them to work alongside the Allies, alongside a programme of ongoing awareness raising across the broader organization.

Allies get together regularly as a group to share experiences, building their knowledge and confidence, driving awareness across the organization, and running events such as Mental Health Awareness Week and 'risk-watching' for language and actions which might re-enforce stigma. During the COVID-19 crisis, Allies played a vital role in ensuring wellbeing checks across the firm's workforce which overnight moved to a virtual operation – encouraging conversation around the impact the crisis was inevitably having on employees' mental health, risk-watching for those who may be unusually quiet or in lockdown alone, and facilitating any support that might be required.

Thanks to these efforts, MediaCom achieved Silver level in the Mind Workplace Wellbeing Index, with 89 per cent of employees stating that MediaCom encourages openness – against a UK workplace norm of 20 per cent. As a result, 68 per cent of employees are now disclosing a mental health issue to their manager, but only 13 per cent are coming to HR – indicating that conversations around mental health are more open and normalized and seen as part of a usual work conversation with line management.

AWARENESS TO ACTION FOR LEADERSHIP AT ALL LEVELS

Leaders cannot remove every source of stress in an environment of rapid change – 'We are not living an era of change but a change of era' as one leader of organization change, Pope Francis, commented.[264] Many organizations are still at the 'awareness' stage – sharing experiences to remove stigma and looking at the facts of the epidemic. It is difficult – and possibly unhelpful – to leap immediately into a whole programme of action. But there are some clearly positive and low-risk actions to be taken by leaders at all levels:

Do engage in real work that promotes mental health

- *Be yourself*
  Leaders are subject to the same potential stressors of
  increasing demands, shortage of resources, overwork
  and insecurity as anyone within the organization.
  Accepted wisdom suggests leaders suffer less stress
  because of their discretion to shape their situation,[265]
  but leaders are often disempowered by organizational
  restructuring and constant monitoring, accentuated by
  modern technology. Every leader's mental well-being
  requires coherence across their personal and organizational lives. Leaders need to share personal stressors and
  stories of thriving rather than merely surviving.

- *Recognize that people cope in different ways*
  Your ways of coping with stress and maintaining
  internal balance may not be the same as the person next
  to you – at a basic level, some people need company
  to unwind, others need solitude. Just look at how
  differently people experienced the lockdown.
     Language matters – talk about 'our lost potential' rather
  than othering 'those stressed people' in your organization.
     Support faith groups and other activities around the
  workplace as part of enabling people to bring all of
  themselves to work and avoid stress of 'non normal'
  characteristics.

- *Equip yourself as a line manager*
  Managers need to be talking with their people when
  40 per cent of them, at some point in any year,
  are coping with anxiety or depression. Introduce
  mechanisms tailored to your organization's situation.[266]
  Make clear that you as a leader or manager *cannot* be
  expected to deliver 'therapy' – but you *can and will* be
  capable and motivated to provide 'therapeutic actions'
  for your people: providing more listening than acting,

but tackling stressors, providing encouragement to share and resolve issues, and making the workplace human.

Don't avoid challenging leadership tasks – done well, they support mental health too

- *Do the real work of change, making difficult choices*
  Keep leadership confident and focused – not made anxious by game-playing, fear of speaking up or stress. Examine objectively, probe for evidence, evaluate competing experiments.

  Don't succumb to the temptation to use disempowerment as a strategy or a tactic – 'I don't have time to explain: just do it'. Encourage candid comment – choking off staff input is a self-inflicted wound.[267]

- *Talk up the basics*
  Promote a common sense approach to mental health: good patterns of sleeping, eating, drinking and exercise; communication and openness; doing good does you good; demand clarity and resources needed to do your job well.

  Don't medicalize the challenges – this is about people at work, not occupational health.

- *Act on bad behaviour*
  Watch turnover rates like a hawk, understand and talk with people leaving – any sign of a talent drain is a flashing red light.[268] Tackle poor behaviour, especially from 'high performers' who may be delivering short-term results by chewing through people, whether staff or customers or suppliers or colleagues, through pressure or discrimination.

It is *not* that organization leaders need to take on the wider socio-economic-environmental factors that drive mental ill health – adverse childhood events, trauma, inequality, discrimination and stigma. Leaders *do* need to take responsibility for what goes on within *their* organizations:

Senior leaders saying...	*We only thrive as an organization when our leaders thrive and when our people bring themselves fully to work.*
	It goes without saying – but we still fall down on this – that unacceptable behaviour is unacceptable.
	Our people have a right to good Mental Health At Work.
Front-line leaders saying...	*Our jobs are about making trade-offs, we manage the stresses by...*
	We support our people to enjoy good Mental Health At Work by...
Management teams saying...	*This is how we identify the priorities to ensure our organization thrives and the actions individuals are empowered to take...*
	We offer training for line managers and encourage people to develop personal resilience to enjoy good Mental Health At Work.

Summary *Work can, and should be positive for mental health. Change at work can be productive and supportive for individuals and organizations, when well led. Strategy and leadership is required to shape mentally healthy outcomes from:*

- *Our changing ways of working and living in the aftermath of the pandemic.*
- *New technology and capabilities.*

Leaders across every sector of society and the economy increasingly talk about their personal experience of mental ill health. Depression and anxiety cause US$1 trillion of lost productivity each year in the global economy with a huge – and avoidable – toll on individuals, families, organizations and society.

Work and change challenge our performance and leaders have to develop and step up. 'Challenge' can give positive results – but 'stress' is only to be coped with.

	Stress is about frustration, overreaction, powerlessness, bullying behaviours, alienation – and unremitting stress can lead to mental ill health in the form of depression and anxiety.
	Legally and morally, leaders at all levels are already obligated to protect their people's health and safety at work – both physically and mentally. The good news is that there is a body of evidence on effective prevention of mental ill health and that investing in mental health has a huge financial pay-off.
Action	*Leaders need to move on from 'awareness' to 'action', creating a supportive workplace culture that promotes mental health. A mentally healthy workplace would:*

- *Build personal resilience and peer support.*
- *Equip line managers – not to become 'therapists' but to suggest 'therapeutic actions'.*
- *Promote leaders as allies for mental health.*
- *Appraise the impact of senior leaders, front-line leaders and management teams in promoting mental health.*

Leaders need to engage with the real work of change – not indulge in the variety of work avoidance games – and tackle poor behaviours in their organizations. Leaders' behaviour must match their words in valuing mentally healthy leadership at all levels.

PROMOTING MENTAL HEALTH AT WORK – RESOURCES
Mental Health Foundation resources
How to… guides, research and COVID-19 resources at www.mentalhealth.org.uk
Mental Health At Work resources[269]
I am Not Working from Home, I am at Home Working and taster sessions at
www.mhaw.uk.com
Samaritans resources
Self-help app, research and approaches at www.samaritans.org
Call free, day or night, 365 days a year on 116 123 or email jo@samaritans.org

Part Six

'ALL THIS? ALL
AT ONCE?'

CHANGE JUST CHANGED

Leading change in organizations was always one of the toughest challenges for leaders at all levels. The traditional model of change management never really fitted what leaders actually did, nor what success called for. Now we face the additional challenges of:

- Change that is up close and personal – and continuous and relentless.
- Many more leaders in more diverse organizations.
- Leading in a more transparent and challenging environment.

However, our shared experiences of change equip us to use a more powerful model of leadership – one that is both more successful and more truly human, because it is grounded in what leaders actually do.

A MORE REALISTIC MODEL WILL ALSO BE A MORE HUMAN MODEL

After reading through the stories of what leaders do, you might be feeling the personal challenge of leadership, stressed at where to start, pressure to *do something now*:

> If you work in a traditional corporate or public service organization, all these expectations may be more than you expected 'when I become the boss'.

> If you work in a non-traditional social enterprise or start-up or community organization, you may be thinking 'I never signed up for all this'.

Clearer thinking about 'what actually works' will help – the old model of thinking about leading change is more stressful because it wrongly describes what leading change is:

'The right answer'	The illusion of scientific method proceeding rationally and linearly to objective truth was never an accurate description, but it lives on in conventional management-speak. In fact, the only *rational* way to think about leading change is to see it as an iterative, experimental process.
'The leader'	The myth of the heroic single leader is deeply embedded in societal thinking. The *reality* is that society and organizations only prosper when leaders at all levels are engaged in working through how they and their communities (and organizations) adapt to change.
'Quick wins'	The pursuit of short-term profit and operating targets ceased to be an accurate description of corporate and public service organizations'

purposes decades ago, but lives on as a dogma. Organizations can and should meet profoundly *human* needs of identity, meaning and promoting mental health – recognizing that doing good does you good.

When thinking about the *reality* of leading change in organizations, it should be clear that you do not need to do all of this, all at once. Above all, you should not try to do it alone. The stories of change and the real-world experience of leaders at every level demonstrates that a more powerful – and less stressful – model of leading change is available:

...already emerging from organizations experiencing successful change in the old world.

...reflecting the continuing consequences of the pandemic and learning from our shared experience.

...building organizational purpose, belonging and mental health.

LEADERSHIP CAN DO BETTER

Leaders can – and do – lead successful change in their organizations. They master the complexity of organizational behaviour without imposing a deceptive simplicity, they do what only they can do, they shape a common language of change and build a community of peers.

The COVID-19 pandemic is the latest in a series of shocks that have changed the context for leading change in our organizations. We continue to change what we do and how we do it as we respond to the new political economy and new expectations of our employers, our governments, our public services, our community groups, our churches, our schools. Although the aftermath of the COVID-19 pandemic continues to be stressful and demanding, it is not wholly negative. We can exercise leadership that is better than what went before by accelerating three recurring themes:

Reality brought inside

Organizations defend the status quo by focusing on their internal world of power groups and conforming to established wisdom, limiting change until there is a visible disaster. Designing change that brings the 'outside world' into the organization...

> ...injects both optimism and realism by providing evidence of real-world change and experience – and reduces risk by learning from others....changes the culture by including the experiences of everyone within the organization.

Language matters

Words are a key currency of leadership and it is typically debased in management-speak and especially its overuse of military analogies.[270] Delivering change requires learning and creating a new common language that...

> ...focuses leaders on what really matters....emphasizes participation, rather than coercion....tells stories that reinforce purpose and belonging.

Leadership at all levels

The tacit model where some are 'leaders' and the rest are 'led' to change is a huge constraint on human potential and organizational effectiveness. Leadership is exercised at all levels in every organization and encouraging it...

> ...avoids the obfuscation and the traps of 'having all the answers'....encourages innovation at the front line....supports a thriving and mentally healthy organization.

246

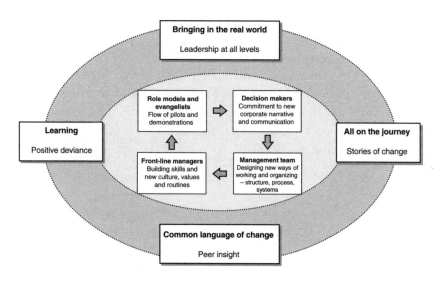

OUR SOCIETIES DEPEND ON LEADERS ASKING POWERFUL QUESTIONS

Successfully leading change is not just about good stewardship, personal fulfilment and organizational effectiveness – it is also about social, economic and institutional recovery.

Improving economic performance matters

Investment in national infrastructure and public services will only be affordable if organizations can successfully change and improve their productivity. London School of Economics analysis of productivity variations across the G7 economies attributes 30 per cent of the gap between the average and the most productive (the US) to management practice and leadership.[271] All too often, discussions of productivity focus on fixed investment, automation and IT, regulatory and taxation differences. The LSE analysis goes on to highlight the potential for improving transparency, open communication, encouragement, integrity, humility and trust in poor-performing economies. In other words, most of the factors underpinning successful leadership of change.

247

Restoring trust in institutions matters

During the last two decades, leadership scandals hit institutions across big business, government, churches, health, human services and charities in many countries. These institutions will only regain trust and influence after demonstrating that they have changed. Change is in part about delivering positive results – doing what the organization is meant to do – but it is just as much about demonstrating leadership behaviours, purpose, belonging and mental health.

'JUST DO IT' WON'T DO

The temptation for leaders is to launch a programme based on what worked for them in the past, provide the answers directly, push for rapid results and drive the programme from the centre – setting up a cycle of failure:

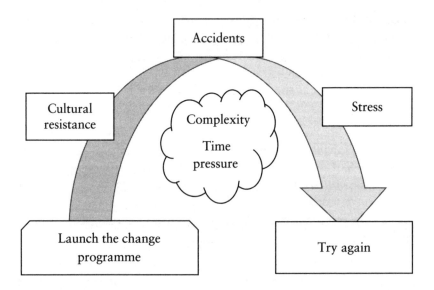

Similarly, you can't bully an organization into change. Sometimes a leader will think that if they behave unreasonably, then they can shock their organization and bend it to their will. Ultimately, organizations work out how to frustrate the unreasonable leader. Fear is not a sustained motivator of performance – key people leave and those who stay merely comply and defend their position.

Busyness and the 'just do it' mentality are pernicious leadership traps. They are substitutes for thinking and they are barriers to engaging leaders across the organization.

The only exception, when you should issue orders like a commander, is during a short-term crisis – as we saw during the pandemic in the first few weeks before and after the imposition of lockdown. Very quickly, the commander has to give way to the leader, who engages people in adapting to the new post-crisis context. Leadership is then about asking the right questions, not providing smart ready-made answers.

ASKING POWERFUL QUESTIONS IS THE SMART THING TO DO FIRST...

The classic example of 'getting too smart' when telling people what to do is cited in *Seeing like a state*,[272] when, in 1849, the Spanish Governor of the Philippines required all Filipinos to adopt Hispanic surnames to facilitate taxation and property registration, which had been impossible when the population could not be distinctly identified. The Governor collected a catalogue of approved names drawn from history, saints' names, flowers etc. He then ordered each mayor to allocate surnames from this approved catalogue to the population so everyone would have a distinct identifier – and told his regional officials to make sure the mayors did as they were told. In practice, though, the disenfranchised regional officials did not bother mixing up the names for variety within each town – they simply tore a number of pages from the alphabetized catalogue and handed a few to each mayor, producing whole towns with every family's surname beginning with the same letter – still perfectly visible 150 years later.

We are back where we began: one measure of success in reading this book is whether you are now equipped to ask a better class of question as a leader:

Asking about the current situation	*'I see this happening – this is my interpretation – what is yours?'* *'In your view, where is this taking us?'* *'What are the trade-offs we are making? How do we keep the operation stable?'* *'Where do you feel you belong here?'*
Asking about potential change	*'This is where we want to get to – how should we get there? What are the steps or phases we shall have to get through?'* *'Who is already achieving some of this – and what can we copy and improve? Who could be allies?'* *'What is the real purpose of what we are trying to do here?'* *'How does this help you lead?'* *'What is the minimum infrastructure and process we need to fill in as we go?'*
Asking about the people in the organization	*'Who are the people who need to be in the room?'* *'How can this be made to work for you and your team? What is the overall story? What do you need from me?'* *'How will people react – what happened last time we did something like this? How should we manage the stresses this will cause?'* *'What does this mean for you? How do you feel about it?'*

...BEFORE CHOOSING A FIRST STEP THAT ENGAGES PEOPLE

Perhaps my all-time favourite piece of advice as a consultant was to propose to one of the Boards of the Church of Scotland that they 'Pray more'.[273] It was true that they were the only Board of the Church that did not open their meetings in prayer. Although it surprised them that prayer was the first recommendation from the world's most famous management consultancy, it connected with everyone around the table – and we all took the first step together.

We spend roughly a third of our waking hours at work – and much more than that engaging with organizations of all kinds as consumers, families and communities. We feel better and work better when we have a say, when we are included in decisions and when our contribution is valued. In fact, it is not just that we *feel* better, we *are* mentally healthier. If you alone take on the task of having all the answers, then you are bound to end up feeling stressed with 'All this? All at once?'

The saving grace in leading change is that you need to share the load and engage people. Do what only you can do and ask others to do what they do best. Then you – and those around you upon whom you depend – will be fulfilled in leadership and successful.

THE AUTHOR

Keith Leslie is a leadership mentor, speaker and writer, living and working in London and Bristol. Keith has devoted extensive time to the voluntary sector. He is now Chair of Samaritans in the UK & Ireland and Chair of Mental Health At Work CIC; from 2014 to 2020 he was Chair of the board at the Mental Health Foundation. He also served as Chair of Build Africa 2010–14 and as a non-executive director of The Tablet Publishing Company Ltd 2006–14. He has been a fellow at Windsor Leadership since 2010.

Keith began his career with Shell, working in New Zealand, Sweden, Cyprus and the UK in a series of front-line and general management roles. He joined McKinsey in 1993, becoming a partner in 1998, and served clients in a wide range of industrial sectors and government. He moved to Deloitte as a partner in 2006 and retired in 2017, having focused on organization and leadership challenges at senior levels in industry and government.

Based on his experience working with senior management teams, Keith has published more than 50 articles in *European Management Journal, McKinsey Quarterly, The Times, Wall Street Journal, The Tablet* and many other professional journals. He also speaks regularly at conferences and development programmes for senior leaders.

Keith grew up in Kirkcaldy, Scotland. He graduated with a first class honours degree in law from the University of Edinburgh in 1980, where he was elected President of the Students' Association. He then took an MBA *summa cum laude* from the Wharton School at the University of Pennsylvania in 1982, where he was a Thouron Fellow.

ACKNOWLEDGEMENTS AND SOURCES

I have sought to reference public-domain data and analyses throughout the text when referring to organizations I dealt with as a consultant or non-executive director, in order to avoid relying on confidential information or private conversations. I have not referenced stories from my time at Shell because they represent solely my personal observations on events as a participant.

To the best of my ability, I have referenced all quotations from other writers and I have sought to draw out explicitly my reliance on eminent academic thinkers, including the handful of academic books on leadership that I think repay regular rereading – Heifetz's *Leadership Without Easy Answers*, Mintzberg's *The Nature of Managerial Work*, Kahneman's *Thinking, Fast and Slow*, Woods et al *Behind Human Error*, Kuhn's *The Structure of Scientific Revolutions*, David Whyte's *The Heart Aroused* and the work of Keith Grint.

Otherwise, the personal judgements expressed in the text – whether credible or accurate or not – are solely mine.

Forming my views over the years and drafting them into this text would not have been possible without the input of former colleagues with many lifetimes of experiences – notably Alex Massey, Joel Bellman, Adam King, Sam Unger, Julian Holmes, Jay Bevington, Anna Brown, Basab Mitra, Mary Meaney, Mike Carson, Tera Allas, Emily Lawson, Jonathan Day, Caroline Webb, Kirstan Marnane. Friends and clients, especially Will Storrar when at the Church of Scotland, provided all my learning! Advice and suggestions came from James Lahey at the University of Ottawa, Sir Peter Housden, Kate Lye at KLI who read early drafts; and wise mentoring and ideas over the years from Sir David Varney of Shell, British Gas and HMRC. Thanks are due to them and to family who read and challenged and encouraged numerous drafts.

And above all, for Senna, who kept the faith.

REFERENCES

1 *Leading people* – for example: Edmondson's *Teaming: How Organizations Learn, Innovate and Compete in the Knowledge Economy* (2012, Harvard Business School Press) and *The Fearless Organization* (2019, Wiley) is a much broader treatment of teaming and creating a psychologically safe space to enable rapid teaming to deliver extraordinary results. I focus on a crucial subset – the role of management teams in leading change through organizations.

   Organization design – for example: Laloux's *Reinventing Organizations* (2014, Diateino) is a series of ideas to update our organizational options for the 21st century and to propose an ideal organization. Instead, I analyse the behaviour of *all* organizations, with their mix of many positive and some endemically unproductive features.

   Models of change – for example: Kotter's *Leading Change* (1996, Harvard Business School Press) provides a model of change, an eight-stage process and the necessary tools and approaches for project managers and consultants supporting major change projects. Instead, what I cover is the longer view on leadership of change at all levels and especially focusing on understanding and shaping organizational behaviour.

2 Change management is notoriously unsuccessful – most research shows a 60–70% failure rate for change programmes – e.g., 'Change management needs to change', Ashkenas, R., *Harvard Business Review*, April 2013: https://hbr.org/2013/04/change-management-needs-to-cha

3 Others have been punchier in making the same point, like AL Kennedy in *The Observer*, 24 May 2020: 'Who knew it was possible to run so many thought experiments simultaneously in the real world? Don't get me wrong: I'm a huge fan of sci-fi and stories that begin "What if?" But did we have to run *all of this, all at once?* And did we have to make our experiments in thinking involve non-theoretical, living (at the moment) and (currently) breathing human beings?' and Caroline Stockmann, chief executive of the Association of Corporate Treasurers, quoted in the *Sunday Times* 22 March 2020: 'A pandemic is the worst of the worst because it touches on everything. It's not just that the markets are going down like they did in the financial crisis, it's that people are worried about their loved ones dying.'

4   *Complex Organizations*, Perrow, C. (2014, Echo Point Books & Media), pvii. See also *The modern firm*, Roberts, J. (2004, Oxford University Press), pp74–114 and *The nature of the firm*, Coase, R. (1937, Economica), 4:386–405.

5   Review of catastrophic tank failure incidents sourced at https://www.epd.gov.hk/eia/register/report/eiareport/eia_1272006/EIA_Report/appendix/Appendix_H4.pdf; Shell safety statistics in the Shell Sustainability Report 2019 at https://reports.shell.com/sustainability-report/2019/responsible-business/safety/managing-safety.html

6   Akin to W. Edwards Deming's concept of operations being 'in statistical process control' – see *Out of the Crisis: Quality, Productivity and Competitive Position* (1982, MIT Press).

7   *Wilful Blindness*, Heffernan, M. (2011, Simon & Schuster), p217;https://www.chron.com/neighborhood/baytown-news/article/BP-s-Manzoni-Serious-concerns-at-Texas-City-came-1604140.php

8   'PPE: Gowns flown from Turkey fail UK safety tests': https://www.bbc.co.uk/news/uk-52569364

9   *File on Four*, Radio 4, 20 May 2020; 'The Times view on the response to coronavirus of Public Health England: Official Failure', *The Times*, 20 May 2020; https://news.sky.com/story/coronavirus-care-home-bosses-accuse-government-of-prioritising-nhs-not-most-vulnerable-people-11991078; https://www.bbc.co.uk/news/52674073, Coronavirus timeline on care homes going into lockdown; '22 Days', *Sunday Times*, 24 May 2020; '33,000 dead', *The Observer*, 10 May 2020; 'Johnson listened to his scientists – but they were slow to respond', *National Post*, 7 April 2020; 'Carehomes were "afterthought" with devastating coronavirus consequences', *The Times*, 12 June 2020; National Audit Office report https://www.nao.org.uk/report/readying-the-nhs-and-adult-social-care-in-england-for-covid-19/

10 *Thinking, Fast and Slow*, Kahneman, D. (2011, Allen Lane), p200–202.

11 For a dramatic account see *The Looming Tower* (Hulu network) which traces the rising threat of Osama bin Laden and al-Qaida in the late 1990s and how a rivalry between the FBI and CIA during the time period may have inadvertently set the path for the attacks of 9/11.

12 See the Francis Report into events at Mid-Staffordshire NHS Trust, where many NHS staff were aware of patient neglect leading to deaths over an extended period; see the case of Dr Hadiza Bawa-Garba, who was restored to the register of medical practitioners following the Court of Appeal decision to overturn the General Medical Council removing her licence to practise, following her conviction for manslaughter by gross negligence. She misdiagnosed a six year old's sepsis but was under considerable pressure in an under-staffed and disorganized hospital – www.bbc.co.uk/news/resources/idt-sh/the_struck_off_doctor and 'Making doctors scapegoats won't save lives', *The Times*, 15 August 2018.

13 World Health Organization https://www.who.int/

14 'Ultimately, a richer language is essential to the skill of constructive criticism... There is a direct link from more precise gossip at the watercooler to better decisions', *Thinking, Fast and Slow*, Kahneman, D. (2011, Allen Lane), p418.

15 For example, https://www.thoughtco.com/what-is-business-jargon-1689043#:~:text=Business%20jargon%20is%20the%20specialized%20language%20used%20by,vogue%20words%2C%20and%20euphemisms.%20Contrast%20with%20plain%20English.

16 Examples: war for talent, war footing, war on drugs, war against crime, analogies with SAS or SEALs or Commandos.

17 See 'The real power of real options', Leslie, K. and Michaels, M., *McKinsey Quarterly*, June 1997.

18 *Reaching for the Moon*, Launius, R.D. (2019, Yale University Press); *First Man: The life of Neil A. Armstrong*, Hansen, J.R. (2005, Simon & Schuster).

19 Spectacular accidents also attract huge public interest – *Air Crash Investigation* and *Car Crash* play repeatedly on TV, *Chernobyl* was a hit for Sky Atlantic and the Boeing 737 MAX crisis led to a Channel 4 documentary titled *Boeing's Killer Plane – what went wrong?*

20 *Accidents like Chernobyl will always happen*, Conway, E., *The Times*, 6 June 2019.

21 The US DoD investment in management sciences was a major contributor to the perceived superior American management of industry in the 1950s and 1960s.

22 Interestingly, the engineering model ignores the Second Law of Thermodynamics: that decay and disorder are intrinsic.

23 *Normal Accidents*, Perrow, C. (1984, Princeton).

24 *Behind Human Error*, Woods, D.D., Dekker, S., Cook, R., Johannesen, L. and Sarter, N., 2nd edition (2010, Ashgate), pxviii.

25 *Behind Human Error*, Woods *et al*, 2nd edition (2010, Ashgate), p62.

26 *Accidents like Chernobyl will always happen*, Conway, E., *The Times*, 6 June 2019.

27 US National Transportation Safety Board report.

28 For an excellent article expounding the challenge, see 'Reality has a surprising amount of detail' by John Salvatier at johnsalvatier.org.

29 The most recent example being the LaMia crash of 2016 that cost the lives of the Chapecoense football team. Notable examples include Tenerife in 1977 when two jumbo jets collided on the runway, Washington in 1982 when an aircraft de-iced inadequately, San Francisco in 2013 when an aircraft attempted to land at low speed.

30 https://www.cbc.ca/news/canada/ottawa/phoenix-federal-government-report-lessons-1.4339476

31 Goss Gilroy report, 4 October 2017.

32   'Pilots "not told" about 737 jet's deadly flaw', Parry, R.L. and Bremner, C., *The Times*, 13 November 2018; 'Boeing could pay a heavy price for crashes', Bremner, C., *The Times*, 21 March 2019; 'FAA is blamed for letting Max jets fly', Bremner, C., *The Times*, 12 October 2019; 'Boeing whistleblower raises doubts over 787 oxygen system', Theo Leggett, *BBC News*, 6 November 2019; 'Boeing defies shareholders' demands for reform at top', Dean, J., *The Times*, 30 April 2019; 'Stabiliser may have tipped fatal flight out of pilot's control', Bremner, C., *The Times*, 12 March 2019; 'Boeing Max 737 crash in Indonesia "caused by pilot error and faulty design"', Bremner, C., *The Times*, 24 September 2019.

33   *Normal Accidents*, Perrow, C. (1984, Princeton); *Behind Human Error*, Woods *et al*, 2nd edition (2010, Ashgate).

34   'No Silver Bullet – Essence and Accident in Software Engineering', Brooks Jr, F.P. 1986, University of North Carolina, www.worrydream. com.

35   Too many examples to quote – including: the 100,000 tests/day target, allocation of local authority funding to cover adult social care costs, comparisons with other countries, deliveries of PPE.

36   A £58m settlement was accompanied by £100m of legal fees. House of Commons Business Select Committee hearings, 10 March 2020.

37   'How complex systems fail', Cook, R.I., 1998, University of Chicago Cognitive Technologies Laboratory.

38   'How complex systems fail', Cook, R.I., 1998, University of Chicago Cognitive Technologies Laboratory.

39   Resetting the cost structure at Shell https://www.strategy-business. com/article/11402

40   *Make overhead cuts that last*, Neuman, J., *Harvard Business Review* 1975 https://hbr.org/1975/05/make-overhead-cuts-that-last; Overhead costs and Overhead Value Analysis https://expertprogrammanage-ment.com/2011/04/overhead-costs-overhead-value-analysis/

41   'Testing times: Double-counting included in official tally' 21 May 2020, https://www.telegraph.co.uk/global-health/science-and-disease/tens-thousands-coronavirus-tests-have-double-counted-officials/; https://www.statisticsauthority.gov.uk/correspondence/sir-david-norgrove-re-sponse-to-matt-hancock-regarding-the-governments-covid-19-testing-data/; 'Testing confusion', *New Scientist*, 13 June 2020, p9; *Coronavirus: The inside story of how UK's 'chaotic' testing regime 'broke all the rules'* Conway, E., Sky News, 9 July 2020.

42   https://forum.wordreference.com/threads/gattopardismo.2042688/

43   Stockbroker AJ Bell calculated that average tenure of CEOs in quoted companies fell to 5.4 years in 2018 compared to 8.3 years in 2010.

44   'What really caused the great crash of 2008?', Leslie, K., *The Tablet*, 2008.

45   '22 Days', *Sunday Times*, 24 May 2020; '33,000 dead', *The Observer*, 10 May 2020; 'Johnson listened to his scientists – but they were slow

to respond', *National Post,* 7 April 2020; 'How it all went wrong in the UK', *New Scientist,* 6 June 2020.

46 Randomized Control Trials, the gold standard in scientific and medical evidence.

47 See *How to Have a Good Day,* Webb, C. (2016, Macmillan) for the best set of practical steps to combat the personal pressures of fragmentation.

48 https://data.gov.uk/data/contracts-finder-archive/contract/1071880/

49 *desider* (DE&S monthly magazine) Issue 67 December 2013 p7, Issue 70 March 2014 p38, Issue 71 April 2014 p6, Issue 72 May 2014 p13.

50 *The nature of managerial work,* Mintzberg, H. (1973, Harper & Row), p5.

51 *Ibid.,* p113.

52 *Managing,* Mintzberg, H. (2011, Financial Times Series).

53 *Thinking, Fast and Slow,* Kahneman, D. (2011, Allen Lane), p219. As an example of recognizing this flawed thinking from experience, Shell recruited its head of oil price forecasting from line management and kept them in post only two years – so they came unsullied to the task, built their mental model and moved on before it became time-expired.

54 '22 Days', *Sunday Times,* 24 May 2020; '33,000 dead', *The Observer,* 10 May 2020; 'Johnson listened to his scientists – but they were slow to respond', *National Post,* 7 April 2020; 'How it all went wrong in the UK', *New Scientist,* 6 June 2020.

55 *Why Smart Executives Fail,* Finkelstein, S. (2004, Portfolio Penguin).

56 See *The modern firm,* Roberts, J. (2004, Oxford University Press), pp180–190.

57 See *Right on target,* Leslie, K. and George, R., *The Tablet,* 2007.

58 See *The modern firm,* Roberts, J. (2004, Oxford University Press), pp214–230.

59 'Building the healthy corporation', Leslie, K., Dobbs, R. and Mendonca, L.T., *McKinsey Quarterly,* 2005; 'Manage your organization by the evidence', Leslie, K., Loch, M.A. and Schaningar, W., *McKinsey Quarterly,* 2006; 'Evidence-based decisions on organization, process and people', Leslie, K., Deloitte, 2015.

60 *Complex Organizations,* Perrow, C. (2014, Echo Point Books & Media), p179.

61 *Complex Organizations,* Perrow, C. (2014, Echo Point Books & Media), p263.

62 'Beware of targets that come with temptation', Alex Massie, *The Times,* 1 January 2020 accessed from thetimesonline.co.uk

63 *Wilful blindness,* Heffernan, M. (2011, Simon & Schuster).

64 https://www.forbes.com/sites/forbesleadershipforum/2013/11/13/heres-to-the-death-of-microsofts-rank-and-yank/#56f467b2777b

65 See *Right on target,* Leslie, K. and George, R., *The Tablet,* 2007.

66   'Health service is dysfunctional says NHS boss', *The Times*, 15 February 2019 accessed from thetimesonline.co.uk; https://www.daily-mail.co.uk/health/article-6708639/NHS-dysfunctional-doctors-running-like-headless-chickens.html

67   *The Organization of al-Qaida in the Islamic Maghreb* Shura Council released by CIA and accessed in 2012 from the *Daily Telegraph* website. Similarly, IS issued thousands of mundane regulations through multiple departments from motor vehicles through health and pricing of fruit. Observers of IS' governmental behaviour comment that it was more concerned with orderliness than with scripturally correct governance, perhaps because it drew inspiration from a 13th-century treatise on Islamic governance – *How to Run a Caliphate* by Tom Stevenson, *London Review of Books*, 20 June 2019, p9.

68   GOCO was the acronym for Government Owned Contractor Operated concept for the entire DE&S operation to be outsourced under contract to a commercial consortium. In practice, the sheer scale and complexity meant that virtually no commercial organization in the world could take on the task. When the bidders all withdrew, DE&S rushed to sign up commercial partners for subsets of its operation – a strategy that was clearly available years earlier, but rejected in favour of the one big move.

69   http://knowledge.wharton.upenn.edu/article/home-unimprovement-was-nardellis-tenure-at-home-depot-a-blueprint-for-failure/ and https://www.seattletimes.com/business/mcnerneyrsquos-impact-at-ge-3m-also-stirs-debate/

70   *Thinking, Fast and Slow*, Kahneman, D. (2011, Allen Lane), p304.

71   Windrush Lessons Learned Review, *The Times*, 20 March 2020; Catalogue of Failure and Neglect, *The Tablet*, 7 March 2020, p2.

72   *Wilful blindness*, Heffernan, M. (2011, Simon & Schuster).

73   Described in *Opening Skinner's Box: Great psychological experiments of the twentieth century*, Lauren Slater, L. (2004, Bloomsbury), p32 and *The Lucifer Effect*, Philip Zimbardo (2007, Penguin).

74   *What really caused the great crash of 2008?*, Leslie, K., *The Tablet*, 2008.

75   *Complex Organizations*, Perrow, C. (2014, Echo Point Books & Media), p126.

76   *The Economist* lauded Pierre Wack (1922–1997) as an unconventional French oil executive who developed the use of scenario planning at Royal Dutch Shell's London headquarters in the 1970s. "So successful was he that the Anglo-Dutch oil giant was able to anticipate not just one Arab-induced oil shock during that decade, but two." https://www.economist.com/news/2008/08/29/pierre-wack.   Example reference to Wack as court jester in Fuelling the War by Louis Wesseling accessed via https://journals.sagepub.com/doi/pdf/10.1260/0144598001

492049. The British Airways example is quoted in *Wilful blindness*, Heffernan, M. (2011, Simon & Schuster), p303.

77   See *Boyd: The fighter pilot who changed the art of war*, Robert Coram (2002, Back Bay Books) for several examples of the career risks when challenging groupthink.

78   See *The Manager*, Carson, M. (2013, Bloomsbury) for illustrations from the tough world of Premier League football managers: p58 on steel expressed through values, p76 on setting and enforcing boundaries and *The Fearless Organization*, Edmondson, A. (2019, Wiley) for extensive examples from corporate organizations.

79   *Games People Play*, Berne, E. (1964, Penguin).

80   *Gaudete et exsultate*, Pope Francis (2018), p41.

81   *Thinking, Fast and Slow*, Kahneman, D. (2011, Allen Lane), p255–260.

82   *Ibid.*

83   See http://www.company-histories.com/English-China-Clays-Ltd-Company-History.html

84   Imperial College and London School of Hygiene & Tropical Medicine, 6 March 2020.

85   *Thinking, Fast and Slow*, Kahneman, D. (2011, Allen Lane), p247–251 and *Megaprojects and risk*, Flyvbjerg, B. (2003, Cambridge University Press).

86   See http://www.masteringthemerger.com/masteringthemerger/case_example_bmw_rover.asp

87   'PPE: Gowns flown from Turkey fail UK safety tests', https://www.bbc.co.uk/news/uk-52569364; 'Coronavirus: PPE stocks were in chaos . . . then army got a grip', *The Times*, 11 June 2020.

88   *Change and people – 5 myths and 5 realities*, Leslie, K., Windsor Leadership, 2015.

89   https://www.mckinsey.com/business-functions/organization/our-insights/how-to-demonstrate-calm-and-optimism-in-a-crisis

90   *Complex Organizations*, Perrow, C. (2014, Echo Point Books & Media), pvii. See also *The modern firm*, Roberts, J. (2004, Oxford University Press), pp74–114 and *The nature of the firm*, Coase, R. (1937, Economica), 4:386–405.

91   'Wicked problems and clumsy solutions', Grint, K., 2008, Clinical leader, British Association of Medical Managers; 'Dilemmas in a general theory of planning', Rittell, H.W.J. and Webber, M.M., *Policy Sciences*, 1973.

92   As documented in *Surfing the edge of chaos: The laws of nature and the new laws of business*, Pascale, R.T., Milleman, M. and Gioja, L. and *The modern firm*, Roberts, J. (2004, Oxford University Press), pp24–26 and 182–190.

93   See *The Outsider: Pope Francis and his battle to reform the Church*, Lamb, C. (2020, Orbis), pp125–132.

94 *Narrative therapy with couples... and a whole lot more!*, Freedman and Gene Combs (2002, Dulwich Centre Publications), pp205–207.
95 *Ibid.*, pp187–189.
96 *The Healing Power of Stories*, Taylor, D. (1996, Doubleday Books).
97 *The Manager*, Carson, M. (2013, Bloomsbury), pp35–36.
98 www.mentalhealth.org.uk/news/millions-uk-adults-have-felt-panicked-afraid-and-unprepared-result-coronavirus-pandemic-new
99 *A Failure of Nerve: Leadership in the age of the quick fix*, Friedman, E. (2007, Seabury).
100 See *Out of the Crisis: Quality, Productivity and Competitive Position*, Edwards Deming, W. (1982, MIT).
101 This was not a consultant-led project – only one full-time McKinsey consultant led by Basab Mitra supported the HMRC staff and trained them in lean techniques. It has remained, for me, the archetype of how to enable front-line leaders to deliver change for themselves.
102 For HMRC's own description of the ups and downs in its journey to lean, see: https://www.buckingham.ac.uk/wp-content/uploads/2015/12/European-Lean-Educators-Paper_HMRC_final.pdf
   For analysis by many commentators on HMRC and lean, see *inter alia:* http://clok.uclan.ac.uk/16890/3/__lha-033_pers- _00061E 14_My%20Documents_My%20Publications_La%20Nouvelle%20 Revue%20du%20Travail_La%20Nouvelle%20Revue%20du%20 Travail%20English%20version.pdf   https://publications.parliament. uk/pa/cm201011/cmselect/cmtreasy/memo/hmrc/27.htm https://www. questia.com/magazine/1P3-2588830541/lean-management-failure-at-hmrc http://www.bobemiliani.com/goodies/emiliani_hmrc.pdf and https://www.leanblog.org/2007/02/bad-lean5s-hits-uk-media/
103 See 'The delivery challenge for the next Government', Leslie, James and Hancock, Deloitte, 2007.
104 *The nature of managerial work*, Mintzberg, H. (1973, Harper & Row).
105 https://news.sky.com/story/coronavirus-inside-the-northern-ireland-care-home-where-staff-believe-they-are-beating-covid-19-11989176
106 The Hawthorne effect was observed at Western Electric's telephone-manufacturing factory in Hawthorne, Illinois during the 1920s, when productivity improved as different and contradictory measures were tried (better lighting, worse lighting) and the workforce responded to management attention, almost regardless of how it was applied.
107 For the NHS examples, see nhsManagers.net; https://survivingwork-inhealth.org/
108 https://news.sky.com/story/coronavirus-inside-the-northern-ireland-care-home-where-staff-believe-they-are-beating-covid-19-11989176; 'Coronavirus: Care home residents account for more than half of NI deaths', 30 May 2020 https://www.bbc.co.uk/news/uk-northern-ireland-52774149

109 *Daily Record*, 22 April 2020.
110 https://www.mentalhealth.org.uk/campaigns/mental-health-aware-ness-week/why-kindness-theme
111 https://www.mentalhealth.org.uk/campaigns/mental-health-aware-ness-week/why-kindness-theme;   https://www.cbi.org.uk/articles/kindness-matters-1/
112 *Change or die*, Deutschman, A. (2005, Fast Company 52).
113 *Leadership at all levels*, Leslie, K. and Canwell, A., *European Management Journal*, August 2010.
114 See *Teams that work*, Leslie, K. and Crowley, D., Deloitte, 2007 and *Teamwork at the top*, Leslie, K., Herb, E. and Price, C., *McKinsey Quarterly*, 2001 for further examples and approaches to improving the performance of management teams.
115 *Grooming, gossip and the evolution of language*, Dunbar, R. (1996, Harvard University Press); 'Neocortex size, group size, and the evolution of language', Aiello, L.C. and Dunbar, R.I.M., *Current Anthropology* 34:2 (1993), p189; 'Comparing two methods for estimating network size', McCarthy, C. *et al*, *Human Organization* 60:1 (2001), p32; 'Social Network Size in Humans', Hill, R.A. and Dunbar, R.I.M.: *Human Nature* 14:1 (2003), p65.
116 *The wisdom of teams*, Katzenbach, J.R. and Smith, D.K. (1992, Harvard Business School Press).
117 *Why corporate team-building events can be terrible*, Green, A., 23 August 2018, www.bbc.co.uk/news/business-45260246
118 *Simple sabotage field manual*, 1944, Office of Strategic Services (now CIA) Declassified Strategic Services Manual No3.
119 See *Teams that work* Leslie, K. and Crowley, D., Deloitte, 2007 and *Teamwork at the top*, Leslie, K., Herb, E. and Price, C., *McKinsey Quarterly*, 2001.
120 *The Guardian*, 16 May 2020; Tussell Report on strategic suppliers to Government 2020.
121 Community Interest Company whose shares are owned by the Mental Health Foundation, the UK's oldest mental health charity.
122 See research by LinkedIn and the Mental Health Foundation on the burnout and mental health effects of the lockdown and tips to avoid burnout: www.mentalhealth.org.uk/coronavirus
123 *Twelfth Night* Act III Scene I, Shakespeare.
124 An honourable exception is *Wilful blindness*, Heffernan, M. (2011, Simon & Schuster).
125 See *The rise and fall of Enron* http://www.sjsu.edu/faculty/watkins/enron.htm and *The smartest guys in the room*, McLean, B. and Elkind, P. (2004, Penguin).
126 *The resourceful leader*, Leslie, K., Canwell A., Longfils, H., Edwards, A. and Hannan, S., 2011, National College for Leadership at https://

dera.ioe.ac.uk//2564/; *Child protection services near crisis as demand rises*, bbc.co.uk, 6 November 2018; https://www.bbc.co.uk/news/education-46049154

127 For current programmes, see www.adcs.org.uk and Aspirant Directors of Childrens Services Programme https://thestaffcollege.uk/what-we-do/core-provision/aspirant-dcs-programme/. For the Baby P case, see *Baby Peter care in Haringey*, Garboden, M. in *Child Safeguarding*, 12 November 2008; *The Story of Baby P: Setting the Record Straight*, Jones, R. (2014, Policy Press).

128 Private conversations with the author.

129 See *How safe are our children*, NSPCC; *Safeguarding Pressures*, Research Phase 6 ADCS; *Baby P: can training prevent another?*, Michael Shaw, *Times Educational Supplement (Tes)*, 23 January 2009.

130 *Pilots "not told" about jet's deadly flaw*, Parry, R.L. and Bremner, C., *The Times*, 13 November 2018; *Boeing could pay a heavy price for crashes*, Bremner, C., *The Times*, 21 March 2019; *FAA is blamed for letting Max jets fly*, Bremner, C., *The Times*, 12 October 2019; *Boeing whistleblower raises doubts over 787 oxygen system*, BBC News, 6 November 2019; *Boeing defies shareholders' demands for reform at top*, Dean, J., *The Times*, 30 April 2019; *Stabiliser may have tipped flight out of pilot's control*, Bremner, C., *The Times*, 12 March 2019; *Boeing Max 737 crash in Indonesia "caused by pilot error and faulty design"*, Bremner, C., *The Times*, 24 September 2019; *Test pilot case turns up problems to Max*, Dean, J., *The Times*, 14 March 2020.

131 *Crossrail: National Audit Office to investigate delay and rising costs* https://www.bbc.co.uk/news/uk-england-london-46316587; *Mayor "knew about delay to Crossrail"*, Collingridge, J. *Sunday Times Business & Money*, 25 November 2018, pp1–2; *HS2 faces big challenges, says chairman facing the sack*, Paton, G. and *Sacking HS2's chairman won't solve its problems*, Wolmar, C., both in *The Times*, 4 December 2018.

132 See numerous articles in *The Times* exposing the Oxfam scandal 2017–19.

133 *The Fifth Risk*, Lewis, M. (2018, Allen Lane).

134 Credited to John Wanamaker (1838–1922), the successful Philadelphia retailer, religious leader and politician whose stores became part of Macy's.

135 'Using the fish tank as a metaphor for the organization, people see the fish. They want the fish to shine and perform. What they don't see, and are inclined to neglect, is the quality of what surrounds the fish – hierarchy, rules, incentives, and so on. If managers are taken out for training, they are then plopped back in the same dirty environment and we are surprised when they revert to old habits. As fast as leadership talent (new and retrained) is poured in, it leaks away.

Waste is the winner. Leadership doesn't stand a chance. Nor does the organization.' Bill Tate, Institute for Systemic Leadership, www.systemicleadershipinstitute.org

136 *The resourceful leader*, Leslie, K., Canwell A., Longfils, H., Edwards, A. and Hannan, S., 2011, National College for Leadership at https://dera.ioe.ac.uk//2564/

137 www.gov.uk/government/publications/major-projects-leadership-academy-mpla-handbook

138 See *Mistakes were made (but not by me)*, Tavris, C. and Aronson, E. (2016 updated edition, Pinter & Martin).

139 www.allbrightcollective.com – learning and networks for women.

140 *The Manager*, Carson, M. (2013, Bloomsbury), p75.

141 Also illustrated on the £20 banknote.

142 *Thinking, Fast and Slow*, Kahneman, D. (2011, Allen Lane), pp247–251 and *Megaprojects and risk*, Flyvbjerg, B. (2003, Cambridge University Press).

143 Documented in National Audit Office reports and quoted *inter alia* in *Megaprojects and risk*, Flyvbjerg, B. (2003, Cambridge University Press).

144 https://www.usnews.com/news/politics/articles/2020-05-15/pandemic-planning-becomes-political-weapon-as-deaths-mount

145 *Thinking, Fast and Slow*, Kahneman, D. (2011, Allen Lane), p220.

146 This is not as surprising as one might think: many defence projects have feature after feature added as they go through design, until the overall design fails to deliver as planned at the start. In the case of the submarine, adding weight of extra equipment meant the overall buoyancy calculation was no longer valid. Then, to rescue the project, a major correction is made but, like any complex system, the knock-on consequences add cost and delay somewhere else. In the case of the submarine, buoyancy was restored by adding hull length, but it was then too big to fit in an original constraint – that is, its planned home port docks. 'Spain's €1bn S-80 Plus submarine won't fit in its own port', Graham Keeley, *The Times*, 19 July 2018.

147 *Jackspeak – a guide to British naval slang and usage*, Jolly, R. (1989, Conway).

148 See 'Turning up the heat in electricity: managing through deregulation', Leslie, K., Kausman, D. and Bard, G., *McKinsey Quarterly*, Winter 1999; 'What utilities are good for', Leslie and Jenna, *Wall Street Journal*, 1999.

149 Powergen employed around 12,000 staff and supplied 5 million customers across its residential and business markets within the UK. For a fuller description, see http://www.company-histories.com/Powergen-PLC-Company-History.html and http://www.company-histories.com/Nationalpower-PLC-Company-History.html

150   As an aside, it is reasonable to ask why this vital, relatively slow-moving industry went through (and continues to go through) successive inconsistent waves of change. The answers lie in the fundamental structure and technology of the industry: (1) *Long-lived capital assets that require deep-pocketed investors to invest substantial amounts at regular intervals – power stations can have a 40-year life.* They are highly sensitive to government and regulators' stance across a range of policies, including subsidies, consumer protection, industry structure and investment incentives. (2) *Elements of the electricity industry are monopolies – the wires and transforming stations of the grid and distribution networks cannot be operated by competing companies.* This means that government has a constant opportunity to intervene to influence suppliers' and consumers' behaviours, although interventions can easily be obscured in consumers' bills. (3) *The combination of capital-intensity and government intervention stimulates companies to continually manage these risks and minimise uncontrolled competition.* Vertical integration and deals with government and regulators are welcomed because they minimize potential downsides. In general, companies will sacrifice profitability to maximize long-term stability.

151   See *Boyd: The fighter pilot who changed the art of war*, Coram, R. (2002, Back Bay Books).

152   *Competitive Strategy*, Porter, M. (1980, Free Press).

153   For a full discussion of complementarity, see *The modern firm*, Roberts, J. (2004, Oxford University Press), pp33–51, 67–73, 182–190.

154   'When reorganization works', Leslie, K., Day, J. and Lawson, E., *McKinsey Quarterly*, Winter 2003.

155   https://www.gov.uk/government/organisations/defence-infrastructure-organisation/about

156   For the chief executive's view, see https://insidedio.blog.gov.uk/2013/11/11/welcome-from-andrew-manley-dio-chief-executive-2/

157   See https://www.nao.org.uk/report/delivering-the-defence-estate/

158   See https://www.telegraph.co.uk/news/uknews/1339789/Marconi-from-boom-to-bust-in-a-year.html

159   See https://www.telegraph.co.uk/finance/newsbysector/supportservices/2781922/ICI-finally-consigned-to-history.html

160   See http://www.masteringthemerger.com/masteringthemerger/case_example_bmw_rover.asp

161   *Inside America's Dysfunctional Trillion-Dollar Fighter-Jet Program*, Insinna, V. *New York Times*, 21 August 2019.

162   https://publications.parliament.uk/pa/cm200607/cmselect/cmdfence/56/5606.htm

163   See http://www.company-histories.com/English-China-Clays-Ltd-Company-History.html

164 Chancellor of the Duchy of Lancaster and Secretary of State for Education, 17 May 2020.

165 *File on Four*, Radio 4, 20 May 2020; 'The Times view on the response to coronavirus of Public Health England: Official Failure, *The Times*, 20 May 2020; https://news.sky.com/story/coronavirus-care-home-bosses-accuse-government-of-prioritising-nhs-not-most-vulnerable-people-11991078; https://www.bbc.co.uk/news/52674073, Coronavirus timeline on care homes going into lockdown.

166 *Obliquity*, Kay, J. (2010, Profile).

167 https://thebristolmayor.com/2020/04/22/food-poverty-a-sad-reality-of-life/

168 *140,000 NHS volunteers left idle*, Gregory, A., *Sunday Times*, 5 July 2020.

169 *Communities versus Coronavirus – the rise of mutual aid*, Tiratelli, L. and Kaye, S., New Local Government Network July 2020; Power to change, 5 June 2020.

170 Big Society Impact Report 2020.

171 *Independent review of the effectiveness of Big Society Capital*, Leslie, K., Sherlock, N. and Brown, C., The Oversight Trust, July 2020.

172 For the best and latest take on the entire field, see *Impact: Reshaping capitalism to drive real change*, Cohen, R. (2020, Ebury Press).

173 https://blogs.deloitte.co.uk/mondaybriefing/2019/11/whats-the-purpose-of-a-company.html

174 https://www.ey.com/en_gl/podcasts/better-question/2019/09/episode-0-how-will-personal-purpose-shape-the-future-of-work

175 An interesting potential research study would be to correlate experience/exposure to military/sporting heroes/leaders and the default leadership styles of male and female leaders – accepting that there would always be outliers and exceptions.

176 *Anna Karenina* opening sentence.

177 Consistent with the impact of isolation and disempowerment on health – see *The health gap*, Marmot, M. (2016, Bloomsbury), p228. For Samaritans data, see www.samaritans.org

178 Not least because a narcissistic leader's self-belief does not waver in the face of evidence. 'Narcissism and self-belief', *The Times*, 30 October 2019 highlights that narcissistic leaders may have grandiose delusions of their importance but they remain mentally tough. https://www.the-times.co.uk/article/narcissists-are-happier-than-the-rest-of-us-after-all-it-s-all-about-them-zt9kkpdch (29 October)

179 Nielsen research, June 2020.

180 Freelancing platform Upwork.

181 www.samaritans.org

182 'Jobs after COVID-19', Deloitte Monday briefing, 1 June 2020; Institute for Social and Economic Research, 5 June 2020; https://www.

itv.com/news/2020-06-09/peston-why-the-coronavirus-recovery-is-worsening-hideous-inequalities/

183 Examples: mckinsey.com/featured-insights/leadership/from-think-
ing-about-the-next-normal-to-making-it-work-what-to-stop-start-
and-accelerate;   ey.com/en_au/covid-19/how-to-build-resilient-work-
forces-and-workspaces; Deloitte Monday Briefing, 25 May 2020;
corporate-rebels.com/corona-virus-separating-the-good-from-
the-bad/

184 *Newsnight*, BBC2, 6 May 2020.

185 Examples drawn from 'We must seize the chance for real change',
The Tablet, 9 May 2020; 'Why kindness matters in public policy',
www.mentalhealth.org.uk; 'A deepening crisis?' Jubilee-plus.org; 'As
we emerge from crisis, we need a revolution for a born-again world',
The Observer, 24 May 2020; 'Will Covid-19 help us to design hap-
pier, greener, better cities?', *The Observer*, 24 May 2020; 'Inside story
– prisons under quarantine', *The Tablet*, 9 May 2020; 'Don't put
rough sleepers back on the street after lockdown', *The Observer*, 17
May 2020; 'We cannot go back to what was normal in the past', *The
Tablet*, 9 May 2020.

186 'As we emerge from crisis, we need a revolution for a born-again world',
https://www.theguardian.com/commentisfree/2020/may/24/covid-19-
has-changed-everything-now-we-need-a-revolution-for-a-born-again-
world.

187 *The Heart Aroused: Poetry and the preservation of the soul in corporate America*, Whyte, D. (1994, Currency-Doubleday), p10.

188 *Ibid.*, p21.

189 *Ibid.*, p271.

190 *Ibid.*, pp228–229.

191 *Ibid.*, pp263–265.

192 *The Fearless Organization*, Edmondson, A., (2019, Wiley), pxvi.

193 Royal Dutch/Shell Group was created in 1907 by a merger of Royal
Dutch Petroleum of the Netherlands and Shell Transport and Trading
of the UK.

194 *Perspective on McKinsey*, Bower, M. (1979 and 2004, McKinsey and
Company), p162, reprinted in *The Times*, 15 June 2019.

195 *Surviving the Enron fallout*, interview with David Sproul by Madison
Marriage, *Financial Times*, 2 December 2018.

196 For example, see *The modern firm*, Roberts, J. (2004, Oxford University Press), pp18 and 284–285.

197 *Rolls-Royce revamp rolls on and on*, Osborn, A., *The Times*, 15 June
2018.

198 *Complex Organizations*, Perrow, C. (2014, Echo Point Books & Media), p128.

199 www.jaygalbraith.com

200 https://www.mckinsey.com/business-functions/strategy-and-corporate-finance/our-insights/enduring-ideas-the-7-s-framework#

201 'Coming to a New Awareness of Organizational Culture', Schein, E.H., *Sloan Management Review* 25:2, Winter 1984.

202 See *The undoing project*, Lewis, M. (2016, Allen Lane) for the story of Tversky, Kahneman, Thaler and the other major contributors.

203 *Thinking, Fast and Slow*, Kahneman, D. (2011, Allen Lane), p387.

204 *Nudge: Improving Decisions about Health, Wealth and Happiness*, Thaler, R. and Sunstein, C. (2008, Yale University Press).

205 The fame of Shell's scenario planning was carefully cultivated – for example *The Economist* lauded Pierre Wack (1922–1997) as an unconventional French oil executive who developed the use of scenario planning at Royal Dutch Shell's London headquarters in the 1970s. *The Economist* stated "So successful was he that the Anglo-Dutch oil giant was able to anticipate not just one Arab-induced oil shock during that decade, but two." https://www.economist.com/news/2008/08/29/pierre-wack.

206 It was this blindness to unfamiliar options that caused J.M. Keynes to comment in *The General Theory* that 'Practical men, who believe themselves to be quite exempt from any intellectual influences, are usually slaves of some defunct economist'. It also underpinned Taleb's 'black swan' analysis of how flawed stories of the past shape our views of the world and our expectations for the future, arising inevitably from our continuous attempt to make sense of the world – see *The Black Swan: The impact of the highly improbable*, Taleb, N.N. (2007, NY Random House).

207 See *How the best bosses interrupt bias on their teams*, Williams, J.C. and Mihaylo, S., *Harvard Business Review*, November–December 2019.

208 *Thirteen Days: A memoir of the Cuban Missile Crisis*, Kennedy, R.F. (1969, Norton).

209 *The modern firm*, Roberts, J. (2004, Oxford University Press), pp24–26 and 182–190.

210 https://www.gov.uk/government/organisations/civil-service-project-delivery-profession; Jesse Norman: My revolutionary experiment with other Ministers today in delivering better value for taxpayers, ConservativeHome.com 17 July 2020; https://www.cranfield.ac.uk/som/research-centres/centre-for-business-performance/project-leadership-programme-plp-fact-sheet

211 See *Deloitte has fired 20 UK partners for inappropriate behaviour*, Marriage, M., FT.com, 9 December 2018.

212 Examples include: 'we shall beat the virus' and call upon leadership urges to control situations, to appeal to nativism and to exclude outsiders.

213　See survey data in mckinsey.com/featured-insights/diversity-and-in-clusion/diversity-wins-how-inclusion-matters; https://hbr.org/2019/11 /getting-over-your-fear-of-talking-about-diversity?utm_campaign=-hbr&utm_source=twitter&utm_medium=social

214　It is a truism that most mental illness is also a physical illness, but we cannot assume that causation flows from the physical to the mental. For example, the experience of abuse is evident in changed physical characteristics of the brains of survivors – the abuse caused physical changes. Research led by Si-Qiong June Liu, MD, Ph.D., Professor of Cell Biology and Anatomy at LSU Health New Orleans School of Medicine, has shown how stress changes the structure of the brain and reveals a potential therapeutic target to prevent or reverse it. The findings are published in the *Journal of Neuroscience* and sum-marized at https://medicalxpress.com/news/2020-04-stress-remod-els-brain.html

215　*Sunday Times*, 7 October 2018, p7 and 24 November 2019, p8.

216　https://www.bbc.co.uk/news/business-51201550

217　'Baker McKenzie chair to take time out', Max Walters, www.lawgaz-ette.co.uk, 22 October 2018; 'BigLaw global chairman's death after leave for health issues highlights stress of law practice', Debra Cassens Weiss, www.abajournal.com, 16 April 2019; 'Baker McKenzie's growth lags City rivals', *The Times*, 30 August 2019. The inquest in June 2020 concluded that it was suicide following 'acute depressive illness'.

218　For example, 'Whitehall strikes back', Oliver Wright and Sam Coates, *The Times*, 31 Mar 2019, p1 www.thetimes.co.uk/article/white-hall-strikes-back-at-brexiteers-lcknwj9z0. 20 October 2018 and 'Brexit: Civil Service leader Sir Mark Sedwill hits back after criti-cism by Eurosceptics', Oliver Wright, *The Times*, 2 April 2019. Brexit conflicts and workload are adding to the planned 'transformation' of public services, including improving delivery of 350+ major pro-jects – defined as £1+ billion project value – see 'Organising for ef-fectiveness in the public sector', Leslie, K. and Tilley, C., *McKinsey Quarterly*, November 2004 and *The Times*. The Civil Service shrank significantly 2010–16 but has rapidly added over 20,000 Brexit posts across Whitehall 2016–18, with 'any warm body' being recruited – often within days of first interview – see NAO report on Brexit pre-paration 2018. Work pressure becomes stress when ministers reject impartial analysis that does not fit political needs and promote press attacks on work they have themselves commissioned. The acting Cabinet Secretary has publicly reprimanded government backbench-ers and media who attack civil servants and accuse them of pursuing their own political agenda – see '"Sniping" Tories told to stop attacks on PM's Brexit negotiator', *The Times*, 16 October 2018. Political pressures discourage collaborative working in line with Civil Service values in order to control information. In fear of leaks, meetings within departments follow a standard process: agendas and papers are not circulated, attendees are permitted 30 minutes in a locked room to read papers. As a result, major issues are discussed only at senior levels, consensus is not built, decisions are not communicated, and cross-government policy does not emerge fully tested. Senior civil servants question the 'new normal' behaviours that recruits are acquiring – running contrary to the established Civil Service values of honesty, integrity, impartiality and objectivity.

219 'Stressed Whitehall staff at "breaking point" over Brexit', Michael Savage, *The Observer*, 17 November 2019.

220 'Breaking the leadership mould', Susie Bailey and Saffron Cordery, King's Fund and NHS Providers, August 2018.

221 *The Times*, 15 September 2018.

222 *The Observer*, 10 May 2020. In UK secondary schools there were 70,000 self-harm incidents (panic attacks, self-cutting, overdoses, eating disorders) in 2017, double those reported in 2012, *The Times*, 9 June 2018; in UK universities, students declaring anxiety or depression increased 73% to 12,773 from 2014–15 academic year to 2017–18.

223 See 'Trust issues', *Charity Times* cover story June/July 2018, p20.

224 *The Tablet,* 21/28 December 2019, p49.

225 Our World in Data website: https://ourworldindata.org/global-mental-health

226 National Alliance on Mental Illness https://www.nami.org/learn-more/mental-health-by-the-numbers

227 National Alliance on Mental Illness https://www.nami.org/learn-more/mental-health-by-the-numbers

228 Canadian Mental Health Association website: https://cmha.ca/fast-facts-about-mental-illness

229 Australian Institute for Health and Welfare website: https://www.aihw.gov.au/reports/mental-health-services/mental-health-services-in-australia/report-contents/summary-of-mental-health-services-in-australia/prevalence-impact-and-burden

230 OECD: http://www.oecd.org/health/health-systems/OECD-Factsheet-Mental-Health-Health-at-a-Glance-Europe-2018.pdf

231 OECD 'Sick on the job? Myths and realities about Mental Health and Work', 2010. For Samaritans data see www.samaritans.org

232 National Alliance on Mental Illness: https://www.nami.org/learn-more/mental-health-by-the-numbers

233 Canadian Mental Health Association website: https://cmha.ca/fast-facts-about-mental-illness

234 *The Observer*, 16 September 2018, p22 reporting a ministerial written answer: Health Minister Jackie Doyle-Price in reply to Paula Sherriff

MP. 23,686 mental health staff left the NHS in England between June 2017 and May 2018. The total number of posts is budgeted at 209,233 full-time equivalent staff, but only 187,215 were in post in May 2018.

235 The hidden health crisis of COVID-19 in Europe https://www.mckinsey.com/industries/healthcare-systems-and-services/our-insights/understanding-and-managing-the-hidden-health-crisis-of-covid-19-in-europe

236 www.mentalhealth.org.uk/news/millions-uk-adults-have-felt-panicked-afraid-and-unprepared-result-coronavirus-pandemic-new

237 Two women are killed every week in England and Wales by current and former partners, Office for National Statistics. See also www.samaritans.org

238 https://assets.publishing.service.gov.uk/government/uploads/system/uploads/attachment_data/file/892085/disparities_review.pdf

239 Reported by BBC South West during the lockdown.

240 https://www.gov.scot/publications/adverse-childhood-experiences/ for a brief description of ACEs and their lifelong impact – in summary, they are abuse, neglect and growing up in a disadvantaged or violent household.

241 https://www.mentalhealth.org.uk/news/mental-health-foundation-publishes-major-new-report-social-inequalities-and-mental-health

242 For a devastating and compelling account of the impact of poverty on the mental health of families across the UK, see *Poverty Safari*, Darren McGarvey (2017, Luath Press); for the inequalities in the impact of the pandemic, see www.mentalhealth.org.uk for Covid-19-inequality-briefing

243 https://edition.cnn.com/2020/05/14/health/un-coronavirus-mental-health/index.html; mentalhealth.org.uk/campaigns/mental-health-awareness-week/kindness-research; mentalhealth.org.uk/campaigns/mental-health-awareness-week/kindness-policy-asks; www.kingsfund.org.uk/blog/2020/04/ethnic-minority-deaths-covid-19

244 'Five Year Forward View for Mental Health', Mental Health Taskforce, 2016; 'Don't suffer in silence', Good University Guide 2019, *Sunday Times*, 23 September 2018, p11.

245 'The Marmot Review' www.local.gov.uk/marmot-review-report-fair-society-healthy-lives

246 See 'What is depression and why is it rising?', Juliette Jowit, *The Guardian*, 4 June 2018, p10; 'Stress: are we coping?', Mental Health Foundation, 2018.

247 Health Executive Agency (2017) Work-related stress, depression or anxiety statistics in Great Britain 2017.

248 CIPD Absence Management Report, 2015.

249 Annual Injury and Ill Health Statistics, Health & Safety Executive, 31 October 2018.

250 Work-related stress statistics in Great Britain 2019, www.hse.gov.uk/
     statistics; 'Civil servants take thousands of days off sick', *The Times*,
     16 October 2018. https://www.thetimes.co.uk/article/mental-ill-
     health-costs-whitehall-300-000-sick-days-jvgwfwggv
251 See 'Mental health: 10 charts on the scale of the problem' https://
     www.bbc.co.uk/news/health-41125009
252 'Stress: Are we coping?' Mental Health Foundation, May 2018, p11;
     available at www.mentalhealth.org.uk/publications/stress-are-we-coping
253 'Will the gig economy prevail?', Colin Crouch (2019, Polity).
254 'Jobs after COVID-19', Deloitte Monday briefing, 1 June 2020; ht-
     tps://www.mckinsey.com/featured-insights/future-of-work/the-fu-
     ture-of-work-in-europe
255 See 'Mental Health: Stress and the start-up', https://www.theguard-
     ian.com/society/2018/oct/20/tech-startups-stress-pressure-macho-
     approach-to-coping
256 Ann Francke, chief executive of the Chartered Management Institute,
     Sunday Times, 24 November 2019.
257 *The Times*, 15 September, 2018
258 'Insecure Overachievers: How personal insecurity is used to drive ex-
     ceptional performance in elite City workplaces', Laura Empson, Cass
     Business School, Radio 4, 29 September 2018; *Perspective on McKin-
     sey*, Marvin Bower (1979 and 2004, McKinsey and Company), p220,
     reprinted in *The Times*, 17 June 2019; https://www.bbc.co.uk/pro-
     grammes/b0bkqy1l
259 'Better Mental Health for All – a public health approach', Mental
     Health Foundation, www.mentalhealth.org.uk/publications/better-
     mental-health-all-public-health-approach-mental-health-improvement
260 https://www.mckinsey.com/business-functions/organization/our-in-
     sights/tuning-in-turning-outward-cultivating-compassionate-leader-
     ship-in-a-crisis?cid=eml-web; https://www.ey.com/en_au/covid-19/
     how-to-build-resilient-workforces-and-workspaces
261 See 'Mental health and employers: refreshing the case for investment'.
     Deloitte, January 2020, https://www2.deloitte.com/uk/en/pages/con-
     sulting/articles/mental-health-and-employers-refreshing-the-case-for-
     investment.html
262 As criticized by Dame Sally Davies, England's Chief Medical Officer
     2011–2019, in her first report on mental health.
263 'Mental Health At Work', Business in the Community, 2014.
264 *The Tablet*, 11 November 2015.
265 See *The health gap*, Michael Marmot (2016, Bloomsbury) for discus-
     sion of the research into civil servants and the health outcomes for
     different levels of leadership and the original research in Marmot,
     M.G., Davey Smith, G., Stansfeld, S., Patel, C. *et al* (1991) *Health*

inequalities among British civil servants: the Whitehall II study, *The Lancet*, June 1991, 337, 1387–1393.

266   For example, Schwartz Rounds, which were developed to provide health professionals (clinical and non-clinical) with a structured forum to discuss the social and emotional aspects of working in healthcare, and where the evidence shows that staff who attend feel less stress and less isolated.

267   Catastrophic mistakes have pushed some organizations into launching policies of candour and appointing champions – notably the NHS following the Francis Report into events at Mid-Staffordshire NHS Trust, where many NHS staff were aware of patient neglect leading to deaths over an extended period.

268   *Leading organizations: Ten timeless truths*, Scott Keller and Mary Meaney (2017, Bloomsbury).

269   Mental Health At Work plc is a community interest company (owned by the Mental Health Foundation, a charity registered in England & Wales and in Scotland) that provides insight and training for line managers on how to have the conversations with their people that help them maintain mental health and handle the stress-related incidence of anxiety and depression that can be expected in the workplace.

270   Examples: war for talent, war footing, war on drugs, war against crime, analogies with SAS or SEALs or Commandos.

271   Centre for Economic Performance, London School of Economics

G7 economy	Relative productivity
US	3.31
Japan	3.23
Germany	3.21
Canada	3.14
UK	3.03
France	3.01
Italy	2.99

'Accidental managers behind Britain's poor productivity', Alexandra Frean, *The Times*, 1 September 2019. https://www.thetimes.co.uk/article/rise-of-the-accidental-manager-lies-behind-uks-low-productivity-0wc9rl6ph

272   *Seeing like a state*, James C. Scott (1998, Yale University), p69.

273   McKinsey were nicknamed the 'Jesuits of capitalism' and this appealed to the Kirk's sense of humour and history.

Index

accidents during change   23
  assigning blame   26–7, 29–30,
    40, 44
  clusters around non-routine
    tasks   26, 28, 43
  'designing out' human error   33–6
  focus on capacity to remedy   39, 40,
    45
  front-line leaders   27, 28, 39, 42
  instability of complex systems
    32–41, 43
  IT system transitions   37–9, 43
  obscuring the system view   28–9,
    34–5, 39, 42
  oil industry   23–7, 28–9
  senior management   27, 36, 39, 42
adaptive leadership   75, 76, 87, 88,
  89–90, 92, 95
agile approaches to change   102, 103
Air France   447 plane crash   38
al-Qaida   61
aligning direction   58, 121–3, 129
AllBright   145
American Business Roundtable   181
Andersen, Arthur   201
anxiety and depression   187, 219, 220,
  222, 235, 236, 241, 242
Apollo space flights   31–2
apprenticeships, leaders   195–6
Ardern, Jacinda   186
Atlee, Clement   86
automation, future of   38–9

Baby Boomers   183
Baby P   136
Baker McKenzie   219
Bay of Pigs invasion   212
behavioural science   52, 87, 127–8

belonging see purpose and belonging,
  organizational
Big Society Capital   123, 169, 179–80,
  225
Black Lives Matter   212
Blair, Tony   54–5
blame, assigning   26–7, 29–30, 44,
  68, 69
BMW and Rover Group   79–80, 148,
  165
Boeing   737 MAX   38, 137
Bower, Marvin   200
BP   27, 54, 60, 64, 151, 233
British Airways   68
Browne, John   54
BT   63
bullying, tackling   233, 236

Cialdini, Robert   127–8
Canadian Air Force   33
candour, organizational   69
Carillion   62
Carson, Mike   91
Carstairs, Kenny   97
catalytic events, non-harmful   168–9,
  171
Central Electricity Generating Board
  (CEGB)   155
Central Intelligence Agency (CIA)   65,
  117
Chernobyl nuclear disaster   35
Church of Scotland   211, 251
Churchill, Winston   86, 186
Civil Service   213, 219, 230
Community Interest Companies
  (CICs)   180
community support   179–80, 225
competing strategy teams   69

contained change 3–5
corporate social responsibility
    (CSR) 179
cost reduction programmes 42, 45–7
Covid-19 global pandemic (2020) 1,
    6–9, 16, 17, 28, 29, 30, 47, 50, 59,
    70, 79, 80–1, 85–6, 88–9, 92, 101–2,
    107–9, 124–5, 167–8, 173, 178–9,
    185, 186, 187–8, 209, 211, 245–6
  global economic impact 187–9
  lockdown advice from former
    hostage 225–6
  mental health issues 222–5, 238
  social impact of 189–90
Crossrail 137–8
culture, organizational 175
  attempts to impose and police 204–6,
    216
  changing peer groups and
    affiliations 212–13, 216
  different thinking systems 206–8
  inclusivity and discretionary
    effort 213–15
  informal organizational behavioural
    norms 203–4, 216
  new assumptions 208–9, 215, 216
  nudging towards change 208–13,
    215, 216
  and restructuring 202–3
  source of alienation and barrier to
    change 202
  stories told to new joiners 198–202
  telling new stories 210–12, 215,
    216
customers, challenges 67, 149

Defence Equipment & Support
    (DE&S), Ministry of Defence 51,
    56, 63, 166–7
Defence Infrastructure Organisation
    (DIO) 163–4
Deloitte 181, 201, 214
Department of Defense, US 32, 69,
    165–6
depression and anxiety 187, 219, 220,
    222, 235, 236, 241, 242
Deutschman, Alan 109–10
'devil's advocate' 68

Dieppe, Paul 225–6
Dimon, Jamie 190
discretionary energy 183

Electricity Act (1989) 155
Emanuel, Rahm 168
English China Clays plc 79, 148,
    167
Enron 62, 135–6, 201
Environmental and Sustainability
    Governance (ESG) 181
Eon 156
Ernst & Young 181
external restructuring 56

F-35 Joint Strike Fighter
    programme 165–6
FAA 137
failure see accidents during change;
    mistakes, dealing with
false certainty, creating 29, 30, 32,
    39, 44
Feeding Bristol 178
financial crash (2008) 49–50, 66, 173,
    185, 186
fourth industrial revolution 38
fragmented time 49, 50–1
Francis, Pope 78, 85, 238
front-line leaders
  on accident probability 28
  agile change 102, 103–4
  bringing realistic perspective 149
  day-to-day operational
    judgements 27
  delivering change 41, 42–3, 70
  developing networks 74
  experiments and pilot operations 75,
    94, 105, 111, 112, 113
  going along with senior leaders
    games 65
  inclusive leadership language 196
  innovation and learning 107–9
  keeping the system view clear 28–9,
    39
  maintaining core operations 74, 75
  mistrust of performance 53–4
  new/crisis experiences 101
  real perspective/speaking out 67

senior leaders testing 69–70
story telling 94, 154, 215
technology-enabled change 102–7, 108, 110, 111, 112–13
trade-offs 12, 13, 20, 27, 30, 39, 41, 42, 43, 54, 69, 74, 75, 107, 119, 128, 129
waterfall approach to change 102–3, 104
see also culture, organizational; language, developing a common; learning programmes, shared; mental health
FTSE-50 management team 114–16
Fukushima nuclear accident 35

game playing, organizational 46–9, 71
 arising from misapplied experience 54–9
 conforming with senior leaders 58–60, 64–7
 controls and KPIs 54–5, 60–1
 cost reduction 46–7
 external reality - bringing in 67–8
 external reality - ignoring 66
 guarding against groupthink 68–9
 making the 'big change' 56, 63
 managing against a plan 55, 61–2
 pivotal developments 57
 process and system transformation 56
 target setting and chasing 47–8
 trust issues 65–6, 71
gattopardismo 48
GE (General Electric) 61, 64
gender equality 213
Geneen, Harold 55
Global Impact Investing Network (GIIN) 180–1
goal displacement 60
government, UK 47, 54–5, 59, 64, 65, 70, 80, 88–9, 104, 148, 179
government, US 50
Grenfell Tower fire, London 29, 211
Grint, Keith 83
group learning *see* learning programmes, shared
groupthink 69–9, 71, 212

Hanford Site 138
Hayek, Friedrich 159
Health and Social Care Act (2012) 164–5
Heifetz, Ronald A. 89–90
Her Majesty's Revenue and Customs 96–9
'heroic leader' propaganda 80–1, 86, 244
hindsight bias 29–30, 44, 207
Home Depot 64
HSBC 49–50
human error, 'designing out' 33–6

ICI plc 56
Immelt, Jeff 64
'impact investing' 180
inclusive culture 213–15
individualistic model of change 81
inequality, racial 188, 211, 223
influencing behaviour 109–10, 127
infodemics 167–8
internal restructuring 56
investment and social impact 174–5
investor pressure 49, 62
IT systems transitions 37–9, 43

Jay Galbraith's Star Model 203
job security and low earners 232
Johnson, Boris 88
JP Morgan 190

Kahneman, Daniel 79, 206–8
Katzenbach, Jon 116
Kay, John 169
Kennedy, John. F 212
KPIs 54–5, 60–1
Krichefski, Josh 237
Kuhn, Thomas S. 158–9

language, developing a common 132–3, 150–1, 152, 153, 246
language of organizational belonging 196, 197
language, using ordinary 9, 14–15, 30–2, 39, 44, 233–4
leadership capabilities, learning new 142–7

lean thinking and practices 96–9
learning programmes, shared 14, 15,
    131, 132, 133–4, 142–7, 149–50,
    151–2, 196
Lion Air Boeing 737 crash 38
Lloyds Banking Group 123, 210, 219
Lloyds/TSB 37, 102
long-term thinking 155–9, 171
    see also waves of change, creating

Major Projects Leadership Academy
    (Cabinet Office) 143–4, 151, 213
'management science' 32
management-speak 30–2, 150–1, 214,
    233, 244
management teams
    action and reflection 120–1
    delivering change 41, 42–3, 70
    developing a story of change 94,
        128
    doing 'real work' 116–17, 128
    enabling technological change 105,
        106
    FTSE-50 114–16
    inclusivity 196, 215
    internal coherence 74
    mobilizing 68, 71
    planning and optimizing 74, 112
    resource allocation 74, 112
    team alignment 76, 121–2
    team-improvement investments
        118–19
    trust in 117–18
    see also culture, organizational;
        language, developing a common;
        learning programmes, shared;
        mental health; team work
Manhattan Project 31
manoeuvring characteristics
    augmentation system (MCAS) 38,
        137
Manzoni, John 27
Marconi plc 164
McKinsey 57–8, 145, 200, 203
McNerney, Jeff 64
media, the 50, 59, 66, 70, 139
MediaCom 237–8
meeting agendas, managing 120

mental health 9, 17, 108–9, 124–5,
    174, 175, 186, 187, 217–18
    about stress 227–30, 235–6,
        239–40, 241–2
    Covid-19 pandemic 222–5, 238
    economic cost of mental ill
        health 220–1
    and leadership in the
        workplace 231–6, 238–41
    MediaCom's story 237–8
    need for more than medical
        treatment 221–2
    positive and negative impact of
        work 227
    stories of organizational
        challenges 218–19
    supporting and protecting staff
        234–6, 242
Mental Health Allies Programme,
    MediaCom 237–8
Mental Health At Work Community
    Interest Company (CIC) 124–5
mentoring and coaching 196–7
    see also learning programmes, shared;
        peer support
Merkel, Angela 186
Microsoft 61
Mid-Staffordshire Hospital Trust 69
Ministry of Defence (MOD) 51, 69,
    166–7
Mintzberg, Henry 51–2, 58
mistakes, dealing with 14–15, 131–2
    addressing leadership fails 139–40
    adjusting strategy 131
    bringing in the real world 132
    pace and waves of change 133, 134
    shared learning 131, 132, 133–4
    using effective language 132–3
    see also learning programmes, shared;
        reality, bringing in

Nardelli, Bob 64
National Health Service (NHS) 28,
    29, 50, 54–5, 59, 61, 62, 69, 80,
    104, 107–8, 164–5, 167–8, 178,
    211, 219, 221, 230, 233
National Lottery 225
National Power 155–6

9/11 terrorist attacks 29
Normal Accident Theory 32–3
nuclear industry 34, 35, 138
nudge theory/nudging 208–13, 215, 216

obliquity concept 169
Office of Strategic Services/CIA 65
Ogilvy, David 140
oil industry *see* BP; Shell
operations research 32–3
optimism bias 78–9, 147–8, 207
organizational vocabulary *see* language, developing a common
outsourcing 56, 63
over-relying on experience 52–3
  case of General Electric (GE) 64
  controls and performance indicators 54–5, 60–1
  managing against a plan 55, 61–2
  mistrust of front-line leaders 53–4
  moves to change everything 56–7, 63–4
  see also game playing, organizational
Overhead Value Analysis (OVA) 46–7
Oxfam 138
Oxford Saïd Business School 143, 145
Ozersk, Russia 138

pandemic (2020), Coronavirus *see* Covid-19 global pandemic (2020)
partners, challenges from business 67, 149
Patient Protection and Affordable Care Act (2010), US 164–5
peer support 138, 143, 144–5, 146, 151–3, 177, 213, 235, 242
performance management 233–4
performance pressure 49–50, 52–3, 80, 219
perspective, bringing in *see* reality, bringing in
Phoenix payroll system 37
planning fallacy 79–80, 147–8, 207
plans, managing against 55, 61–2
poetic imagination in corporate environment 190–1
Popper, Karl 159

positive deviants 75, 105, 111, 132
power-based leadership 186–7, 248–9
Powergen 111, 145, 155–8, 170
PPI scandal 65
Premiership Football 91
Principles for Purposeful Business report (British Academy) 181
Prior, Lord 61
productive vs unproductive distress 92–4
programmatic management approach 75, 87, 88, 89, 91, 95
'project' language 31–2, 39, 44
psychological safety 69, 176, 194, 195, 197
public enquiries 139
purpose and belonging, organizational 9, 16–17, 174–5, 176
  belonging and effort invested in change 194
  corporate traps 190
  inclusive language 196, 197
  influence of leaders' behaviour 194–5
  leadership apprenticeships 194, 195–6, 197
  need for/expectations of 181–3, 197
  need for real-world connection 191, 197
  organizations with purpose 178–81
  pace of change and trust erosion 183–6, 197
  poetic imagination in corporate environment 190–1
  power-based leadership 186–7
  social impact of Covid-19 pandemic 189–90
  social investment and impact 179–81
  surviving or thriving with change 192–4, 197

'real work' 116–17, 119–20, 129, 149–50, 177
reality, bringing in 67–8, 246
  from business sources 149
  from external observers and experts 149
  from internal sources 149

shared learning programmes 149–50
unrealistic leadership mindset 147–8
reflection, team work and 120–1
regulators, outside 139–40
resilience, building personal 177, 235, 242
retention, staff 183
Rolls Royce 202
Royal Air Force 28, 33
Royal Navy 150

safety officers 28–9
safety reports 24–5
Samaritans 178, 187
scapegoats 66, 139
Schein, Ed 203
school system, UK 167–8
'scientific management' 33
Scottish Parliament 148
Second World War 33, 86, 185, 186
senior leaders 243–51
  adaptive approach 75, 76, 87, 88, 89–90, 92, 95
  aligning direction 122–3
  asking the right questions 74, 75, 111, 112, 152, 249–50
  being unrealistic 147–8
  cognitive traps 78–81, 147–8, 207
  conforming management 58–60, 64–7
  critical, tame and wicked problems 83–6, 95
  defining context and goals 74
  delivering change 41–4, 70
  fragmented time 49, 50–2
  guarding against groupthink 68–9
  'heroic leader' propaganda 80–1, 86, 244
  how time is actually spent 51–2
  improving economic performance 247
  inclusive leadership language 196, 197
  influencing stakeholders 74
  mastering organizational complexities 69–70
  mistrusting the front-line 53–4
  need for visible action 57–8
  obscuring the system view 42
  optimism bias 78–9, 80, 147–8, 207
  organizational candour 69, 71
  over-relying on experience/game playing 52–71
  passive resistance of 59–60
  performance pressure 49–50, 52–3
  planning fallacy 79–80, 147–8, 207
  power-based leadership 186–7, 248–9
  productive vs unproductive distress 92–4
  programmatic approach 75, 87, 88, 91, 95
  questioning and listening 69–70
  quick wins 244–5
  reframing the task 94, 95
  safety problems 27, 36, 39, 42
  selecting and backing initiatives 106, 113
  situation dependent style 82–6
  sources of external reality 67–8, 71, 75, 149
  story telling 90–2, 94, 128, 154, 196, 210–12, 215
  see also culture, organizational; game-playing, organizational; learning programmes, shared; mental health; mistakes, dealing with; purpose and belonging, organizational; reality, bringing in; waves of change
Shell 23–5, 45–7, 68, 99–100, 198–9, 209–10, 233
sickness and absences 183, 220–1, 229–30
silo behaviour 59–60, 67, 141, 147
Six Sigma 64
Smith, Adam 147, 192
social investment and impact 179–80
social media 50, 92
space shuttle accidents 34
story telling 90–2, 94, 95, 124–7, 128, 134, 154, 176, 194, 196, 197, 210–12
strategy, changing see waves of change, creating

strategy teams, competing   69
stress   175, 186, 187, 219, 227–30,
    235, 239–40, 241–2
Sturgeon, Nicola   186
sub-prime mortgage market   49–50
suppliers, challenges from   67, 149

target setting and chasing   47–8, 59
team work
    action and reflection   120–1
    aligning direction   121–3, 129
    persuasion   127–8
    'real work'   116–17, 119–20, 128,
        129, 149–50
    sharing stories   124–7, 128, 129
    team-improvement investment
        118–19
    teams defined   116
    trust   117–18
    see also learning programmes,
        shared; management teams
tech start-up plans   62
technology-enabled change   102–7,
    108, 110, 111–13
Texas City refinery deaths, BP   23, 27
Thaler, Richard   208
thinking systems, Kahneman and
    Tversky's   206–8
3M   64
Three Mile Island nuclear accident   34,
    35
time pressure   49, 50–2
Tolstoy, Leo   186
toxic leaders   186–7, 194, 236, 248–9
training see learning programmes,
    shared
trust issues   53–4, 65–6, 71, 117–18,
    182–6, 219, 248
Tversky, Amos   206–8
24-hour news cycle   50

uncontained change   6–9
United States Air Force   33
United States Navy   35–6

visible action, preference for   57–8
volunteers   178–9, 220

Wack, Pierre   68
waterfall approaches to change   102–3,
    104
waves of change, creating   155–8
    building capability at each step   170,
        171
    'change everything' approach   163–6,
        171
    considering ambition, capabilities,
        decision making and legacy   161
    context and complementarity drive
        change   161–8
    creating non-harmful catalytic
        events   168–9, 171
    dividing up the long term   169, 171
    infodemics in the system   167–8, 171
    isolated projects   166–7, 171
    scientific advances in
        knowledge   158–9
    'tacking' towards goal/'aiming
        off'   169–70, 171
    timing and scope of change   160–8,
        171
    wisdom of long-term thinking   155–9,
        171
Weinstock, Arnold   55
Welch, Jack   64
Whyte, David   190–1
Windrush official enquiry   65
Windscale nuclear powerplant   35,
    138
work avoidance and sabotage   117
WYSIATI thinking   79, 147, 207, 210